ANAMNESIS AS DANGEROUS MEMORY

ANAMNESIS AS DANGEROUS MEMORY

Political and
Liturgical Theology in Dialogue

Bruce T. Morrill, S.J.

A PUEBLO BOOK

The Liturgical Press Collegeville, Minnesota

A Pueblo Book published by The Liturgical Press

Design by Frank Kacmarcik, Obl.S.B.

Library of Congress Cataloging-in-Publication Data

Morrill, Bruce T.
    Anamnesis as dangerous memory : political and liturgical theology in dialogue / Bruce T. Morrill.
        p.   cm.
    "A Pueblo book."
    Includes bibliographical references and index.
    ISBN 0-8146-6183-1 (alk. paper)
    1. Catholic Church—Liturgy.   2. Metz, Johannes Baptist, 1928–
3. Schmemann, Alexander, 1921–1983.   4. Political theology.   5. Liturgics.
I. Title.

BX1970.M69   2000
264'.02'001—dc21   00-021135

To my parents,
Helen Beck Morrill and Henry Burnett Morrill,
with love
and in honor of their many years of service in the
Russian Orthodox and Roman Catholic Churches, respectively

Contents

Acknowledgments

The author wishes to thank The Liturgical Press for permission to quote from several of their books, as well as to acknowledge gratefully the following other publishers:

Bishop Colin Buchanan, proprieter of Grove Books, for permission to quote from *Anamnesis in the Eucharist* by David Gregg.

Continuum International Publishing Group for permission to quote from *Dialectic of Enlightenment* by Max Horkheimer and Theodore Adorno.

Oxford University Press, Inc., and Methodist Publishing House for U.S./Canadian and World Rights, respectively, for quoting from *Eucharist and Eschatology* by Geoffrey Wainwright.

Paulist Press for permission to quote from *Followers of Christ* by Johannes B. Metz © 1978 by Burnes & Oates and Paulist Press, and *Sharing the Eucharistic Bread* by Xavier Leon-Dufour, S.J. © 1987 by The Missionary Society of St. Paul the Apostle in the State of New York.

Saint Vladimir's Seminary Press, 575 Scarsdale Road, Crestwood, NY 10707, for permission to quote from the books of Father Alexander Schmemann.

Introduction

To state at the turn of the twenty-first century that the Christian theological academy, across departmental and denominational lines, remains preoccupied with the question of method is to utter a truism. Issues of theological methodology at present owe their complexity and persistence to two factors: (1) the Enlightenment's irreversible impact on all theoretical endeavors and (2) burgeoning awareness, now also irreversible, among theologians that their work's adequacy, even legitimacy, depends upon direct attention to actual forms of Christian practice. While Immanuel Kant opened the way for necessary attention to the freedom of the human subject, the ensuing philosophical movements gave rise to a transcendental idealism that major "schools" of both Protestant and Catholic theology came to appropriate. Although this modern turn in Christian theology included an invaluable discovery and use of history, its transcendental idealism impeded critical attention to the historical (social, political, embodied) realities of contemporary human subjects, operating instead out of abstract notions of "the person" and "experience." While Protestant Neo-Orthodox theologians prophetically recognized the duplicity of modern transcendentalism in oppressive sociopolitical systems, I would argue that their foremost figure, Karl Barth, remained mired in modernity by his insistence that the one "real man" is Jesus Christ and that all other present, historical "men" are merely "phenomenal."[1]

Over the past few decades in North Atlantic countries two types of theology have emerged which look to the concrete circumstances and practices of contemporary Christians and wider society as primary sources for their theoretical work—liturgical theology and political theology. As Peter Fink explains, the current work of liturgical theology is to move "beyond" the systematic sacramental theology initiated by Edward Schillebeeckx and Karl Rahner in the early 1960s. Both writers

[1] See Karl Barth, *Church Dogmatics* III/2, trans. G. W. Bromiley (Edinburgh: T. & T. Clark, 1960) 41–4, 75–6.

abandoned the regnant scholastic view of sacraments as "objective realities" and oriented the discipline in terms of "meaning in experiential categories." Fink argues that the enterprise must continue to shift from sacramental to liturgical theology so as to recover "the liturgical act itself as a theological locus."[2] As for political theology, Rebecca Chopp explains that its theological method interprets, protects, explains, and criticizes the narratives of Christian praxis, "the bringing together of action and reflection, transformation and understanding," in a way that is "fundamentally practical."[3] Both theologies have inherited modern theology's agenda of freedom and human subjectivity while insisting, in distinctive fashions, on attendance to the particular practices of Christian communities in determinate sociocultural matrices.

The objective of this present study, stated most broadly, is to explore how liturgical theology and political theology, as disciplines making normative theological claims in relation to concrete Christian practices, can benefit from a dialogue with each other. This brief introduction has sought to establish the theoretical circumstances and the historical moment that the two types of theology share as they pursue distinct efforts at methodology and content. The comparison is especially compelling since leading theologians in both areas judge the present situation of Christian theory and practice to be in a state of crisis.

Liturgical theologian David Power has explicitly used the language of "crisis,"[4] "emergency," and "ruins"[5] when describing two crucial facts: the struggle of the Roman Church to make a fundamental shift away from scholastic sacramental theology and post-Tridentine ritual and piety, and the threatened societal and global context in which the Church performs the liturgy. Similarly, Aidan Kavanagh has written on the theological principles essential to liturgical reform, while not mincing words about the crisis-level proportions he perceives American society's individualism and consumerism and, thus, human alienation to

[2] Peter E. Fink, "Sacramental Theology after Vatican II," *The New Dictionary of Sacramental Worship,* ed. Peter E. Fink (Collegeville: The Liturgical Press, 1990) 1111.

[3] Rebecca S. Chopp, *The Praxis of Suffering: An Interpretation of Liberation and Political Theologies* (Maryknoll, N.Y.: Orbis Books, 1986) 36–7, 44–5.

[4] David N. Power, *Unsearchable Riches: The Symbolic Nature of Liturgy* (New York: Pueblo, 1984) 1.

[5] David N. Power, *The Eucharistic Mystery: Revitalizing the Tradition* (New York: Crossroad, 1992) vii, 13.

have reached.[6] What Kavanagh and other liturgical theologians have demonstrated in rhetorical skill or pastoral perceptiveness, however, I believe could still benefit from the theoretical acumen of theologians who have studied more concertedly the present sociopolitical context.

In the field of political theology Johann Baptist Metz has emerged as the preeminent Roman Catholic author. Metz has formulated a penetrating critique of the social and economic systems in North Atlantic nations, analyzing the impact of their overall world view upon the religious subjects within those societies. Metz argues that an analysis of this political or social situation is essential to theology, which must then explore the message and viability of the faith precisely in relation to the present historical context. Metz judges Christianity in late modernity[7] to be in a crisis of identity, both in its subjects and its institutions.[8] He proposes a method by which theology must recover the salvific and emancipatory content of Christianity's traditions for contemporary humanity, with special concern for the suffering and the victims of injustice.

Metz's political theology is compelling and has deservedly won a wide, albeit critical, readership by theologians in a variety of specializations. Liturgical theologians, given their burgeoning interest in memorial or *anamnesis*, often refer to Metz's concept of "dangerous memory." However, they have done so most often in either the introductions or concluding sections or endnotes of their writings, only touching on Metz's powerful phrase and its significance or implications

[6] See Aidan Kavanagh, *On Liturgical Theology* (New York: Pueblo, 1984).

[7] A note on terminology: In discussing the present social context in his more recent writings Metz has shifted from the term "modernity" to "late modernity." For my part, I choose to modify the term "modernity" with the adjective "late" in order to indicate that modernity has reached what would seem to be its last stages, as marked by the crises that Metz identifies in modern societies at this point in history (see Chapter 2). The term "postmodern" does not seem to serve this purpose, since, in my estimation, the subjects and institutions of society continue to function in modern ways, even though with increasing difficulty. For Metz, "postmodern" has definite negative connotations, indicating thought and practices in the academy, Church, and society problematically characterized by regressions to myth and ritualism that ignore the difficult crises of history. See Johann Baptist Metz, *A Passion for God: The Mystical-Political Dimension of Christianity*, trans. J. Matthew Ashley (New York: Paulist Press, 1998) 103, 127.

[8] See Johann Baptist Metz, *Faith in History and Society: Toward a Practical Fundamental Theology*, trans. David Smith (New York: Seabury Press, 1980) ix–x, 169.

for liturgy.[9] I find it striking, however, that none have engaged at length his broader concept of "mysticism," which he argues is integral to the faith. Moreover, while Metz has arrived at his most succinct thesis for political theology as the definition and promotion of "a praxis of faith in mystical and political imitation,"[10] the secondary literature on Metz has not addressed in detail the "mystical" side of this definition—the exception being the recently published work of J. Matthew Ashley.[11] Scholars have tended to analyze along epistemological lines what Metz means by positing his political theology as a practical fundamental theology. As a student and practitioner of the liturgy, I have found myself drawn into the question of what Metz implies and argues for in his concept of mysticism. My struggle with that question will comprise a significant part of this book's second chapter, offered as one particular reading and critique of Metz's political theology.

The analysis of various aspects of mysticism in Metz's theology will lead to questions begging for assistance from liturgical theology. In an admittedly surprising move, one that I myself would not have initially predicted, I have chosen to explore the work of Russian Orthodox liturgical theologian Alexander Schmemann in light of the challenges raised by Metz's theological project. Schmemann (d. 1983) produced a significant corpus of writings which comprise a major contribution to liturgical theology in this century. The main reason for my choosing Schmemann among other liturgical theologians is the passionate concern in his writings, not unlike that of Metz, for the Church's mission and viability at present. Schmemann shares with Metz not only a penchant for passionate prose and a clarity of insight on the fundamental topic of faith, but also some stimulating affinities with Metz's critical evaluation of the situation of the Church (its subjects, traditions, and institutions) in the late modern world. There are, as one might expect, strong differences between the two theologians

---

[9] See, for example, William R. Crockett, *Eucharist: Symbol of Transformation* (New York: Pueblo, 1989) 258; Klemens Richter, "Liturgical Reform as the Means for Church Renewal," *The Meaning of the Liturgy,* ed. Angelus A. Häussling, trans. Linda M. Maloney (Collegeville: The Liturgical Press, 1994) 119–20; and Power, *Unsearchable Riches,* 34, n. 27; 81, n. 21; 141, n. 18.

[10] Metz, *Faith in History and Society,* 77.

[11] See J. Matthew Ashley, *Interruptions: Mysticism, Politics, and Theology in the Work of Johann Baptist Metz* (Notre Dame, Ind.: University of Notre Dame Press, 1998).

as well. In my judgment, such are the makings for a feisty if not fruitful dialogue in Chapter 3.

That dialogue will, nonetheless, lead to the recognition that Metz and Schmemann need assistance from the wider field of scholarship concerning a concept crucial to both their theologies: anamnesis. In the fourth chapter, study of the early Christian and Jewish sources of the concept of anamnesis will seek to understand how the Church's liturgical commemoration of God's salvific deeds in history (especially in Jesus) allows for neither a timeless form of religious piety and theology nor a ritualism detached from the commerce of life in the world. I shall rely on the work of several Scripture scholars in order to weave the anamnetic strands of *remembrance* of the paschal mystery, *anticipation* of Christ's parousia, and the *present* call to ritual and ethical praxis. In the concluding chapter a closer investigation of the tensive relationship between anamnesis and eschatology will lead to further considerations about the dialectical character of the praxis of faith.

There is a certain awkwardness to writing in the abstract genre of a scholarly text about theologies critically committed to the particularities and contexts of the practice of faith. Indeed, as practical theologian Don Browning has argued, theory is never simply distinct from practice, no matter how much that may seem to be the case in an academic enterprise.[12] Thus, before moving into the theoretical dialogue between Metz's political theology and Schmemann's liturgical theology, I shall in Chapter 1 provide a brief introduction to the practical reform of the Church and its liturgy which the Second Vatican Council officially set in motion over thirty years ago. The council inaugurated an era of volatile change in the Church. In North America and Europe this change has perhaps been most evident to both Church members and wider society in the area of liturgical practice. Having studied both theology and anthropology at the graduate level, and possessing my own passionate concern for ecclesial reform, I would have liked to open this study with some form of my own participant-observation analysis of contemporary liturgy and parochial life in the United States. Unfortunately, such an undertaking was beyond the bounds of this project. Fortunately, however, in the recent past a study of fifteen American parishes was conducted and the data subjected to analysis by a group

---

[12] See Don S. Browning, *A Fundamental Practical Theology: Descriptive and Strategic Proposals* (Minneapolis: Fortress Press, 1991) 5–7, 47–9.

of theologians and one ritual theorist. In the first chapter, then, I shall avail myself of the published essays of that study in order to animate the ensuing dialogue between liturgical and political theology.

This book originated as my doctoral dissertation at Emory University, and I remain grateful to the professors who with great competence and compassion guided me in the work: Don Saliers (director), Rebecca Chopp, Theodore Runyon, and Walter Lowe. I had the opportunity to present pieces of the project's research at group sessions during the annual meetings of The College Theology Society, The Catholic Theological Society of America, and the North American Academy of Liturgy (N.A.A.L.). I am especially grateful to Kevin Seasoltz, O.S.B., who as convener of the liturgical theology seminar of the N.A.A.L. not only provided me the forum to present my material but also thereafter persistently encouraged me to pursue its publication. The Jesuit community at The Aquinas Center, University of Connecticut, Storrs, kindly welcomed me with office and living space for the better part of a summer as I undertook revising the manuscript for possible publication. My gratitude extends to the several people who read all or parts of the manuscript, but especially to my fellow Jesuits, Robert Daly, Roger Haight, and William Reiser, who took time and care to provide specific comments on content and style. The Department of Theology and The Institute of Religious Education and Pastoral Ministry at Boston College, under the leadership of Donald Dietrich and Claire Lowery, respectively, have provided support in numerous ways. To these and many friends, family members, and colleagues, whose numbers exceed what I dare list here, I give my heartfelt thanks.

Chapter 1

The Promise and Challenges in the Renewal of the Eucharistic Liturgy

THE COUNCIL'S VISION FOR THE LITURGY IN THE CHURCH

Sacrosanctum concilium, the Second Vatican Council's Constitution on the Sacred Liturgy, opens with the following statement:

"The sacred council has set out to impart an ever-increasing vigor to the Christian life of the faithful; to adapt more closely to the needs of our age those institutions which are subject to change; to encourage whatever can promote the union of all who believe in Christ; to strengthen whatever serves to call all of humanity into the church's fold."[1]

In decreeing at its second session in 1963 what would prove to be the first of sixteen documents, the council set the course not only for liturgical renewal but also for a broader vision of the Church itself. This concern with the nature and mission of the Church was already being debated in the form of a draft for a Dogmatic Constitution on the Church, *Lumen gentium,* which the council would ratify at its third session in the following year. The discussions and drafting of that and numerous other documents gave rise to the council fathers' decision also to produce a Pastoral Constitution on the Church in the Modern World. While *Lumen gentium* articulated the Church's mission in relation to all peoples, still the focus was on clarifying the distinctive roles of the hierarchy and laity and the variety of institutional structures whereby the Church is both the "People of God" and the "Mystical Body of Christ."

---

[1] All quotes from the Documents of Vatican II, translated from the original Latin into English, are taken from *Vatican Council II: Constitutions, Decrees, Declarations,* rev. trans., ed. Austin Flannery (Northport, N.Y.: Costello Publishing Co., 1996). Following conventional methods for citing Roman documents, this study shall give the name and paragraph number of the quoted document. The present quote is from *Sacrosanctum concilium,* no. 1.

The last of the council's documents, *Gaudium et spes*, on the other hand, undertook concertedly the pastoral agenda of both identifying the progress and troubles that peoples have realized in modernity and placing the Church at the service of the "modern world."[2]

The Constitution on the Sacred Liturgy provides explicit treatment of the relationship between the Church's sacramental worship and its life and mission in contemporary societies. While acknowledging that the "sacred liturgy is not the church's only activity"[3] and, moreover, highlighting the Church's mission of evangelization, *Sacrosanctum concilium* proceeds to one of its most crucial statements:

"Nevertheless, the liturgy is the summit toward which the activity of the church is directed; it is also the source from which all its power flows. For the goal of apostolic endeavor is that all who are made children of God by faith and Baptism should come together to praise God in the midst of his church, to take part in the sacrifice and to eat the Lord's Supper."[4]

Sacrosanctum concilium presents the liturgical practice of the Church as the source from which its members are able to engage the world to the glory of God and for the salvation of people. Divine worship and human sanctification, in turn, attain their greatest realization in this world in the Church's sacramental ritual. This tenth paragraph further identifies the Eucharist as holding pride of place and purpose in the liturgical economy of salvation, as does an earlier passage: "For the liturgy, through which 'the work of our redemption takes place,' especially in the divine sacrifice of the Eucharist, is supremely effective in enabling the faithful to express in their lives and portray to others the mystery of Christ and the real nature of the true church."[5] The document affirms a position long held by the officials of the Roman Catholic Church and a great number of its laity: the celebration of the Eucharist is the most crucial of all the Church's practices.

While thus affirming the Eucharist's priority in the life of the Church the council also acknowledged that the manner in which this crucial ritual was being performed (i.e., the Mass of Pius V) was in

---

[2] See *Gaudium et spes*, no. 2.
[3] *Sacrosanctum concilium*, no. 9.
[4] *Sacrosanctum concilium*, no. 10.
[5] *Sacrosanctum concilium*, no. 2.

need of extensive revision. An entire chapter of *Sacrosanctum concilium* is dedicated to the reform and simplification of the eucharistic liturgy, with a view to both removing burdensome accretions and recovering other crucial elements from early Christian traditions "which were lost through the vicissitudes of history."[6] The purpose of the revision is clearly stated at the outset of those decrees: "that devout and active participation by the faithful may be more easily achieved."[7] This goal for the Eucharist reiterates the council's fundamental principle for the promotion of the Church's liturgical life:

"It is very much the wish of the church that all the faithful should be led to take that full, conscious, and active part in liturgical celebrations which is demanded by the very nature of the liturgy, and to which the Christian people, 'a chosen race, a royal priesthood, a holy nation, a redeemed people' (1 Pet 2:9, 4-5) have a right and to which they are bound by reason of their Baptism."[8]

While practical (pastoral) in character, this statement contributes to a theological argument that pervades the constitution, namely, that the viability of the Christian life depends intrinsically upon participation in the Church's sacramental rituals, especially the Eucharist. The "nature of the liturgy" places a demand upon all believers, which demand is nothing less than their birthright and the means by which they realize in the context of this world and their place in history the full dignity of that (baptismal) birth.

As if such theological claims for the liturgy's authority, for which a long tradition can be traced especially in the Christian East but also the West, were not enough, *Sacrosanctum concilium* makes a further assertion about the present moment in history:

"Enthusiasm for the promotion and restoration of the sacred liturgy is rightly held to be a sign of the providential dispositions of God in our time, and as a movement of the holy Spirit in his church. It is today a distinguishing mark of the life of the church, and, indeed, of the whole tenor of contemporary religious thought and action."[9]

---

[6] *Sacrosanctum concilium*, no. 50.
[7] *Sacrosanctum concilium*, no. 50.
[8] *Sacrosanctum concilium*, no. 14.
[9] *Sacrosanctum concilium*, no. 43.

The council thus claimed to have discerned the activity of God's Spirit and will for the Church. Commitment to the theory and practice of the liturgy, to its renewal and adaptation for the modern world "in the light of sound tradition,"[10] was henceforth to be seen as a sign of the Church's faithfulness to God, as a response to God's gracious desire for God's people. This act of discernment on the council's part was, in effect, an official confirmation of the work that the liturgical movement, based in Benedictine monasteries in Germany, France, and the Low Countries, had been pursuing for over one hundred years—a combined effort of scholarly study of early Christian liturgical traditions and the performance of experimental rites based on that scholarship.[11]

As soon as the council ratified *Sacrosanctum concilium* in 1963 many dioceses in the United States began immediate and, thus, necessarily piecemeal changes in their parishes' celebrations of the eucharistic liturgy, setting in motion the complex endeavor of altering their most centrally symbolic ritual activity.[12] While promulgation of the Mass of

---

[10] *Sacrosanctum concilium*, no. 4.

[11] For concise histories of the liturgical movement, along with current bibliographies, see Keith F. Pecklers, *The Unread Vision: The Liturgical Movement in the United States of America: 1926–1955* (Collegeville: The Liturgical Press, 1998) 1–23; Virgil C. Funk, "The Liturgical Movement," *The New Dictionary of Sacramental Worship*, ed. Peter E. Fink (Collegeville: The Liturgical Press, 1990) 695–715; and H. Ellsworth Chandlee, "The Liturgical Movement," *The New Westminster Dictionary of Liturgy and Worship*, ed. J. G. Davies (Philadelphia: Westminster Press, 1986) 307–14.

[12] Writing in the middle of the 1960s, Jesuit commentator C. J. McNaspy provided the following enthusiastic evaluation of the impact which the sudden and rapid changes in the liturgy had upon American Catholicism:

"In a very short time after [*Sacrosanctum concilium*'s] promulgation, Catholics began to participate in a more meaningful, more communal celebration of the Holy Sacrifice. This had the added effect of dramatizing in a concrete way (a sacramental way, one might say) the reality of Church renewal, or *aggiornamento*. The Council quickly ceased to be something remote, occupying the bishops gathered in Rome and the newspaper columnists who tried to give it vivid treatment. The Constitution made a difference right in the parishes. By sharing actively in worship, even the ordinary Catholic began to take part in the great work launched by Pope John and continued by Pope Paul."

C. J. McNaspy, "Liturgy: Introduction," *The Documents of Vatican II*, gen. ed. Walter M. Abbott, trans. and ed. Joseph Gallagher (New York: America Press, 1966) 135.

Pope Paul VI in 1969 brought comprehensive and official form to the liturgy's renewal, the daunting complexity of the endeavor remained—the effort of holding respect for religious tradition(s) together with openness to a modern society characterized by an ambivalence (heightened in the late 1960s) toward tradition in whatever cultural forms it might take. Moreover, much of the "renewed" liturgy was a recovery of traditions long suppressed or forgotten in the Roman Church, including perhaps most notably the roles and relations of various liturgical ministers and the proper functions of the entire people (the laity) in the liturgical celebration. Difficult as the task might prove to be, Vatican II had set the local churches on this course of renewal and *aggiornamento* with the conviction that God's Spirit was animating the endeavor.

EVALUATING POST-CONCILIAR LITURGICAL PRACTICE

More than three decades have passed since pastoral implementation of the council's vision for the liturgy began. In continuity with the earlier liturgical movement, liturgical scholarship in this period has sought to establish normative claims about liturgy based on historical studies of the rites. In addition to this scholarly service to the council's mandate for the retrieval of buried treasures from ancient tradition, liturgical theologians began in the 1980s to publish works giving direct and central attention to the practice of the reformed rites in the modern context. In their commitment to the council's understanding of "sound" tradition as the meeting of ancient doctrine and practices with contemporary circumstances, liturgical theologians have had to enlist the resources of scholars specializing in the analysis of the wider contemporary context: social scientists, philosophers, historians, as well as theologians who have concertedly worked with those disciplines. Attention to actual liturgical practice in contemporary contexts has, of course, made the work of liturgical theologians more complex, requiring decisions about not only the methodology for accumulating data but also the theoretical (theological) criteria and commitments they bring to the data.[13] One relatively recent study of American

[13] For a first-person account of one liturgical theologian's wrestling with the theoretical presuppositions that he and his colleagues have endorsed in assessing contemporary American Catholic practice, along with a constructive proposal, see Regis A. Duffy, *An American Emmaus: Faith and Sacrament in the American Culture* (New York: Crossroad, 1995) 9–13, 25–32, 54–67, 72–88.

liturgy resulted in a body of essays that reveal major questions and challenges liturgical theologians face in developing theological theory adequate to and in service of the current practice of tradition.

As the twenty-fifth anniversary of *Sacrosanctum concilium*'s promulgation approached in 1988, four centers for liturgical studies in the United States undertook a cooperative effort to evaluate the extent of progress being made in the renewal of the celebration of Sunday Mass. The centers identified fifteen parishes (all English-speaking) around the country committed to the Vatican II reforms. Research teams collected background information on each parish, described the parish's liturgical planning and programming, and had two observers attend a Sunday liturgy and produce reports of their own descriptions of the liturgy, interviews with two lay participants, and interviews with the presider, the parish liturgy director, and the director of music. These reports were compiled into what the project's directors called an "insight stimulation" study, an 802-page document characterized not by statistical data but by descriptions of liturgical spaces and celebrations, comments by participants, and observations by the researchers. The "insight stimulation" was then directed to nine scholars (mostly theologians) who each studied the data from a particular theoretical perspective so as "to attempt to judge the degree of success or lack thereof of the liturgical reforms of the council in American parishes."[14] At a conference at Georgetown University the theorists presented papers which were later published as a book entitled *The Awakening Church.*

In evaluating the data they had received the theologians of *The Awakening Church* project did not have to concern themselves with the question of whether the formal structures of the renewal of the Mass which the council envisioned were being realized, since the parishes studied were among those most strongly committed to that effort.[15] Therefore, their criteria for judging the "degree of success or lack

---

[14] *The Awakening Church: Twenty-five Years of Liturgical Renewal*, ed. Lawrence J. Madden (Collegeville: The Liturgical Press, 1992) 1.

[15] An article based on observation of a larger number of English-speaking Roman Catholic parishes in the United States confirms the general appraisal that the structural elements of the Mass of Paul VI have been put into practice throughout the country. The 1981–82 University of Notre Dame Study of Catholic Parish Life included participant-observer studies of seventy Sunday liturgies in thirty-six parishes distributed among six regions. In evaluating the reports of that fieldwork, liturgical theologian Mark Searle states the following:

thereof" in the American Catholic liturgical renewal lie in fundamental (and at times tacit) positions each author takes concerning such issues as: the relationship between liturgy—or even "religion" in general—and society; the question of what liturgical "participation" actually means; the relation between the Sunday liturgy and the daily lives of believers; the importance of establishing, affirming, and augmenting the laity's ministries in the Church; and the predominant characteristics of middle-class society and its members. The collected essays betray marked differences in how the theologians approach and even prioritize those sorts of questions and, thus, the "success" of the reformed liturgy. Most notable for the purposes of our present study are two issues: (1) the middle-class ethos of the English-speaking American parish and (2) the qualities and functions of symbolic ritual action.

One particular set of practices evidenced in the fifteen parishes reported gave rise to a variety of assessments on the part of the theologians. Comparison and contrast of their reactions to this data provides insight into similarities and differences in the theorists' appraisal of the impact of middle-class sensibilities upon liturgical celebration and, moreover, the relation between the Church's liturgy and the economy of salvation taking place in the wider world. The practices noted are those whereby people are made to feel welcomed at the liturgy, personally greeted or given a sense of belonging. One such set of practices cluster around the beginning of the liturgy and include some combination of ministers who greet arriving worshipers as they enter the building; lectors, commentators, and/or cantors who "introduce" the liturgy with words of welcome to the assembly; and, in some cases, the invitation for

---

"First and foremost, it is worth recording the well-known fact that, two decades after the promulgation of the Constitution on the Liturgy, the celebration of the eucharist in Roman Catholic churches has undergone a complete transformation. Latin has disappeared, the lectionary is universally in use, a homily is preached at almost every Sunday Mass (it was omitted at two Saturday evening Masses), the *Ordo Missae* is observed more or less intact, and the vast majority of participants go to communion. As the recent [1985] Roman Synod observed: 'the liturgical renewal is the most visible fruit of the whole conciliar effort.'"

Mark Searle, "The Notre Dame Study of Catholic Parish Life," *Worship* 60 (July 1986) 316.

See also Jim Castelli and Joseph Gremillion, *The Emerging Parish: The Notre Dame Study of Catholic Life Since Vatican II* (New York: Harper & Row, 1987).

all to turn to people around them and introduce themselves or extend some greeting. Another noted practice is the ritual exchange of peace, which some of the parishioners interviewed described as the highpoint of the liturgy. Finally, many parishes hold some form of a social with refreshments (most often coffee and doughnuts) after the liturgy.

Systematic theologian Roger Haight evaluates this and all the data of the report from the perspective of Karl Rahner's theology of grace, which he identifies as the Second Vatican Council's theology as well. From the Rahnerian theory of the unthematic presence of God in the lives of all people Haight draws as axiomatic the universal and egalitarian qualities of this "grace," which "must imply that the ordinary and most radical means for responding to God's grace consists in the everyday events that make up any given person's personal history. . . . Every other manifestation of spirituality and response to God derives from there and leads back to it."[16] Just mentioning the "social" aspect of grace, Haight goes on to say that Christians thematize or make grace conscious through the "primary tangible historical symbol" of "the event and whole life of Jesus."[17]

On the basis of this theory of grace Haight gleans from the study's data several theses, the first of which is that liturgy, by nature, is people bringing grace into an assembly. The data from which Haight infers this thesis are (1) the extent to which "welcoming," to the point of becoming a "ministry of hospitality," has become a distinctive element of these parishes' liturgies, and (2) the social gatherings before and after the liturgy which in some parishes "are no longer really the before and after of the liturgy but parts of it."[18] Haight makes the inference from these data to his theological principle in the following way:

"There are, of course, many intentionalities at work in these new practices. But from a theological perspective one has to be a recognition of any and every person, even the outside visitor, as one whose being and value are defined by his or her being an object, subject, and bearer of God's grace."[19]

[16] Roger Haight, "Liturgy as Community Consciousness of Grace," *The Awakening Church: Twenty-five Years of Liturgical Renewal*, ed. Lawrence J. Madden (Collegeville: The Liturgical Press, 1992) 28.
[17] Ibid., 29.
[18] Ibid., 35.
[19] Ibid., 31.

At this point one is left asking on what "level" of Haight's theology of grace this perspective is being exercised and, moreover, by whom. Is Haight arguing that people thus engaged in welcoming and gathering are explicitly conscious of others as grace-bearing objects and subjects? Or is this not more often a subconscious awareness? Perhaps this "theological perspective" only occurs thematically at the "level" at which Haight performs his theology. There is a risk in the abstractness of Haight's theology in that it seems to struggle in the effort to let the data speak for themselves. The other "many intentionalities at work in these new practices" require attention in a theological exercise that claims to wrestle with the actual practices of Christians at liturgy.

Liturgical theologian Aidan Kavanagh performs a radically different assessment of the same data, at least in part on the basis of a different starting point for his theological (and social) analysis. Kavanagh approaches the "gathering rites" which have developed in the parishes in terms of the structure and elements of the official liturgy itself. Far from affirming the tendency of the informal gatherings before and after the liturgy to blur the boundaries between the time of worship and the time of "everyday life," Kavanagh perceives in these a "gathering syndrome" that threatens fundamental aspects of liturgy's purpose and function. On the basis of a brief historical review of the origins and development of the entry rites of the growing churches of the fourth to eighth centuries, Kavanagh analyzes these rites as primarily processional and prayerful, placing the assembled believers in a radical stance of obedience before God for the messianic benefit of the world. Kavanagh judges the welcoming activities reported in the study as countering and, he fears, overshadowing the "traditional and deeply theological attitude" of liturgical *eisodos* or *introit*:

"There is no prayer or Godward direction in this new 'rite of gathering'; it is a set of activities not ritually very different from the same procedures used when persons of middle-class society gather for any purpose. If it bespeaks any ecclesiology, it seems to be a therapeutic one devoid of any sense of separation from ordinariness; to put it in terms used in the study, the procedure is, in fact, *horizontal* rather than vertical."[20]

---

[20] Aidan Kavanagh, "Reflections on the Study from the Viewpoint of Liturgical History," *The Awakening Church: Twenty-five Years of Liturgical Renewal*, ed. Lawrence J. Madden (Collegeville: The Liturgical Press, 1992) 87.

In so analyzing the situation Kavanagh introduces the other criterion for his evaluation of the reported parish liturgies, namely, the extent to which various practices introduce and impose middle-class attitudes and patterns of social performance and organization upon liturgical celebration.

As Kavanagh reflects further upon the phenomenon of the "gatherings" that precede and follow the Sunday liturgy he perceives further encroachment of middle-class society upon the overall liturgical performance, as well as what this portends. First, Kavanagh notes the number of different ministries that are mentioned in relation to these activities and wonders, despite their appearance of spontaneity, about the extent to which these roles and actions force social conventions upon those who come to worship. Second, he ventures to say that all the extra activity at either end of the liturgy proper belies a distaste for the official and rule-governed characteristics of religious performance. Religion needs to be made more informal, vivacious, and bright through the efforts of cheerful, welcoming presiders and liturgy committees that introduce various artistic and dramatic innovations.[21] Kavanagh perceives in all this the triumph of middle-class culture and a probable reason for why poorer and non-white Roman Catholics in the United States are turning elsewhere. Meanwhile, the parishes are stuck perpetuating what is already around them: "Liberality *can* turn into a subtle form of tyranny, manipulating people into approved conformities to social convention rather than liberating them by some sharp-edged counterculturalism. I see very little that is countercultural in the parish liturgies reported in the study."[22] Whereas Haight prescinds from any form of social analysis as he theorizes about the personal and interpersonal characteristics of the grace actualized in liturgy, Kavanagh basically posits the mores of middle-class society as a threat to the future viability of liturgy in the United States. Since *leitourgia* is a work for the benefit of the people, the depletion of liturgy can only result in a grave loss to the society which it would serve. The society (the "world") is left to itself.

[21] Concern over a lost sense of transcendence in the contemporary liturgy remains important for many theologians. See Stanislaus Campbell, "The Sense of Transcendence in Liturgy: What Is Appropriate for Engagement in Mystery?" *Liturgical Ministry* 8 (Summer 1999) 123–35.

[22] Kavanagh, "Reflections on the Study from the Viewpoint of Liturgical History," 88.

Kavanagh, however, does not directly address what is so problematic, perhaps sinful (in theological terms), about middle-class society. The object of the "sharp counterculturalism" for which he calls is only implied throughout his essay.[23]

Systematic theologian Monika Hellwig assesses the same data primarily in terms of the Roman Catholic Church itself as a society in need of transformation and critique, although she does not neglect the Church's mission in relation to wider society. Hellwig understands Vatican II as having set an agenda for "a more vital, collegial, active, and prophetic ecclesiology."[24] Collegiality is a matter of shifting the Church from clerical domination to lay involvement which, with regard to sacramental worship, corrects the view of clergy as doing the primary work of the Church and laity receiving the benefits therefrom. Hellwig considers the act of gathering for liturgy to be the "concrete event" whereby people "become aware that they are the Church."[25] That lay people should be the ministers of this act of gathering Hellwig finds to be a far more powerful proclamation of the people's self-identification as the Church than any sermon that could be preached on the topic. Hellwig lauds the "extensive teamwork" taking place in all areas of planning and implementing the liturgies of local parishes, noting nonetheless that in many places a small circle of laity are involved and, thus, form a sort of "paraclergy" (a parallel to Kavanagh's fear of a new form of elitism among liturgical participants).[26] Taken altogether, Hellwig does not consider these developments to be a concession to modern democratic sensibilities but, rather, a redemptive alternative pattern to the often dominating or controlling relational patterns in society.

While churches are becoming "diaconal" communities wherein the laity serve each other, Hellwig finds them much slower to broaden

[23] This is not, by any means, to say that Kavanagh has not provided description and analysis of middle-class society elsewhere. In the first part of his attempt at a comprehensive liturgical theology Kavanagh continuously criticizes suburban American culture, but does so on a (scathing) rhetorical level. See Aidan Kavanagh, *On Liturgical Theology* (New York: Pueblo, 1984) 1–69.

[24] Monika K. Hellwig, "Twenty-five Years of a Wakening Church: Liturgy and Ecclesiology," *The Awakening Church: Twenty-five Years of Liturgical Renewal,* ed. Lawrence J. Madden (Collegeville: The Liturgical Press, 1992) 67.

[25] Ibid., 56.

[26] Ibid., 57.

this sense of service to wider society. Needed is a "political under-standing of the redemptive and ecclesial task," which must include "the understanding that their faith and Church membership may pit them against prevailing national and cultural values."[27] Hellwig con-siders the current practice and reflection on liturgical worship to be a key hindrance to that transformation:

"In the parishes of the survey, just as in the current practice of theol-ogy and catechesis of the Church at large, there still seems to be the sense that liturgical worship is the real business of the Church and that healing, reconciliation, and the service of practical human needs in all their forms are optional additions for those with that particular charism or inclination."[28]

Hellwig then calls for further reflection, by means of the liturgy, on the nature of ministries in the Church. That call amounts to an inquiry into how liturgical practice forms not only Christians' identities as agents of reconciling service but also their fundamental perceptions about their society and culture. These questions point to the second issue with which this present study approaches *The Awakening Church* essays: the functions and qualities of Christian symbolic ritual action.

Liturgical theologian John Baldovin also notes problems in the way American Catholic worship does not foster the mission of the Church into the world. He does so, however, not from the perspective of how the liturgy gives rise to *ministries* for the laity but, rather, by consider-ing the type of sacramental and symbolic sensibilities liturgical prac-tice fosters. Combing the study's many interviews, Baldovin searches

[27] Ibid., 58, 67.

[28] Ibid., 66. Social ethicist Peter Henriot finds Hellwig's remarks here appli-cable to *The Awakening Church* project itself:

"There is a disturbing absence of attention in this colloquium to the link be-tween liturgy and social concerns. It is a key question to be studied in any thorough examination of parishes, yet it is inadequately represented in the as-sessment of liturgical renewal, done in fifteen places across the country. The question was not explicitly asked in the interview instrument, nor was it ex-plicitly reflected on in the eight major presentations."

Peter J. Henriot, "Liturgy and Social Concerns," *The Awakening Church: Twenty-five Years of Liturgical Renewal,* ed. Lawrence J. Madden (Collegeville: The Liturgical Press, 1992) 117.

for some impression of a "general sacramental vision" amongst the liturgical leaders and other participants. The recurrent words and phrases he notes include: "warmth," "comfortable," "community," "to feel good," "closeness," and "togetherness."[29] These reflections lead him to be uneasy with the fact that the majority of the people interviewed named the Sign of Peace and/or holding hands during the recitation of the Lord's Prayer as the high point of the Sunday liturgy. Baldovin realizes that analysis of these data must take into account the shift away from an individualistic view of salvation long regnant in Roman Catholicism. He perceives, however, another sociocultural phenomenon at work: Americans' feelings of social isolation. Nevertheless, the expectation of liturgy itself to create a sense of community where it does not otherwise exist confuses the relationship between liturgy's symbolic action and daily life, to the detriment of both:

"One of the results is that people are tempted to look to liturgy for immediate gratification and that when communal identity is accentuated to such a degree, the element of mission is underemphasized. Overattention to intimacy and warmth also inhibits worshipers from experiencing sacramental action as God's gift rather than their own creation. Part and parcel of the overblown expectations that are brought to worship is the perverse notion that worship is somehow our good idea in the first place."[30]

Drawing on Newman's concept of "illative sense," Baldovin argues that liturgy entails "a sense of 'thatness,' an intuition of the inexplicable but nonetheless real truth of the object of belief, which demands commitment as well as intellectual agreement."[31] The diminishment

---

[29] John F. Baldovin, "Pastoral Liturgical Reflections on the Study," *The Awakening Church: Twenty-five Years of Liturgical Renewal,* ed. Lawrence J. Madden (Collegeville: The Liturgical Press, 1992) 104.

[30] Ibid., 104–5. In an even more recent essay, Richard Gaillardetz argues that the sort of individualism and privatism pervasive in middle-class American parishes tends to reduce the concept of communal "solidarity" to "warmth, informality, and intimacy" and results in a "'thin theory' of community [that] could not possibly support the liturgical reforms of the Council." Richard R. Gaillardetz, "North American Culture and the Liturgical Life of the Church: The Separation of the Quests for Transcendence and Community," *Worship* 68 (September 1994) 409–10.

[31] Baldovin, "Pastoral Liturgical Reflections on the Study," 112.

of that sense of mystery in liturgical practice serves neither Church nor society well.

Don Saliers, a liturgical theologian known for his multidisciplinary approach to the question of symbolism, pursues the same issue:

"It is the otherness of symbol and the demand of the liturgy itself as symbolic common action that I miss most in the gestalt of the data in the survey. The overwhelming impression is that these communities have focused on the 'expressive' dimensions of participation rather than the inner relations between the formative and expressive power of primary symbol."[32]

Saliers' introduction of the notion of "primary symbol" brings into focus Kavanagh and Baldovin's concerns, which he himself shares. Primary to the Sunday liturgy is the mystery of God's self-gift in Christ to humanity and humanity's response through ritual words and actions of praise and thanks, penitence and intercession, on be-half of the world. For so much attention to be given to gestures of hospitality and friendliness, while few of those interviewed found participation in the Eucharistic Prayer memorable, is an indication to Saliers that the "demand and the otherness of the primary symbols," the "sense of history and mysterion . . . embedded in the ritual ac-tions of the liturgy," are severely diminished in the liturgical practice and reflection in these American parishes.[33]

Saliers wisely does not assume that the deeper levels of symbolic participation were utterly absent from the liturgies observed and the participants interviewed. An adequate theoretical appreciation for the complexity and multivalence of ritual's words and symbolic ac-tions must guide the manner in which one performs a participant-observation study, both in terms of description and analysis of a given liturgy itself and the types of questions one directly asks its partici-pants. In other words, Saliers is gently suspicious of some of the types of questions that the observers in the fifteen parishes asked of the par-

---

[32] Don E. Saliers, "Symbol in Liturgy, Liturgy as Symbol: The Domestication of Liturgical Experience," *The Awakening Church: Twenty-five Years of Liturgical Renewal*, ed. Lawrence J. Madden (Collegeville: The Liturgical Press, 1992) 71. See also Don E. Saliers, *Worship as Theology: Foretaste of Glory Divine* (Nashville: Abingdon Press, 1994) 139–53.

[33] Saliers, "Symbol in Liturgy, Liturgy as Symbol," 72, 76.

ticipants they interviewed and the elements of the liturgical performances to which they more closely attended:

"My point simply is this: We should be cautious about assigning too
much valence to the experienced 'immediacies of feeling.' Even when
asked, 'What was most meaningful, or what were you feeling during
the Communion rite?' we can only speak from a first level of awareness. . . . Thus, immediacy of feeling must be distinguished from
depth of emotion."[34]

Saliers thus touches upon the many difficulties and challenges faced
by ritual theorists (which cannot be underestimated, nor rehearsed
here).[35] Pertinent to this present study is Saliers' indication of the importance of theoretical assumptions or questions with which an ob-
server of the liturgy goes about the task. More specifically, it is notable
that the people studying the fifteen parishes were equipped with
questions that tended to yield analyses in terms of immediate feelings, friendliness, efficiency, and logical coherence. In other words,
not only the parishioners described in the fifteen field studies but also
the liturgical theorists who planned and implemented those studies
seem to have dispositions which impede their fuller attentiveness to
the "otherness" and "demanding" qualities within religious ritual
symbols and their performance.[36]

---

[34] Ibid., 77–8.

[35] For an introduction to methodological problems faced by ritual theorists,
one felicitously provided in the context of the current project being cited, see
Ronald L. Grimes, "Liturgical Renewal and Ritual Criticism," *The Awakening
Church: Twenty-five Years of Liturgical Renewal,* ed. Lawrence J. Madden (Collegeville: The Liturgical Press, 1992) 11–25. For further study of the burgeoning field of ritual studies, see the following of Grimes' works: *Beginnings in
Ritual Studies,* rev. ed. (Columbia: University of South Carolina Press, 1995);
Research in Ritual Studies (Metuchen, N.J.: Scarecrow Press and the American
Theological Library Association, 1985); and *Ritual Criticism* (Columbia: University of South Carolina Press, 1990). See also Catherine Bell, *Ritual: Perspectives and Dimensions* (New York: Oxford University Press, 1997).

[36] In an essay comprised of observations about the teaching (primarily in
seminaries) of theological and practical aspects of liturgy in the North American context, liturgical historian James White notes the dissonance between
what professors of liturgical theology and American parishioners hold to be
of greatest importance in the Sunday celebration:

Curtailing this selective rehearsal of *The Awakening Church* essays, this present study asks: How does one explain the seemingly deficient symbolic perception on the part of the American Catholics observed and interviewed? Are some of these theologians' awarenesses and criticisms of the middle-class ethos of the parishes related to the people's apparent resistance to being confronted by an otherness or non-identity in the words and actions of the liturgy? It would seem that the Second Vatican Council's agendas of both openness and adaptation to modern society and the recovery of crucial elements of ancient Christian liturgical traditions have not realized equal degrees of success. Indeed, one gets the impression that modern society to some extent directs the adaptation of the liturgy and, thus, suppresses the recovery of traditions.[37] To the extent that this appears to be the case, how does one go about evaluating both that phenomenon itself and its relevance to theological reflection?

AN INVITATION TO THEOLOGICAL INVESTIGATION

From that welter of questions two key issues emerge. The first concerns the relationship between theology—in this case, liturgical theology—and the societal context in which it is performed—in this case, North American middle-class society. In the next chapter I shall rehearse the work of Johann Baptist Metz, among whose unique contri-

---

"There is indeed much bad news for liturgists in the forum *The Awakening Church* (The Liturgical Press, 1992) which shows how little concern Roman Catholic laity have in the type of questions that clergy are trained to answer. Nothing seems of less interest than the Eucharistic prayer, the subject of the greatest amount of liturgical scholarship. Much seems to focus on the importance of being a community, of doing together whatever is done—and it may not matter greatly what that is. Some respondents even spoke of the priest doing his 'magic' at the altar. But few neglected the significance of being together in church."

James F. White, "Forum: Some Lessons in Liturgical Pedagogy," *Worship* 68 (September 1994) 446–7. White pursues a similar line of argument in "How Do We Know It Is Us?" *Liturgy and the Moral Self: Humanity at Full Stretch Before God,* ed. E. Byron Anderson and Bruce T. Morrill (Collegeville: The Liturgical Press, 1998) 55–65.

[37] Henriot states the problem in terms of the difference between "authentic enculturation" of the liturgy and "dangerous acculturation." See Henriot, "Liturgy and Social Concerns," 119.

butions to contemporary theology has been critical analysis of the middle-class subject of theology and modern theology's failure to respond adequately to the challenges that late modern, capitalist, technological society poses to theology and Christianity itself. Metz's theology will point toward the second key issue, namely, the theological characteristics of Christian liturgy that both ground its relation to the world and establish it as the medium wherein faith is manifested and known as redemptive for the world. These questions were of great importance to Alexander Schmemann, whose liturgical theology we shall explore in Chapter 3. Here, as a transition into the following chapter, I shall briefly introduce the scope of Metz's theological project, indicating its theoretical relevance to the issues we have raised at the outset of this study.

Metz is widely known as the Roman Catholic leader in the field of political theology. While certain concepts or themes in his work have been cited in numerous areas of contemporary theology, Metz has been frustrated by the general perception of political theology as just another theme or topic to be added on to theology, rather than as a fundamental theology. Metz bears some of the responsibility for that problem himself, insofar as his writing has been largely fragmentary in nature, always pointing toward a more comprehensive treatment. I find this, however, to be one of the attractive qualities of his work. Its provocative, suggestive qualities, as well as the poignantly honest autobiographical thread that intermittently appears throughout, draw the reader into the problems he is pursuing and altogether lend themselves to the sort of rehearsal I shall undertake in Chapter 2. In other words, in trying to grasp more comprehensively what Metz is arguing for and against in theology, one comes to greater theoretical insight into his work not for its own sake but for the light it sheds on the concerns that the reader places in front of the texts. It is in this way that Metz's practical fundamental theology promises benefits for liturgical theology.

Fundamental theology serves other subdisciplines in the theological academy by methodically reflecting both on the nature of divine revelation as conveyed through Scripture and tradition and on the conditions which dispose human beings to receiving that revelation.[38] Concerning revelation, Metz argues that there is a foundational

---

[38] See Gerald O'Collins, *Fundamental Theology* (New York: Paulist Press, 1981) 22.

character to Christian faith that is practical. This requires taking with utmost seriousness the scriptural claim that God really is a God of history. As opposed to perceptions of God as a "pure" concept, biblical tradition reveals a God with a definite history, a God whom people can know only by practically committing themselves to God's vision for that history. Theology must thereby employ what Metz calls an anamnestic form of reason, rational argumentation that cannot dispense with remembering the content of salvation history as a history of suffering that cries out for justice. This commitment to narrative and praxis is what characterizes political theology. Given his identification of this "narrative-practical character" as foundational to Judeo-Christian tradition, Metz insists that all Christian theology is necessarily (fundamentally) political theology.[39]

The other task of fundamental theology is to investigate how it is that people are able to receive revelation. In this regard Metz finds the Neo-Scholastic and transcendental-idealist theologies of the twentieth century to have proven themselves inadequate. By proceeding abstractly with questions about the anthropological conditions for religious belief, both erroneously presume the existence of the religious human subject, that is, that the practice of faith is indeed of central importance to modern people. As a corrective, Metz makes fundamental to his theology the question of whether and what sort of religion is of actual importance to people today. Heavily influenced by the critical theory of the early Frankfurt School, Metz has identified a pervasive worldview in modernity, one based on the forms of rationality specific to technology and market capitalism, that powerfully conditions the effort of the modern subject to be a religious subject. It is this situation that political, post-idealist theology takes into account. In so doing, there is an apologetic character to the work, addressed not only to nonbelievers but, perhaps more primarily, to believers themselves. With these introductory comments in mind, then, we turn to Metz's political theology as a practical fundamental theology engaging issues of key concern to liturgical theology today.

---

[39] Johann Baptist Metz, *A Passion for God: The Mystical-Political Dimension of Christianity*, trans. J. Matthew Ashley (New York: Paulist Press, 1998) 185, n. 8; see also 190, n. 19.

Chapter 2

Johann Baptist Metz's
Political Theology of the Subject

INTRODUCTION

The pressing question to which this study has arrived concerns whether and to what extent the liturgy is able to shape the life of the Church and its mission in the modern world (as envisioned by the Second Vatican Council). More specifically, can the liturgical practice of the Church actually have such an impact in the social and cultural contexts of the North Atlantic societies, which are the historical origin and ongoing center of late modernity? Liturgical theologians, in other words, cannot think abstractly about the relationship between the elements and overall economy of the eucharistic celebration and the participants in those actions. The council's vision of the liturgy as the source and summit of the Church's life can only become a reality if the liturgy is the source and summit of the lives of actual Christians. While sharing in and seeking to promote the council's desire that the Church, as the sacrament of the risen Christ, be a light and a servant to the world, liturgical theologians must recognize and grapple with the reality that the members of the Church are themselves subjects of the social, economic, political, and intellectual systems of that modern world. To pursue this line of inquiry with specific reference to the Church in North Atlantic societies is to respond to the challenge and resources of political theologian Johann Baptist Metz.

In his attempt to establish political theology as a fundamental practical theology Metz argues that it must be a "political theology of the subject."[1] Metz makes his claim as a corrective to the transcendental fundamental theology of his mentor and friend, Karl Rahner. Metz

---

[1] Johann Baptist Metz, *Faith in History and Society: Toward a Practical Fundamental Theology*, trans. David Smith (New York: Seabury Press, 1980) 30. This is an often-awkward translation of the second of five editions of Metz's *Glaube in Geschichte und Gesellschaft*.

considers Rahner's theological anthropology to be the finest exercise in exploring the depths of the "formal Enlightenment or contemporary principle of the subject."[2] In systematically reflecting upon such abstract concepts as existence, person, subject, or "man," Rahner's theology is the height of the belated achievement in which Roman Catholic theology finally responds to the transcendental philosophy initiated by Immanuel Kant. However, the problem is the level of abstraction. Modern theology has failed to ask whether such a religious subject actually exists, that is, whether or to what extent actual people in modern society approach their lives in that society on the basis and priority of the Christian concepts of reason, freedom, and autonomy. Given the extent to which this is not the case in capitalist technological society, "the breakthrough of the new man or middle-class citizen" constitutes an "extreme crisis" for the Church and theology. Theology has failed to grasp "that religion no longer belongs to the social constitution of the identity of the subject, but is rather added to it."[3]

Metz's basic, general evaluation of the middle-class practice of religion (bürgerliche Religion) would indeed seem to amount to a crisis for Church's liturgical renewal, especially with regard to the council's vision of the eucharistic liturgy as the source and summit of the Church's life. Metz is arguing that liturgical theologians must be aware of how that message would sound in the ears of Christian citizens of modern capitalist societies. Do they identify themselves with "the Church's life"? If so, what is the scope of that life? While this line of inquiry into the contemporary social conditions for believers figures prominently throughout Metz's writings from the 1970s to the present, he brought it into clearest conceptual focus in his most noted book, *Faith in History and Society*. This study shall proceed, then, with a rehearsal of the six "central elements" by which Metz performs a theological criticism of middle-class religion in that text. Metz understands his task as a "theological enlightenment of the Enlightenment," that is,

---

[2] Ibid., 32.

[3] Ibid., 33. Elsewhere in his writings Metz makes a similar point and presses its implications: "More and more, Catholicism itself has become [in Europe] a form of bourgeois religion in which 'Christian values' arch over a bourgeois identity without really affecting it in terms of a possible transformation or a promised fulfillment." Johann Baptist Metz, *The Emergent Church: The Future of Christianity in a Post-Bourgeois World*, trans. Peter Mann (New York: Crossroad, 1987) 76; see also 83.

a reexamination of the Enlightenment in terms of the actual socio-historical situation for religion which has resulted from the convergence of the Enlightenment's principles of human reason, freedom, and autonomy with the emergence of the middle-class in capitalist society.[4] Rehearsal of Metz's critical agenda will lead into a selective treatment of his constructive project, whereby he seeks to establish Christian faith as a praxis of mysticism and politics. Those considerations will invite initial points for dialogue with liturgical theology.

THEOLOGICAL CRITIQUE OF MIDDLE-CLASS RELIGION

Privatization

Metz considers privatization to be the most important aspect of the crisis caused by the Enlightenment. While the Enlightenment's distinction between public and private spheres (through the abolition of religiously sanctioned feudal and absolutist socioeconomic structures) contributed to a more humane society, the concept has developed into problematic proportions: "The way of life of the middle-class citizen is ultimately contained within the concept of 'private.'"[5] This is due to the fact that social values are regulated by the (market's) principle of exchange: production, trade, consumption. All other values, many previously considered integral to society, function in the private domain of individual freedom. The basis of such freedom, however, is the possession of property. Religion, with its traditions, is no longer a

---

[4] Metz, *Faith in History and Society,* 34. Here I must note that Metz has acknowledged the distinctive ways that the relationship between religion and politics in the Enlightenment has come about in specific North Atlantic contexts—German, French, American, British. Still, his comprehensive evaluation of the key features of the late modern subject of religion bears relevance across national lines, and seems to do so all the more as the forces of market capitalism and technology function internationally. See Johann Baptist Metz, *A Passion for God: The Mystical-Political Dimension of Christianity* (New York: Paulist Press, 1998) 35, 76–7, 139–41. For another comparison of the continental and Anglo-Saxon forms of interaction between religious faith and modern Enlightenment, with special attention to the type of individualism that has emerged in the United States, see Matthew L. Lamb, "Modernism and Americanism Revisited Dialectically: A Challenge for Evangelization," *Communio* 21 (Winter 1994) 631–62, esp. 646–7.

[5] Metz, *Faith in History and Society,* 35.

primary factor constituting the middle-class subject but, rather, a "cultural" and private one.

The Crisis of Tradition

Having alluded to the predicament in which the Enlightenment placed tradition, Metz addresses it directly as tradition's loss of power in people's decisions for action and direction in life. Intellectually, the establishment of the technical and scientific approach to history and tradition called "historicism" proved to have serious consequences: "Obligation and normativity can no longer be based on historical reason as a medium of tradition—historical knowledge is a medium by which history is made relative and less important."[6] The result for the Christian religion, as Lessing observed, was the establishment of a great chasm between the origins of Christianity and its present claims, which are necessarily historically mediated. Metz judges theologians' attempts to enlist hermeneutics as ineffective because the problem is not confined abstractly to theology but, rather, is based on the fact that tradition itself no longer holds authority in middle-class society. Societal value is exchange value; whatever lies outside the parameters of instrumental (calculating) reason and economic success is relegated to the discretion of the private individual.

Moreover, while middle-class society claims to be conservative of traditions, Metz observes that private individuals most often compromise their conservation of traditions when these conflict with the rules of exchange. With Kierkegaard, Metz especially notes the loss of the tradition of remembering the dead, which loss diminishes such traditional social values as friendliness, thankfulness, and mourning. All together this amounts to the loss of memory, the crucial "inner element of the critical consciousness"[7] desperately needed by society today. Given the constitutive role of tradition in Christianity, the Church must combat its loss among middle-class subjects not simply for religion's sake, but for all humanity (living and dead) and the world, to which the Church is missioned as servant.

The Crisis of Authority

Authority is inseparable from tradition, and the Kantian notion of Enlightenment, namely, a person's use of reason without another's

---

[6] Ibid., 36.
[7] Ibid., 39.

guidance, endangers both. Moreover, in the middle-class concept of exchange *the* authority is competence exercised on an equal playing field. Lost is the authority *in* a tradition. Lost as well is the authority of *subjects*, the authority of freedom, justice, and suffering, which has no exchange value. This is the authority which Metz says theology must defend. Sadly, the Church has tended either to retrench into authoritarian postures or to assume the type of authority that middle-class society permits: overgrown bureaucracy, unapproachable administration, and "authority as a management of truth without any social basis."[8] An authority based on "religious competence," the competence of free and suffering subjects in solidarity for justice, would offer criticism and liberation to middle-class society.

The Crisis of (Metaphysical) Reason

Metz explains that while Kant's Enlightenment had the correct force of banishing tyrannical forms of metaphysics that obscured social and political realities, still the only persons able to explore and exercise such reason were those who already possessed some measure of social power (education, property). The ethics of Enlightenment, accordingly, became a matter of individual moralism, concerned with laziness, cowardice, complacency in comfort. The Enlightenment program was not concerned with the betterment of those below the propertied class. On the contrary, it produced "a new elite or a new aristocracy," whose praxis became "control of nature in the interest of the market."[9] Such technical reason reduces all to the marketable and profitable. Metz insists that the Church and its theology must recognize this force of technical reason (to be discussed in more detail in the next section of this chapter) or else support it by silence.

Religion in a State of Crisis

Along with the criticism of metaphysics and authority inevitably came the Enlightenment's criticism of religion as ideology. On the other hand, the Enlightenment also affirmed a *religio naturalis,* a religion consonant with all people's needs, consistent with reason, and discernible in the history of humanity. Contrary to its claim of universality, however, this "natural religion of reason" belongs to the elitist

---

[8] Ibid., 41.
[9] Ibid., 43.

preserve of the educated, propertied citizen, where it functions as an "inner feeling" incapable of protest in the "society of exchange."[10] Metz observes that much of contemporary German theology and Church practice has been absorbed into this religion of the natural and rational and middle-class.

The Need for a Political Theology of the Subject

Metz summarizes the Enlightenment as the process of making religion the private affair of the middle-class. The middle-class subject, however, is not truly the human subject, for the human subject is the subject in the presence of God. Political theology's task is critically to uncover the contradictions in today's subject, not in order to perform an "abstract negation of the individual" but to "stand up for all [people] as subjects in the face of violent oppression and of a caricature of solidarity in a violent absorption by the mass or an institutionalized hatred."[11] Thus, Metz's concern (as well as my own) is neither to denigrate people as they negotiate their interpersonal and social lives within these societal conditions nor to dismiss the positive social changes that have come with the emergence of modernity. Rather, he seeks to establish the true but threatened values of the subject within the actual social circumstances of today.

[10] Ibid., 45.

[11] Metz adds: "This theological criticism of middle-class religion does not in any sense amount to an abstract devaluation of middle-class values." Ibid., 47. He appends the following note: "This seems to me to be the case of the dialectics of the Enlightenment as outlined by members of the Frankfurt school such as [Max] Horkheimer and [Theodore] Adorno." Ibid., 48, n. 14. Metz learned a great deal from the critical theory of the Frankfurt School, especially with regard to the deleterious impact of the instrumental reason of technology and the market upon modern society and its subjects. Here, however, Metz is apparently voicing a criticism of those philosophers that is not unlike many others' evaluations of their thought: The degree of abstraction in the Frankfurt philosophers' own theories causes them to diminish the potential and resistance that emerges through inter-subjectivity, various social organizations, and individual creativity, thus leaving the reader with a despairing landscape. See Axel Honneth, *The Critique of Power: Reflective Stages in a Critical Social Theory*, trans. Kenneth Baynes (Cambridge, Mass.: MIT Press, 1991) 74–5, 80–1, 89, 94–5. See also, Paul Connerton, *The Tragedy of Enlightenment: An Essay on the Frankfurt School* (Cambridge: Cambridge University Press, 1980) 71, 77–9.

Metz's six-point critique of middle-class religion ends with the positive affirmation of the genuine human subject as knowing oneself and living with others in the presence of God. In his more recent writings, he has come to articulate what is negatively at stake when Christians lose sight of the specific biblical, narrative revelation of the Jewish and early Christian people's histories as lived in God's presence. In so doing, Metz both introduces an additional element to his critique of the contemporary religious situation and further develops the implications of his theory of the modern world view that he has been developing since the 1970s.

Metz increasingly finds ours to be a time of "postmodern Godless Christianity," by which he means a Christianity practiced without a central, ongoing recourse to the unsettled, and therefore unsettling, history of catastrophe and consolation that comprises the narrative of Judeo-Christian tradition. In place of this bounded history of suffering and salvation, in denial of the contradictions inherent to historical religious awareness, many postmodern Christians have undertaken a new recovery of religious myths, seeking "to unlock the potential for consolation that slumbers in myths and fables."[12] Metz judges this temptation to "mythicism" to be a perduring problem for Christianity since the second century. The recourse to myth, and for the purposes of liturgical theology one could easily add the recourse to a ritualism inordinately opposing the sacred and the profane,[13] has its roots in the Gnostic threat of dividing the order of creation from that of redemption. The problem is one of seeking relief from, as Metz puts it, the apocalyptic cry of Judeo-Christian tradition, "What is God waiting for?"[14] In late modernity we experience this cry breaking out when we accompany the sick in their suffering, those who die too young and those whose infirmity is protracted in old age, when we witness recurrent explosions of violence near and far, when we stagger under the economic burdens of a consumer culture and the images produced by the culture industry. In face of these realities, people are turning more and more to new forms of religious myth and ritual, eclectically mixing and matching them in a manner that has been symbolized by the concept of New Age religion.

[12] Metz, *A Passion for God*, 102.
[13] This will be discussed in detail in Chapter 3.
[14] Metz, *A Passion for God*, 84.

Metz, again, is certainly not unsympathetic to the postmodern subject in these throws. He astutely warns, however, that for Christian churches to respond to the newfound and legitimate need for religious ritual on the postmodern principle of pastiche, rather than the narrative-practical character of the faith, renders a grave disservice to people. For the Church to practice its mission effectively (that is, faithfully to tradition), it must assess how humanity and, thus, the gospel are threatened in the present context. In the "still- or postmodern" world, the religious temptation to myth is actually consistent with and plays into a mythical background that pervades all of society. Metz's ongoing assessment of the predominant social world view finds it to be one of mythical, unbounded timelessness. A study of this further perspective on late modernity will open into Metz's call for a new apocalyptic consciousness in Christianity.

FROM EVOLUTIONARY WORLD VIEW
TO DANGEROUS MEMORY

Metz identifies a pervasive form of practical reason that has emerged through two interrelated processes of the Enlightenment: capitalism's principle of exchange and the instrumental reason of technology and science. The problematic feature these two practices of rationality share is the manner in which they effectively render time as an endless and empty continuum. Metz recognizes an "evolutionary" rationality so pervasive in technological and economic systems, and thus influential throughout society, as to constitute an interpretation of reality and the world itself. This evolutionary logic amounts to an operational world view which qualifies the way in which Western subjects perceive themselves in relation to nature, history (time), fellow-humans, themselves, and, therefore, the way in which they can or cannot (do or do not) receive and live the message of Christianity.

Based as it is on technical or instrumental or calculating rationality, this evolutionary world view is one in which whatever or whomever is encountered can be reduced to the status of an object submissive to some form of scientific analysis or explanation. The purpose of this sort of reasoning is to make the object useful for some precise, technical end. The world, both natural and historical (societal), comes to be perceived as the sum-total of scientific, that is, technological and economic, problems to be solved. Modern humanity exists as those taking part in an ongoing and total domination of nature. Therein lies the evolutionary logic of technological, capitalist society: Humanity's ability to master discrete "problems" is presumed along with the expectation that each successful technical solution inevitably (and unquestionably) contributes to further progress. To the extent that members of Western society have come to accept unquestioningly the pervasiveness of technical rationality itself, without raising the question of what greater end is or is not being achieved, this logic of evolution amounts to "a new form of metaphysics" or "a quasi-religious symbol of scientific knowledge."[15]

The power of this largely tacit evolutionary world view has proven to have negative consequences for society and its subjects. Far from generating the sort of optimistic view of history and nature that characterized the nineteenth century, the present valorization of technical reason has produced deep measures of fatalism and apathy. People find themselves part of an anonymous, inevitable, timeless technological and economic process: "There is a cult today of the makeable—everything can be made. There is also a new cult of fate—everything can be replaced. . . . This understanding of reality excludes all expectation and therefore produces that fatalism that eats away [the

---

[15] Metz, *Faith in History and Society,* 171, 6. Here Metz echoes Horkheimer and Adorno, who argued that Enlightenment has proven itself to be mythological:

"Myth turns into enlightenment, and nature into mere objectivity. Men [*sic*] pay for the increase of their power with alienation from that over which they exercise their power. Enlightenment behaves toward things as a dictator toward men. He knows them in so far as he can manipulate them. The man of science knows things in so far as he can make them. In this way their potentiality is turned to his own ends. In the metamorphosis the nature of things, as a substratum of domination, is revealed as always the same. This identity constitutes the unity of nature. . . . The doctrine of equivalence of action and reaction asserted the power of repetition over reality, long after men had renounced the illusion that by repetition they could identify themselves with the repeated reality and thus escape its power. But as the magical illusion fades away, the more relentlessly in the name of law and repetition imprisons man in the cycle—that cycle whose objectification in the form of natural law he imagines will ensure his action as a free subject. The principle of immanence, the explanation of every event as repetition, that the Enlightenment upholds against mythic imagination, is the principle of myth itself."

Max Horkheimer and Theodore W. Adorno, *Dialectic of Enlightenment,* trans. John Cumming (New York: Continuum, 1972) 9, 12.

person's] soul."[16] The need to conform in these systems, so as to be personally successful in them, depletes people's imaginations, inhibits dreams for the future, and ultimately threatens the loss of their subjectivity and freedom. The ethos of control and technical manipulation has depleted people's openness to mystery and to whatever or whomever does not succumb to the solution of calculating reason or its attendant sociocultural conventions. In its now nearly universal economic form, the exchange mentality inherent to market capitalism integrally influences not only political institutions but also "reaches the foundations of our spiritual life," to the effect that "everything now appears to be exchangeable, and interchangeable, even interpersonal relationships and life commitments."[17] The strains upon interpersonal and social relations overlap. Frustrations, especially economic hardships, in the face of the inadmissible limits of the instrumental reason of technology, the market, and political bureaucracies give rise at times to hateful fanaticism, for which Auschwitz stands as the perduring and haunting witness.[18]

Metz, nonetheless, recognizes positive movements over the past few decades wherein people are losing confidence in the evolutionary world view: "We are becoming ever more conscious of the dangers and antagonisms that arise when technological and economic processes are left to their own nature."[19] The evidence includes the strain upon and even breakdown of legal and social systems, the deterioration of urban centers, threatened and sometimes ruined ecological environments, increased turmoil in the nations of the southern hemisphere, genetic manipulation, and unresolved issues concerning computer technology and advanced communication capabilities. Such evidence has caused people to question the "neutrality" that has been afforded technological and/or economic projects and decisions under the rubric of the "scientific." This growing array of problems points to the fundamental concern for the future of humanity and, specifically, the freedom and subjectivity of every person. Anonymous progress is no longer accepted but, rather, is questioned in terms of *whose*

[16] Metz, *Faith in History and Society,* 170. Elsewhere, Metz discusses how Nietzsche's philosophy exposed this mythical totality that tacitly pervades modernity. See Metz, *A Passion for God,* 78–81, 172–3.

[17] Metz, *A Passion for God,* 166.

[18] See Metz, *The Emergent Church,* 17–33; and Metz, *A Passion for God,* 39.

[19] Metz, *Faith in History and Society,* 100.

progress is being affirmed and at what cost to the freedom of *other* human subjects.

To scrutinize instrumental rationality thus is to strike at the heart of the evolutionary world view. The possibility of change requires some other logic than one based on calculation:

"The question of the future of our technological civilization is a question not primarily of technology, but of the control and application of technology and economico-technological processes; a problem not primarily of means but of ends, and of the establishment of priorities and preferences. This means, however, that it is primarily a political and fundamentally a social problem."[20]

In order for politics to have a mediating influence on technology and economics, politics itself cannot simply be the instrumentalist business of sheer planning. Politics needs a form of reason and imagination which resists absorption into the technological process. Metz, strongly influenced by the work of Theodore Adorno, locates such moral imagination in "the memory of suffering accumulated in history."[21] This form of political consciousness brings to awareness the reality which the evolutionary logic of modern society suppresses— the senseless suffering inflicted upon people in the name of human progress. Even a "trace" of such suffering proves any technological, economic, or political system's teleological claims to justification to be lies, indeed, myths.[22]

Social and political consciousness is necessarily historical consciousness, the remembrance of those who have suffered and died as victims of human efforts to dominate over nature and/or human beings. To remember explicitly the "losers" of history is a negative awareness which demands that their suffering not be in vain but, rather, that it motivate efforts to build a future that is characterized by

---

[20] Ibid., 101. For a parallel passage, see Metz, *The Emergent Church*, 60–1.

[21] Metz, *Faith in History and Society*, 105.

[22] "The slightest trace of senseless suffering in the world of human experience gives the lie to all affirmative ontology and all teleology and is clearly revealed as a modern mythology." Ibid., 108. To this statement Metz appends an endnote, referring the reader to Adorno's "criticism of an ontologization of suffering" in *Negative Dialectics*. Ibid., 118, n. 5. See Theodore W. Adorno, *Negative Dialectics*, trans. E. B. Ashton (New York: Continuum, 1973).

freedom and the vanquishing of such suffering. This memory of and motivation by suffering constitutes the "essential dynamics of history."[23] The definite memory of suffering, therefore, is dangerous in its capacities both (1) to render a critique of the evolutionary world view and (2) to stimulate human imagination for social-political action.[24]

Through critical theory's assessment of the threatened situation of the world and its negative dialectics of suffering in history Metz constructs the hermeneutical key for unlocking the powerful message of Christianity from the modern manacles of privatized religion and institutional power structures. Metz interprets the gospel as the "dangerous memory" of Jesus Christ, the *memoria Jesu Christi*.[25] The importance of this insight for Metz cannot be understated, for he considers it basic and "central" to his entire theological project: "Christianity does not introduce God subsequently as a kind of 'stop-gap' into this conflict about the future; instead, it tries to keep alive the

---

[23] Metz, *Faith in History and Society*, 108.

[24] See ibid., 117. See also Johann Baptist Metz, "Communicating a Dangerous Memory," *Communicating a Dangerous Memory*, ed. Fred Lawrence (Atlanta: Scholars Press, 1987) 42.

[25] I must note here that while Metz explicitly refers to Adorno in the course of the development of his argument in *Faith in History and Society*, the influence of Walter Benjamin is operative throughout as well, especially in Metz's crafting of the phrase, "dangerous memory." One particular passage by Benjamin, wherein he joins the notions of memory, danger, messiah, tradition, and hope for the dead, demonstrates his impact upon Metz's thought and rhetoric:

"To articulate the past historically does not mean to recognize it 'the way it really was' (Ranke). It means to seize hold of a memory as it flashes up at a moment of danger. Historical materialism wishes to retain that image of the past which unexpectedly appears to man [sic] singled out by history at a moment of danger. The danger affects both the content of the tradition and its receivers. The same threat hangs over both: that of becoming a tool of the ruling classes. In every era the attempt must be made anew to wrest tradition away from a conformism that is about to overpower it. The Messiah comes not only as the redeemer, he comes as the subduer of Antichrist. Only that historian will have the gift of fanning the spark of hope in the past who is firmly convinced that even the dead will not be safe from the enemy if he wins. And this enemy has not ceased to be victorious."

Walter Benjamin, "Theses on the Philosophy of History," *Illuminations*, ed. and intro. Hannah Arendt (New York: Harcourt, Brace & World, 1968) 257.

memory of the crucified Lord, this specific *memoria passionis,* as a dangerous memory of freedom in the social systems of our technological civilization."[26] In the *memoria Jesu Christi* Metz is able to identify the history of suffering as a history of freedom. As the eschatological memory that anticipates the promised future of the oppressed, the hopeless and failed, it is at once dangerous and liberating, compelling northern middle-class Christians continuously to change their attitudes and actions with this specific future in mind. This constant change takes the form of a constant concern for other people's suffering. The story of what God has done in the death and resurrection of Jesus is a shocking interruption, a (negative) critique, to any teleological argument justifying economic profit or technological efficiency or ideological power, as well as a (positive) hope which sustains efforts to combat the forces of oppression that arise therefrom. To all such systems the narration of that memory, precisely through the solidarity it inspires, is dangerous.[27]

The concept of the dangerous memory enables Metz to perceive in the nagging and disruptive stories of human oppression and death

[26] Metz, *Faith in History and Society,* 109. For this reason, Metz explains, the project of political theology cannot be considered a sub-discipline of theology but, rather, a fundamental dimension of contemporary theology in general. The goal of political theology is not to frustrate Christians by adding the field of politics as another activity to pursue but, rather, to articulate effectively the Christian tradition in this particular social context as a dangerous memory. This objective for his political theology is at the heart of his argument for its being a fundamental theology. See *Faith in History and Society,* 89.

[27] In developing the "concept" of political theology as a practical fundamental theology Metz adopts and argues for the integrally related categories ("in the widest sense" of the word) of memory, narrative, and solidarity as the three "major" ones for his theological approach. While Metz devotes a chapter to each, he admits to not having yet arrived at their systematic treatment. The latter disclaimer is certainly in keeping with the fragmenting and subverting character of Metz's theology, leaving open the question of whether a "fully elaborated attempt to systematize them" is an effort to which Metz would be genuinely committed. Metz, *Faith in History and Society,* 183. Indeed, James Matthew Ashley reports that Metz adopted Adorno's dictum, "The whole is untrue," indicating that for Metz, "'the system' is not the place to work out theological truth today." James Matthew Ashley, *Interruptions: Mysticism, Politics, and Theology in the Work of Johann Baptist Metz* (Notre Dame, Ind.: University of Notre Dame Press, 1998) 100, 192.

more than a despairing criticism of the ideological deceptions that en-shroud technocratic society. This he is able to do on the basis of a re-source to which the philosophers of the Frankfurt School had no recourse, namely, the dogmatic content of Christian faith:

"At the midpoint of this faith is a specific *memoria passionis*, on which is grounded the promise of future freedom for all. We remember the future of our freedom in the memory of his suffering—this is an escha-tological statement that cannot be made more plausible through any subsequent accommodation, and cannot be generally verified. This statement remains controversial and controvertible: the power to scan-dalize is part of its communicable content. For the truth of the passion of Jesus and the history of human suffering as we remember it in the word 'God' is a truth whose recollection always painfully contradicts the expectations of the individual who tries to conceive it. The eschato-logical truth of the *memoria passionis* cannot be derived from our his-torical, social and psychological compulsions. This is what makes it a liberating truth in the first place. But that also is at the root of its nature and constitutionally alien to our cognitive systems."[28]

In a tone reminiscent of St. Paul, Metz revels in the scandalousness and the irreducibility of belief in the universally salvific death of Christ to any theoretical system.[29] In that sense, the fundamental Christian kerygma is resonant with the startling or dissonant quality (the non-identity) that Adorno considered essential to any "trace" that might challenge and disrupt the steady progress of a system. On the other hand, the very content of that Christian belief is the identity of Christ with every member of the human race. Such "identity think-ing" poses the threat of reconciling all of the pain and disaster of human suffering into the resolution of the resurrection. A teleology that incapacitates critical thought (let alone action) thus threatens the

---

[28] Metz, *Faith in History and Society*, 111–2. Metz puts this thesis another way, stating that only on the basis of their belief in an eschatological meaning for history are Christians able to look into the abyss of historical consciousness and risk remembering the ruined and lost. See Metz, *A Passion for God*, 40.

[29] See Metz, *Faith in History and Society*, 51. "The theology in which this memory is articulated is no theology worked out in system concepts, but rather a theology worked out in subject concepts, with a practical founda-tion." Metz, *A Passion for God*, 40.

viability of the Christian message, as has so tragically been the history of "Christian" nations.[30] For precisely that reason Metz insists that the *memoria passionis* is the "midpoint of this faith" and that the truth of the identity of all human suffering with Christ is essentially "eschatological." Such considerations are, as Metz recognizes, outside the scope of political discourse and, therefore, require that Metz turn the scandalousness of the Christian tradition on the middle-class subjects who claim it for their own.

The task for Metz as a political theologian is to bring the "message" of the gospel to discourse in a way which upends the privatized middle-class possession of Christianity and recovers the tradition's authentic claim to their lives. The memory of Christ's passion, death, and resurrection is indeed "the promise of future freedom for all," but Metz does not want that statement interpreted in an individualistic manner, as only the assurance of spiritual freedom added to the social-economic freedom one already possesses. No, the *memoria passionis* grounds a promise in which believers understand their freedom as related to the future freedom for all, which requires first, that they consider the promise of salvation not in terms of their individual personal histories but in terms of all of human history, including those who have already died, and second, that their belief in that promise fashion a life of solidarity with those now threatened by deadly oppression. "Resurrection faith," Metz argues, "acts 'contra-factually' in making us free to bear in mind the sufferings and hopes of the past and the challenge of the dead."[31] Resurrection faith is not merely the

---

[30] Acute awareness of this pattern, still persistent among their nations, is a hallmark of the liberation theologians in Latin America, among whom Gustavo Gutiérrez is a prominent author. Among his works, two are particularly helpful in analyzing the history of the official Church's duplicity in ruling elites' suppression of the overwhelming majority of their peoples, as well as relaying and analyzing the dramatic ecclesial change undertaken after Vatican II on a grassroots level and promoted by the Councils of Medellín and Pueblo. See *A Theology of Liberation*, rev. ed., trans. and ed. Caridad Inda and John Eagleson (Maryknoll, N.Y.: Orbis Books, 1988), and *The Power of the Poor in History*, trans. Robert Barr (Maryknoll, N.Y.: Orbis Books, 1983).

[31] Metz, *Faith in History and Society*, 113. Metz has continued to emphasize and develop this theme of universalism, noting that while political theology can learn from Marxism's insistence on humanity's self-realization as a historical process, it supersedes Marxism by asserting the reality of human guilt

object of one's contemplation and an assurance of one's salvation but, rather, a call to follow Christ, to imitate Christ by taking on the pattern of his selfless action on behalf of freedom for everyone, living and dead. Bourgeois Christianity is a religion of "purely-believed in faith" or mere contemplation.[32] The christology of the dangerous memory is a "practical knowledge," a praxis, the *imitatio Christi*.

THE CHRISTOLOGY OF IMITATION

Like all areas of modern theology christology, as practiced both in the academy and the Church's leadership and membership, is in need of a shock to its system. Metz finds the power for such a shock within the authority of the Church's christological tradition itself. He understands his christology, then, as a recovery of tradition, "the social counterpart of memory."[33] Metz's christological thesis is that one only knows Christ by imitating him: "It is only when they imitate Christ that Christians know who it is to whom they have given their consent and who saves them."[34] Without citing any specific examples, Metz argues that the narratives of Christ's ministry in the New Testament always contain the element of commandment, that the purpose of the stories is to change the listener into one who willingly follows Christ by doing what he did. In his book *Followers of Christ* Metz sharpens the point by insisting that this evangelical call and command to follow

---

in that process. Only the recognition of guilt as an authentic aspect of human history, as opposed to alienation as a mere derivative of it, affords the possibility of a genuinely universal liberation by prohibiting the absolute division of peoples into the innocent and guilty, the just and unjust, friend and foe, the victorious living and the vanquished dead. See Metz, *A Passion for God*, 36–9.

[32] Metz, "Communicating a Dangerous Memory," 44; see also 46; and Metz, *The Emergent Church*, 3. As Metz's early writing began to take its critical turn he articulated his distrust of the "purely contemplative and conceptual nature of metaphysics." Whether the "objectivistically developed" version of scholasticism or the "transcendental or personal or existential" types after Kant, such metaphysics make the future a mere "correlate of the present" and, thus, play no small role in the modern ambivalence toward history, wherein a definite future and its demand for a genuine exercise of freedom are suppressed. Johann Baptist Metz, *Theology of the World*, trans. William Glen-Doepel (New York: Seabury Press, 1969) 98–9.

[33] Metz, *Faith in History and Society*, 197.

[34] Ibid., 52.

Christ is not only a pastoral but a dogmatic question. Metz, in a manner typical to all his theology, summarizes this dogma in a paraphrase: "Christ himself is not only a supreme being worthy of worship, but also, and always, a way."[35] The point Metz draws from this statement is that the *"logos"* of christology must constitutively include "the practice of following Christ" or else it remains the "purely contemplative Logos of the Greeks, for whom ultimately Christ could only ever be foolishness." The latter phrase implies that Metz is thinking in terms of the christology of the New Testament (St. Paul), but his case would be strengthened by considering the fact that the christological arguments waged from the third to the fifth centuries (and beyond) were motivated in no small part by concern for the practical consequences of how one understands the divinity and humanity of Christ. While the pursuit of this last point is beyond the scope of the present project, the effort would honor Metz's argument that the Church needs to recover the dangerous memories contained in dogmas.[36]

The problem that remains for Metz is to explain in what sense the Jesus whom Christians imitate was himself politically active. On this point the ongoing questions of what Metz means by "political," a question for both Metz and analysts of his thought,[37] becomes evident and perhaps even a bit ironic, in that Metz seems to consider himself to be stating the obvious:

"Clearly the message of Jesus is already political by the mere fact that it proclaims the worth and dignity of the person and the fact that all [people] are independent in the sight of God. Hence those who bear witness to this Gospel must also stand up for this independence whenever it is threatened. They must not only fight so that people remain independent in the face of growing collective pressures, but so that people can be freed from misery and oppression to become independent."[38]

The word "political" does not describe a particular course of action but, rather, a principle for action, a principle of human dignity—the

---

[35] Johann Baptist Metz, *Followers of Christ: The Religious Life and the Church*, trans. Thomas Linton (New York: Paulist Press, 1978) 39.

[36] See Metz, *Faith in History and Society*, 200–4.

[37] See Rebecca S. Chopp, *The Praxis of Suffering: An Interpretation of Liberation and Political Theologies* (Maryknoll, N.Y.: Orbis Books, 1986) 79.

[38] Metz, *Followers of Christ*, 54.

independence of all people as "free agents before God" or, in the language of *Faith in History and Society,* "subject[s] in the presence of God."[39] That last phrase, "in the presence of God," is the crucial qualification that distinguishes Metz's notion of human subjectivity from that of the Enlightenment. Whereas Kant, by presuming the subject of Enlightenment to be educationally and socially established, treated practical reason as the exercise of individual morality (see above), Metz believes that placing the subject in the presence of the God of Jesus allows no such social and political neutrality. The biblical God is the one to whom afflicted people, people without a future, prayed and from whom they received deliverance from their oppressors. The "mysticism" of their prayer and the "politics" of their deliverance together constituted the pattern of their lives "in the presence of God." This pattern realizes its fulfillment and its universality in the mission, death, and resurrection of Jesus.

In the end Metz's christology, sketchy as it is,[40] seems to serve two purposes for his political theology. First, through the identification of all of humanity with the person and history of Jesus, the *memoria passionis, mortis et resurrectionis Jesu Christi* both attests to God's solidarity with all victims of suffering and oppression and assures the final, still unrealized, deliverance of the victims. Christians thereby read history not in affirmation of conquest but in hope for the conquered. Here the eschatological aspect of christology is prominent, a point to which this study must soon return.

Second, through their own identification with Christ (as his "followers" or disciples) Christians take on the mission of obedience-in-

---

[39] Ibid., 58, and Metz, *Faith in History and Society,* 70. In his more recent writings Metz has argued that the contemporary juncture of religion and politics arises out of the need to justify universalist claims for human rights. Metz proposes that the one principle that can ground this political claim is the recognition of the authority of those who suffer. See Metz, *A Passion for God,* 144–5.

[40] Amidst his published articles and talks, including those gathered into books, Metz performs in *Followers of Christ* what is perhaps his most concerted treatment of christology. That being said, one must quickly add that the book is a slender volume based upon lectures Metz gave to a meeting of religious superiors in Germany. In general, Metz's work is characterized by touching upon crucial elements of Christian dogma or doctrine without exploring them in systematic depth. For a discussion of this characteristic of Metz's work, including specific reference to his christology, see Ashley, *Interruptions,* 192.

poverty that he received from God. Here a strongly kenotic element is operative. While Metz does not draw upon that theological term,[41] nonetheless, the christological hymn in the second chapter of Paul's letter to the Philippians anonymously pervades Metz's arguments in *Followers of Christ*. Early in the text (as noted above) Metz states without comment that Christ is "a supreme being worthy of worship." One thinks of the concluding three verses of the hymn. Like the hymn, Metz treats Jesus' obedience to God in a narrative form, expounding on both the "radical hopelessness and contradictoriness" of Jesus' "obedience 'unto death, even death on a cross,'" and the revelation of the "brilliant image of God who raises up and liberates, who releases the guilty and the humiliated into a new future full of promise . . . ."[42] This pattern establishes the definite character of Christian subjectivity and the practical knowledge at the heart of christology. The Christian lives a "passionate obedience" to the God of Jesus, an "uncalculating surrender" which "impels one to stand close to those for whom obedience is not a matter of virtue but the sign of oppression and of being placed in tutelage, and to do so in a practical way."[43] *Kenosis* thereby characterizes not only Jesus' life but also the life that can be salvific for the middle-class Christian.

---

[41] In his earlier writing Metz demonstrates the kenotic character he perceives as essential to a "Christian asceticism," although he uses the Latin equivalent, *descensus:*

"For the God of the Christian faith is found only in the movement of his love towards men [*sic*], the 'least,' as has been revealed to us in Jesus Christ. Christian mysticism finds, therefore, that direct experience of God which it seeks precisely in daring to imitate the unconditional involvement of the divine love for man, in letting itself be drawn into the *descensus* of God, into the descent of his love to the least of his brothers [and sisters]. Only in this movement do we find the supreme nearness, the supreme immediacy of God. And that is why mysticism, which seeks this nearness, has the place not outside, beside, or above responsibility for the world of our brothers [and sisters], but in the center of it."

Metz, *Theology of the World*, 104.

[42] Metz, *Followers of Christ*, 64, 66. In the latter, Metz is quoting a document of the joint synod of the dioceses of the Federal Republic of Germany, *Unsere Hoffnung* ("Our Hope"), which Metz himself had drafted for the bishops.

[43] Ibid., 67. It is interesting to note that *Followers of Christ* is based on a set of lectures Metz was invited to give on the topic of living the vows of religious

Metz seems to draw his kenotic parallel between Jesus and middle-class Christians on the basis of the wealth and autonomy possessed by each. What he does not explicitly note, however, is that the parallel rests at the level of theme and not content. Jesus' wealth is his unique status as the Son of God, but he was, in Metz's reading of the tradition, always financially poor.[44] The wealth of bourgeois Christians is literally financial, being "those who already have, those with secure possessions, the people in this world who already have abundant prospects and a rich future."[45] For such Christians to "stand close" to the oppressed "in a practical way" is a kenotic praxis, but it is a self-emptying of the bourgeois principles of exchange, economic autonomy, and privatism, as well as the reputation attendant upon such social conformity. By joining in solidarity with both those who presently suffer injustice and those who have already died, middle-class Christians can expect both their peers and political leaders to call them rebels and fools, weaklings and traitors—as happened to Jesus.[46]

---

life (poverty, chastity, and obedience). This observation provides evidence for the way in which Metz's theology is practical, in that he is concerned about discovering what is dangerous and transformative in a particular element of Christian tradition, namely, the tradition of consecrated religious life, in the context of contemporary North Atlantic society. One of Metz's main points here is that the vows of poverty, chastity, and obedience place the women and men who profess them in a voluntary solidarity with people for whom dire economic need, radical loneliness, and political tutelage are anything but a choice. I myself find this the basic way to make social sense of vowed religious life (the religious sense being based on belief in a divine call). It is further interesting to observe that membership in the religious orders and congregations who have adopted the practical vision Metz advocates has been on a precipitous decline in the years since he produced these lectures. While the evaluation of causes for this decline is an admittedly complex issue, the fact of the problem would seem to provide evidence for Metz's theoretical assessment of the crisis state of middle-class religion at the end of the twentieth century.

[44] "And of course [Jesus] did not have to go out of his way to show his solidarity with the poor: he was himself poor." Ibid., 57.

[45] Metz, *The Emergent Church*, 2.

[46] See ibid., 15; Metz, *Followers of Christ*, 43, 67; Metz, "Communicating a Dangerous Memory," 45. German Reformed theologian Dorothee Soelle provides a testimony to the accusations of treason and weakness visited upon activists for peace and justice, as well as her reply in a German court of law, in

They can also, however, expect to discover the freedom that is inherent to the tradition and history of those who have followed (and not merely believed in) Christ. Christology thereby opens into a soteriology that amounts to nothing less than an "anthropological revolution" for middle-class Christians.[47] Through "a social and political consciousness in the interest of others' suffering,"[48] they undertake a praxis that can begin to realize their own human and religious capacities for sorrow and joy, pain and play, mourning and expectation, generosity and gratitude, friendship and loyalty, solidarity and individuality. These capacities, which Metz calls "messianic virtues,"[49] are not only behavioral but noetic. They constitute "a kind of anti-knowledge *ex memoria passionis*" that contains "cognitive and critical meaning" over against the instrumental, controlling reason that dominates modern society.[50] The middle-class Christian's social-political *kenosis* thus results in a new freedom for the subject, a transformed self-knowledge through the praxis of messianic virtues, a "postbourgeois principle of individuation inspired essentially by the gospel."[51]

The key to Metz's "political theology of the subject" is for Christians who are formed by the "anticipatory memory" of Jesus' suffering to bring that "new moral imagination" into the arena of politics, "alongside many other often subversive innovative factors in our

---

her text *The Window of Vulnerability: A Political Spirituality,* trans. Linda M. Maloney (Minneapolis: Fortress Press, 1990) 50–7.

[47] Metz, *The Emergent Church,* 34, 36, 41.

[48] Metz, *Faith in History and Society,* 115.

[49] Metz, *The Emergent Church,* 4–8.

[50] Metz, *Faith in History and Society,* 111. Matthew Lamb, a theologian strongly influenced by Metz's work, argues that "agapic praxis" (a prophetic-missionary practice of Christian faith), if it is not to devolve into fideism or fundamentalism, needs the wisdom which comes from the performance of such activities as liturgy, poetry, art, music, and spiritual discernment. These "prophetic-apocalyptic narrative expressions of agapic love" go deep into the "human psyche and spirit" and nurture a wisdom that seeks reflective (intellectual) and "noetic" praxis. The latter gives rise to theology's task as the "reflective noetic praxis" of mediating religious transformative values and narrative to cultures and societies. Matthew L. Lamb, *Solidarity with Victims: Toward a Theology of Social Transformation* (New York: Crossroad, 1982) 13–14.

[51] Metz, *The Emergent Church,* 74.

society."[52] The innovative factor unique to the Christian moral imagination Metz broadly calls "mysticism." Mysticism and politics constitute the dialectical praxis of faith or praxis of imitation. Metz's treatment of mysticism seems to divide thematically or conceptually along two lines of thought which have already appeared in the present rehearsal of his theology: prayer and eschatology. Metz performs here a recovery of traditions; however, he does so in a manner that, although conceptually compelling, begs questions about the actual practice of those traditions. Having mounted an argument for religious tradition as practical knowledge, Metz's theology invites further attention to the practices themselves. Thus, in turning to mysticism I shall begin to point toward the contribution liturgical theology can make to the positive agenda of Metz's political theology. I shall first consider eschatology, which discussion will help to fill out Metz's theological categories of memory, narrative, and solidarity.

MYSTICISM I: APOCALYPTIC ESCHATOLOGY

Metz fully acknowledges the level of danger—the radical demands—that a political praxis of following Christ places upon the middle-class believer. The counter-cultural strain of the *imitatio Christi* cannot be borne indefinitely by the consolation the subject experiences in practicing the messianic virtues. The trouble lies, however, not in the virtues, for these are both redemptive and emancipative, but in the insidious timelessness that is endemic to the evolutionary world view of technocratic society. Only the intrinsically eschatological character of the biblical tradition of the *memoria Jesu Christi,* long confused or ignored in the Church's theory and practice, can break the evolutionary assault of apathy:

"Following Christ is not something that can be lived without the idea of the parousia, without looking forward to the second coming. Anyone who forgets this destroys following Christ or is engaged on silently destroying or mutilating it, since he [sic] cannot repeat actions that are always similar with the same intensity. What corresponds to following Christ is an existence based absolutely on hope: a life with an apocalyptic goad."[53]

[52] Metz, *Faith in History and Society,* 117–8. See also Metz, *A Passion for God,* 142–3.

[53] Metz, *Followers of Christ,* 75–6.

The praxis of imitation needs the interruption of apocalyptic narratives as a source of both challenge and encouragement in the message that the time of this world and its powers are running out. This, Metz notes, was the function of apocalyptic stories for the Jews and Christians who endured persecution and bequeathed that tradition to later generations through the formation of biblical texts and canons.

Metz posits an "apocalyptically-oriented eschatology" as a corrective to contemporary theological discussions of eschatology.[54] Due to an uncritical acceptance of the evolutionary view of time which distorts their reading of biblical texts, theologians tend to discuss eschatology in terms of a "meaningful teleology" in an open-ended future or an "existential" reflection upon an individual's salvation in relation to one's own death.[55] Rudolf Bultmann had dismissed any other reading of the New Testament's apocalyptic literature as "mythical." Such an acceptance of the course of time, however, defeats the very urgency of biblical-apocalyptic Christianity, which does not ask about the

[54] Metz, *Faith in History and Society*, 73. The doctrine of eschatology became an increasingly important category and a central issue for systematic theology in the 1960s. Metz's Protestant colleague, Jürgen Moltmann, made a major contribution to this development in his publication of *Theology of Hope: On the Ground and Implications of a Christian Eschatology*, trans. James W. Leitch (New York: Harper Collins, 1967, 1991). Metz's and Moltmann's approaches to eschatology have followed divergent paths over the years. In his early book Moltmann opposed the "promises for the future" with the experiences of the present, describing humanity as "drawn into the conflict between hope and experience" (see 18). In stark contrast, the later Moltmann has strongly criticized the dialectical theology of Karl Barth and others, proposing instead a theology of experience: "Every true experience of the self becomes also an experience of the divine spirit of life. . . . Every lived moment can be lived in the inconceivable closeness of God in the Spirit." Jürgen Moltmann, *The Spirit of Life: A Universal Affirmation*, trans. Margaret Kohl (Minneapolis: Fortress Press, 1992) 35; see 5–7, 37. Metz, on the other hand, moved away from his initial identification of eschatology with secularized Christianity's brave trust in the undefined future of an evolving world to an apocalyptic eschatology, whose content I shall expound in the following pages of this chapter.

[55] Metz, *Faith in History and Society*, 177, 178. Elsewhere, Metz criticizes this tendency among Christians in terms of the desire to be conventionally normal, rather than "deranged by possibility," that is, given over to the element of "anarchy" in the disturbing message and scandalous actions of Jesus. See *A Passion for God*, 152.

extent to which individual believers are already or not yet saved but, rather, about how much time humanity and the earth as we know it still have left. A practical and truly hopeful Christianity lives not in "constant expectation" but, rather, in "imminent expectation" of a God who, far from drawing believers into timelessness and eternity, interrupts and delimits time, placing the world and history into question.[56]

Once again Metz finds the power of the Christian message to reside in its scandalousness (in contrast, he says, to Bultmann and all theologians who prefer to follow sound theoretical judgment). This scandalousness is not, however, pointless speculation about numbers and signs determining dates for the *eschaton*. The catastrophic images in biblical apocalyptic vision are, rather, "a mystical analogy with an experienced political reality."[57] From this analysis of early apocalyptic faith Metz coins another phrase for a theology which would have a practical impact upon contemporary Christianity. The message of the gospel contains an "apocalyptic naiveté" which "lies in ambush" for, scandalizes, and interrupts the banality and boredom of *bürgerliche Religion,* which in its affirmation of the "common modern consensus" is "rid of danger but also rid of consolation."[58] In an apparent challenge to theologies which employ the hermeneutical theory of Paul Ricoeur, Metz insists that present response to the gospel is not a matter of interpretation which leads to a second naiveté in the process of appropriation. In the hermeneutical dialectic the traditional source tends to bear the burden of modifications to itself. To recover and adhere to the apocalyptic naiveté of the gospel, and thus suspect and reject the modern view of time, is to hold a belief that is sheer nonsense to one's social peers. While the latter may adopt a dismissive attitude toward apocalyptic Christians, the threat of serious conflict (danger) looms in concrete situations where the praxis of faith begins to have tangible impact in a particular political situation. Metz's analysis of the evolutionary world view as a "crypto-religious symbol" or "quasi-religious totality" is insightful. If the apocalyptic naiveté of Christians is able actually to threaten any area of capitalist-technological society,

[56] Metz, *Faith in History and Society,* 74, 174. See also, Metz, *A Passion for God,* 82–4.

[57] Metz, *Faith in History and Society,* 175.

[58] Metz, "Communicating a Dangerous Memory," 48. For Metz's explanation of how a literalist approach to the biblical texts is not to be confused with fundamentalism, see *A Passion for God,* 200, n. 7.

those Christians may find themselves in an experience of persecution analogous to some of the earliest believers, who refused to comply with imperial religious worship. Metz considers this charge of foolishness, already established in relation to christology, to be essential to the praxis of Christian faith.

Metz's purpose, then, in introducing apocalyptic to eschatology is to heighten a sense of urgency that goads Christians in their action, their praxis of solidarity with the poor and oppressed. Apocalyptic vision is the antidote, to use Rebecca Chopp's phrase,[59] to the timelessness of evolution, to its inherent fatalism and apathy, as well as to the theology of "permanent reflection," which can only legitimate these. While that may prove an interesting or even promising move in Metz's theoretical argument, still the question remains as to how "apocalyptic consciousness" avoids producing a "paralyzing fear of catastrophe" that "deprive[s] responsibility of its power."[60] Metz finds the answer not in the catastrophic images themselves—for example, in the Apocalypse of John—but in the story of final judgment in the Gospel of Matthew:

"The well-known last judgment discourse of Matthew 25—where the king separates the just from the unjust according to the criterion: 'As you did it (or did not) to one of the least of these my brethren, you did it (or did it not) to me'—is thoroughly apocalyptic in character, since awareness of the end and of the judgment is linked in it with the idea of the necessity of active commitment to others, of 'the least of the brethren.'"[61]

The kenotic Christ-of-imitation cedes to Christ the king and judge. The theoretical move on Metz's part serves well one of the major goals of his political theology, namely, to recover the ancient Christian sense of a definite future, of an *eschaton* with an urgent and specific content that transforms current praxis.[62]

[59] See Chopp, *The Praxis of Suffering*, 77.

[60] Metz, *Faith in History and Society*, 177.

[61] Metz, *Followers of Christ*, 79.

[62] It is this effort to recover the definite and urgent content of Christianity's early apocalyptic tradition that reveals the monumental change in Metz's approach to eschatology. In his earlier work, Metz wrote of the "eschatological proviso" of Christian faith which asserts a critical attitude toward "the

When one begins, however, to press Metz with the question of *how* apocalyptic-eschatological narratives actually (practically) motivate solidarity with the living and the dead, Metz's program becomes somewhat less clear.[63] Metz locates the apocalyptic motivation for "practical solidarity" with the living in gospel stories that threaten judgment and promise reward; the narrative sparks the imagination of judgment. This is not to say that the final judgment is the only motivation for solidarity. Indeed, Metz presents "following Christ" and "the second coming" as "two sides of a coin."[64] The narratives of Jesus' mission constitute the attractive call to discipleship. Only the "apocalyptic idea of imminent expectation," however, can sustain those who imitate Jesus radically: "an apocalyptic consciousness . . .

---

present condition of society" on the basis of the provisional (but not arbitrary) nature of all efforts at human and social betterment. Metz, *Theology of the World*, 114. Kathryn Tanner demonstrates the inadequacy of this approach:

"Some of these criticisms [of the social order] seem, however, to be fairly useless. . . . For instance, would a social policy of murdering Jews be any less objectionable if it were subject to an 'eschatological proviso,' held onto tentatively as a revisable human project on the part of Christians who hope to do God's will even as they admit their own sin?"

In a footnote to this question Tanner associates the term "eschatological proviso" with Metz's work in *Theology of the World*. She does not, however, cite anything from Metz's later development of an apocalyptic eschatology as she continues her argument in the main body of the text: "For a critique that burrows deeper, the character of relations between persons has to be the explicit subject matter under consideration. Are there any specifically Christian criteria for a critique of that sort?" Kathryn Tanner, *The Politics of God: Christian Theologies and Social Justice* (Minneapolis: Fortress Press, 1992) 129–30.

[63] This observation corroborates a more general one by Joseph Colombo, who considers Metz's treatment of narrative as a category of his fundamental theology even more "fragmentary and suggestive" than his development of the category of memory. Colombo argues that rather than providing a systematic approach to the category of memory, Metz is more concerned to establish narrative's fundamental role in the transmission of religion. Metz's argument for narrative, Colombo explains, is offered as a corrective to "transcendental" and "universalist" theologies. Joseph A. Colombo, *An Essay on Theology and History: Studies in Pannenberg, Metz, and the Frankfurt School*, AAR Studies in Religion 61, ed. Lawrence S. Cunningham (Atlanta: Scholars Press, 1990) 192.

[64] Metz, *Followers of Christ*, 75.

accepts suffering."[65] Precisely on this point, however, Metz's theology becomes abstract: the story of Jesus is complemented by the "idea" of apocalypse. He does not demonstrate how the *narratives* of "apocalyptic catastrophe," not just those depicting individual accountability before God, sustain solidarity, and a solidarity not only among the living but also with the dead.

The problem with which I am confronting Metz certainly is not an easy one. The apocalyptic narratives in both the Old and New Testaments are of a literary genre so foreign to the middle-class Christian as to be utterly bizarre. The magnitude of the problem is accentuated by Metz's heavy reliance on the shock value of apocalypticism for his practical fundamental theology: a political theology *"with an apocalyptic sting."*[66] I must not force biblical apocalypticism into a conceptual resolution in the overall scheme of Metz's practical theology that he himself does not give it. Indeed, Metz introduces his chapter on time and immanent expectation in *Faith in History and Society* with the warning that he is offering a series of theses which are corrections and suggestions, and "often exaggerated" ones, at that.[67] Metz has continued to admit honestly this challenge for his theology: "[Apocalyptic] has exercised me over the years, because it is to a certain degree the hem of my theological approach, although I have not learned to speak consistently and convincingly about it."[68]

The actual, practical shape of Metz's call for an apocalyptic mysticism becomes clearer in an essay published in the late 1980s, in which he performs an "autobiographical" rather than a "systematic" approach to the notion of the dangerous memory.[69] By narrating an autobiographical story Metz demonstrates the (still unsystematic) relationship between the three major categories he had established for his practical fundamental theology: memory, narrative, and solidarity.

[65] Metz, *Faith in History and Society*, 176.

[66] Ibid., 73.

[67] Ibid., 169.

[68] Metz, *A Passion for God*, 47.

[69] Metz, "Communicating a Dangerous Memory," 37. In his overview of the development of Metz's thought, Ashley has also noted the significance of Metz's introducing the narrative of his own biography into his theology. See Ashley, *Interruptions*, 35–6. In his forward to his most recent English-language collection of essays, Metz begins from this autobiographical position. See Metz, *A Passion for God*, 1–2.

The story is a chilling one indeed. Metz recounts how in 1945, at the age of sixteen, he and his schoolmates were conscripted into the army by the (at that point desperate) Nazi regime. Untrained, Metz and his company were sent to the front, through which the American forces were rapidly advancing. One night the company commander sent Metz with a message to the battalion headquarters. Metz recalls the burning villages and farms he traversed, conveying a sense of the fear and disorientation the scenes visited upon the youth. Far more shocking, however, was the discovery upon his return that his company had been completely wiped out:

"I saw only the lifeless faces of my comrades, those same comrades with whom I had but days before shared my childhood fears and my youthful laughter. I remember nothing but a soundless cry. I strayed for hours alone in the forest. Over and over again, just this silent cry! And up until today I see myself so. Behind this memory all my childhood dreams have vanished."[70]

Metz explains that this memory establishes his basic theological question not as "Who saves me?" or "What happens to me when I suffer, when I die?" but, rather, "Who saves you?" and "What happens to you when you suffer, when you die?" The memory and its question also give rise to a "basic form of Christian hope": not "What dare I hope?" but "What dare I hope for you and, in the end, also for me?"[71]

I have recounted Metz's story in full detail for three reasons: first, out of respect for its inherent integrity and power; second, in order to examine the way in which Metz formulates his basic theological questions from it; and third, to allow that reflection to lead into further aspects of the mysticism Metz considers essential to political theology.

The first reason witnesses to Metz's argument for the irreducibility of narratives of suffering, for the manner in which they neither allow themselves to be abridged nor allow their hearers to continue with their lives or arguments (reason) unaffected. What strikes me about this narrative of suffering with which Metz privileges his reader is that, along with his reflections on the impact of Auschwitz on German historical consciousness, it comprises the only detailed, narrative account of "catastrophe" that he actually recounts amidst his many

[70] Metz, "Communicating a Dangerous Memory," 40.
[71] Ibid.

occasional writings.[72] In *Faith in History and Society*, especially, one is left wondering whether Metz intends that the actual biblical apocalyptic books and passages (so utterly foreign if not bizarre in their symbolism and imagery) should themselves exert a shocking impact on middle-class Christians, or whether Metz wants contemporary believers simply to remember that this sort of "consciousness" or "vision" was essential to the earliest believers. It is notable that one of the subheadings in the chapter on time and immanent expectation reads, *"Against the Grip of Timelessness: Memory of the Apocalyptic Vision."*[73] Can one not, then, consider this story to be an apocalyptic narrative, a story that exhibits the features of the biblical apocalyptic passages to which Metz refers at other places in his essays? Metz defines apocalyptic consciousness as consciousness of suffering in history, and as stories which place time and this world into question. Surely, that is the case for his story from the battlefield. What nonetheless is different about Metz's story is that it results in questions about suffering and hope, whereas the ancient apocalyptic literature exudes an assertiveness of God's judgment upon those persecuting or oppressing God's people.

Second, a consideration of the theological questions Metz raises from his story, as well as the theological solution he proposes: As in earlier essays Metz addresses the crucial question of how such overwhelming, catastrophic stories of suffering can avoid leading their hearers into "tragic consciousness" (or what he describes earlier as "paralyzing fear"), thereby failing to be memories "with a practical-political intention."[74] Put another way, how is Metz able to move from the question of suffering and death to the question—and praxis—of hope?

[72] By focusing at such length on Metz's story from his youth I by no means intend to minimize the role that the Holocaust has played in the formation of Metz's theological reflections on memory and suffering. See Johann Baptist Metz, "Facing the Jews: Christian Theology After Auschwitz," *Faith and the Future: Essays on Theology, Solidarity, and Modernity*, Johann Baptist Metz and Jürgen Moltmann (Maryknoll, N.Y.: Orbis Books, 1995) 38–48; and Metz, *A Passion for God*, 3–4, 39–42, 121–32. For commentary on the profound significance of the Holocaust to Metz's theology, see Colombo, *An Essay on Theology and History*, 183–4, and Ashley, *Interruptions*, 32, 122–5.

[73] Metz, *Faith in History and Society*, 175.

[74] Metz, "Communicating a Dangerous Memory," 42.

Metz answers by means of a brief narrative, describing the inspirational impact of his visits to base communities in the Third World:

"I have met in the face of communities of the Third World—but not only there—persons in whose suffering, in whose struggle, in whose sorrow, and in whose courage I can identify the symbols of the kingdom of God. And I can make this identification more easily through them than through my own life. Through my experience of these persons and these communities I can relate the pictures and parables about the kingdom of God finally also to myself."[75]

What Metz seems to recognize in the lives of those poor and persecuted Christians is the impact of not only the catastrophic biblical stories and images but also the promising images of the kingdom of God. The latter is what I find lacking in Metz's earlier treatment of apocalyptic eschatology, where he never draws upon the parables of banquets and generous forgiveness but only upon the one of final judgment. The reason for that lies not only in his agenda for the urgency of time but also in his observation of how bourgeois religion co-opts the consoling images to reinforce the world view of the middle-class subject. Because of their current overt suffering, however, the poor Christians of the southern hemisphere authentically receive the consoling message of the parables of the kingdom of God. Because they know their lives to be in danger they also know the hope of the "vision of rescue or salvation."[76] Metz, who stands as a representative of the northern middle-class subject of theology, seems to have needed the ecclesial experience of the base communities both to return to his own memory of suffering and to orient that memory to a hopefulness inspired by the biblical eschatological narratives of both catastrophe and consolation.

By means of narrative-memories Metz mounts a theological argument for what, at the end of the essay, he calls "an eschatological dialectic" endemic to a praxis of faith grounded in biblical stories:

"Only if we recognize something of the situation of our own Christian hope—our eschatological hope—in the apocalyptic symbols of danger, of crisis and downfall, the images and symbols of the Kingdom

---

[75] Ibid., 41.
[76] Ibid., 52. See also, Metz, *A Passion for God*, 39, 45, 49.

will not decay like wishful thinking. Only when we remain faithful to the symbols of the crisis can the symbols of promise and consolation remain faithful to us: the images and symbols of the great peace, of the home, of the Father, and of the kingdom of freedom, justice, and reconciliation, the images of the tears wiped away, and the images of the laughter of the children of God."[77]

By thus concluding the essay Metz provides a more concrete sense of the mysticism which he has long argued is essential to the praxis of faith. His recognition of a dialectic in the eschatology of the New Testament resonates with the dialectic he recognizes in the *memoria Jesu Christi*, wherein one cannot remember either Jesus' death or resurrection without having the other in mind. Both the definite memory of Christians and the future it anticipates are characterized by a dialectic of crisis and consolation. Notable as well is the prominence of symbols, images, and parables in Metz's more fully developed apocalyptic eschatology (a point to which I shall return later in this chapter).

I wish to return one more time to Metz's story from the battlefield in order to raise a question about the way he formulates his own basic theological questions from the story. The "lifeless faces" of Metz's comrades constitute the shock which leads him to ask about the other's ("your") suffering and hope. The story indicates the personal origins of Metz's theological arguments for solidarity with the dead and for the primary question of suffering as the suffering of others. But how can one not be struck by the suffering that Metz himself endured in 1945 and that, by his own account, continues to endure to this day? He describes the dreams of youth that were stripped from him and, perhaps even more poignantly, the "soundless cry" that remains with him "up until today." I raise these observations in order to move the present study forward along two lines of thought. First, Metz has made a compelling case for how the modern subject of religion needs to be deconstructed by an awareness of suffering in history and reconstructed through a praxis in solidarity with those who now suffer or are dead. Still, if one is to affirm the notion of subjectivity (as Metz does indeed do), then one needs to integrate the concerns for others' suffering with a whole range of one's experiences, memories,

---

[77] Metz, "Communicating a Dangerous Memory," 53.

and emotions—however fragmented they might (necessarily) be. Again, the issue of symbols emerges and, moreover, perhaps a call for a fuller sense of what the Christian tradition has meant by its proclamation, through word and sacrament, of the paschal mystery. Second, the "soundless cry" of the shocked boy on the apocalyptic battlefield autobiographically indicates the other element of mysticism to which Metz has given concerted attention: prayer. The mysticism of apocalyptic eschatology not only shocks timelessness and instills hope amidst suffering, but also takes form in the utterance of longing, the plea for deliverance.

MYSTICISM II: PRAYER

In order for Christians to live in the constant dialectical movement of the dangerous, anticipatory memory, they need, Metz argues, to recover the ancient tradition of prayer. To step outside of the evolutionary stream of progress is to step into an experience of the world and history which is not adequately served by language that is technical, instrumental, controlling, and, therefore, hopeless. Those who join in solidarity with the suffering discover that prayer "is the only form of language that can express our lives and feelings adequately."[78] Drawing on the Hebrew psalms Metz characterizes prayer as the subject's affirmation of faith in God amidst the contradictions of suffering, violence, oppression, and death. In order for this faithful relationship to God not to be a denial or suppression of the contradictions and, thus, in order for prayer to constitute genuine human subjectivity, prayer must be free in form, uninhibited by linguistic constraints, expressive of the whole range of emotions from mourning to celebration. The "extreme emotions" of prayer thereby liberate the subject from the bourgeois ideal of moderation in feelings and the banality of consumerism.[79]

[78] Johann Baptist Metz, "The Courage to Pray," *The Courage to Pray,* Johann Baptist Metz and Karl Rahner, trans. Sarah O'Brien Twohig (New York: Crossroad, 1981) 3.

[79] A "note" in the "Notes and Drafts" of *Dialectic of Enlightenment* is relevant to Metz's argument at this point:

"Individuals are reduced to a mere sequence of instantaneous experiences which leave no trace, or rather whose trace is hated as irrational, superfluous, and 'overtaken' in the literal sense of the word. . . . It is not considered

Metz's argument, nonetheless, is never for an open-ended expressivism or a vague sort of spontaneity. The specific type of experience which prayer must not restrain is the experience of suffering. Prayer must, on the contrary, heighten the sense of suffering's ineffability. The resource and model for the assertive expression of suffering is the Hebrew tradition of lament:

"Again and again prayer is a cry of lament from the depths of the spirit. But this cry is in no sense a vague, rambling moan. It calls out loudly, insistently. Nor is it merely a wish or desire, no matter how fervent. It is a supplication. The language of prayer finds its purpose and justification in the silently concealed face of God. Hence the lament, supplication, crying and protest contained in prayer, as also the silent accusation of the wordless cry, can never simply be translated and dissolved into discourse."[80]

The prayer of lament and supplication addressed to God, even in the form of the silent cry, is a practice of subjectivity Metz recognizes as alien not only to the mainstream of capitalist, technocratic society but also specifically to the Christian religion. The latter has come to assert far too many answers while finding itself too little compelled to raise up passionate and painful questions. With this lack of identification with the suffering the Church has also deprived itself of the paradoxical freedom that the Hebrew tradition has known in the ability truly to seek God's confidence and not to withhold doubts, even doubts about God. This, however, was the culmination of Jesus' life of prayer and obedience, a cry of abandonment by God upon the cross. Metz perceives in Jesus' words of faithfulness (obedience) to God even in death "the mysticism of suffering embodied in the prayers of the Old Testament . . . grasped at its very roots."[81]

---

proper to show emotion, and the girl who proudly described the first-class burial of her grandmother, adding 'a pity that Daddy lost control' (because he shed a few tears), accurately reflects the situation. In reality, the dead suffer a fate which the Jews in olden days considered the worst possible curse: they are expunged from the memory of those who live on."

Horkheimer and Adorno, *Dialectic of Enlightenment*, 215–6.

[80] Metz, "The Courage to Pray," 13.

[81] Ibid., 14.

Typical to the style of his theology, Metz touches upon the figure of Jesus, and thus christology, in a suggestive way.[82] Metz evokes the image of the crucified Jesus so as to disrupt the prevailing Christian attitude and provoke believers to a radically different practice in prayer. Here again, christology for Metz is a christology of imitation. Metz moves dialectically from the faithful Jesus' catastrophic abandonment by God to his consoling knowledge of God as boundlessly merciful and loving. There is a non-identity in Jesus' experience of God in prayer that Metz, far from seeking to resolve in some positive synthesis, highlights for the purpose of defining and encouraging the prayer of Jesus' followers. Having reflected for a moment on the irreducible role of lament before "this silent, faceless God," Metz wards off any image of God as a tyrannical master or ruler—and, therefore, of the follower of Christ as a masochist—by a momentary reflection on the prayer of Jesus during his ministry:

"The God of his prayers is 'our Father' too; his prayers, his whole demeanour, his entire destiny make this evident. From this we can see clearly that the God of his prayers is neither a humiliating tyrant nor the projection of worldly power and authority. Rather, he is the God of insuperable love, the God of a dwelling almost beyond our imagining, the God who wipes away our tears and gathers lost souls into the radiant clasp of his mercy."[83]

[82] Metz's fellow political theologian, Jürgen Moltmann, has pursued the issue of suffering (theodicy) through systematic reflection on christology and trinitarian theology. The following questions prompt Moltmann's work at the outset of a programmatic essay:

"If man [sic], suffering because of injustice, calls the existence of a just God into question, then the reverse also happens and his longing for justice and for the one who guarantees it causes him to question his suffering, so that it becomes a conscious pain. Suffering and protest go beyond theism and atheism to the question of theodicy: if God is just, what is the origin of evil? If the sting in the question 'Why is there suffering?' is 'God,' then the sting in the question, 'Is there a God?' is, of course, 'suffering.'"

Jürgen Moltmann, "The 'Crucified God': God and the Trinity Today," trans. David Smith, *New Questions on God*, Concilium 76, ed. Johann Baptist Metz (New York: Herder and Herder, 1972) 27. See also, Jürgen Moltmann, *The Crucified God*, trans. R. A. Wilson and John Bowden (New York: Harper & Row, 1974).

[83] Metz, "The Courage to Pray," 21.

The practical conclusion Metz draws from this reflection is that Christians must imitate Jesus by seeking this "liberating, edifying" God in prayer and making precisely this God evident in the world by their attitudes (of merciful love and hopefulness), words (of public prayer and proclamation), and actions (of direct care for the poor and oppressed).

While Metz's essay on prayer is, by his own admission, offered as an exhortation to fellow middle-class Christians, the brief analysis just performed has discovered therein a heightened sense of the dialectical quality of Metz's theology of imitation. It is a sort of negative dialectics in that the nonidentity of suffering, at the center of the *memoria Jesu Christi*, does not allow any synthetic resolution in the mysticism of Christian prayer. The life of faith, the praxis of discipleship, is lived in the gaps between moments of lament and praise, suffering and consolation. The prayer that rises up in the gaps is the urgent plea that Christ return: "Hence, Christianity's oldest prayer is simultaneously the most up-to-date: 'Come, Lord Jesus!' (Rev. 22:20)."[84] Prayer must be apocalyptically eschatological, resisting both hopelessness amidst evolutionary time and self-absorption in a personalistic view of salvation.

Metz's reflections on prayer give further substance to his assertion that the modern subject must become the "subject in the presence of God." This language of presence includes an irreducible absence and thus avoids idealist tendencies in transcendental theologies. Of special note is Metz's construction of the subject as mediated by the encounter with not only the consoling but also the startling, disconcerting, even painful otherness of God. This experience of God, mediated by *memoria Jesu*, opens out into a life of solidarity with the suffering. Christian mysticism, therefore, can never have an individualist or exclusively personalist bent; rather, mystical praxis entails a universal solidarity with all of humanity, especially a solidarity in remembrance of the dead. The "anamnesis or the memory of the sacrifices of history" serves as "an apocalyptic stimulus" for particular acts of political solidarity with the suffering and oppressed in the present.[85] In his more recent work Metz has come to conceptualize this convergence of apocalypticism, prayer, and social action as *Leiden an Gott*, suffering

---

[84] Ibid., 28. See also Metz, *Followers of Christ*, 75; and Metz, *Faith in History and Society*, 176.

[85] Metz, *Faith in History and Society*, 58, 231.

unto God.[86] To know oneself as a subject in God's presence is a practical knowledge in mystical and political solidarity.

The practice of mysticism, as an experience of universal solidarity, is not only disconcerting—as a form of the apocalyptic goad—but also consoling. For all his argumentation for the middle-class subject's need for conversion to a concern for the other person's suffering, Metz nonetheless demonstrates sensitivity to the fragile condition of the bourgeois subject. The forces of instrumental reason of technology and the capitalist market isolate the middle class, and the frenetic qualities of professional work and even entertainment only repress burdensome feelings of loneliness and discourage self-awareness.[87] Given those cultural pressures Metz is not surprised that the inclination to prayer is weak and requires genuine courage. Those who venture into the practice of prayer, however, discover that they "are not alone; they form part of a great historical company; prayer is a matter of solidarity."[88] Metz's reflections on this point remain general and prompt questions as to how one's awareness of the historical company comes about, let alone grows and deepens. The answer in terms of his practical fundamental theology resides in the diffuse category of narrative, but his reflections on prayer indicate the need for closer attention to specific resources in the tradition, of which liturgy, especially in its anamnestic qualities, is no small part.

Metz's primary interest, nonetheless, is to argue for the compelling sense of responsibility that prayer should impart. In one of the few instances in which he critiques a specific practice of Christian prayer,

[86] See Metz, *A Passion for God*, 42, 66–71; Ashley, *Interruptions*, 126–9, 160.

[87] In their devastating critique of "The Culture Industry," Horkheimer and Adorno argue that amusement in late capitalist society is a "prolongation of work," wherein "pleasure hardens into boredom" as the "bloated pleasure apparatus" provides forms of entertainment which neither demand any effort on the part of the recipients nor encourage any resistance or thought. The conformity expected in the workplace is replicated in the amusements of leisure time. Even the surprise-elements in the story-lines of films (and now television) follow formulaic patterns while, nonetheless, reaching ever greater degrees of sensationalism. The culture industry is at once "pornographic and prudish," unlike genuine art, which is "ascetic and unashamed." In the process, "inwardness, the subjectively restricted form of truth," is utterly trivialized. Horkheimer and Adorno, *Dialectic of Enlightenment*, 137, 139, 140, 144.

[88] Metz, "The Courage to Pray," 9.

and a liturgical one at that, Metz argues for the transformation that must occur in the Church's "official prayer" so that it might impart a dangerous power for political praxis:

"Let us consider the language of our 'modern' prayers of petition which often purport to be 'explicit' and 'social' in intent. Are they really prayers or merely excuses by which we take the easy option, with little risk of responsibility? 'Lord help drug addicts back to a "normal" life' or 'Lord help prevent racial discrimination, and give food to the poor countries of the third world. . . .' Surely the only practical effect of such prayers can be to appease our consciences."[89]

The problem with such prayers is that they function as a "eulogistic evasion" of the responsibility that a "mature attitude towards prayer presupposes." The Church's concern for institutional stability and, thus, its own uncritical participation in modern society have allowed prayer to be co-opted as "a useful social tool to ensure the smooth running of society."[90] The question arises, however, as to whether prayer itself, in its form and content (its "language"), can generate among believers the mature attitude it requires. Metz alludes to the possibility in saying that prayer "feeds on the contradictory, painful feelings which necessarily accompany the acceptance and fulfillment

---

[89] Ibid., 20.

[90] Ibid., 22. Elsewhere, Metz notes "the historical conscience of generations who are aware of the Church's dubious alliances with the power structures of society," and makes the following judgment:

"It is indeed the most pressing historical and hermeneutical problem confronting contemporary ecclesiology and far more important than, for example, that of finding historical evidence for the foundation of the Church and the apostolic succession. This problem cannot, moreover, be solved by providing a better or more subtle interpretation of the Church's past history. It can only be solved by a painful process of change involving proof of the spirit and strength of a new praxis."

Metz, *Faith in History and Society*, 93. One wonders whether Metz, when criticizing theological efforts at a "more subtle interpretation" of Church history, has in mind (at least in part) his teacher and mentor, Karl Rahner, whose work included many exercises in retrieving dogmatic tenets of the faith that seem dubious in light of contemporary historical-critical and social-philosophical views.

of this responsibility."[91] He does not, however, explain how this can happen: whether, for example, it is a matter of changing the actual words or their manner of delivery or, to think more liturgically, of changing other aspects of the rite in which the petitions are situated.

Metz's more direct answer, on the other hand, seems to focus on the liturgical assembly itself: The Church must stop praying *for* the poor and the outcast and start praying *with* them. The actual social location of the Church establishes the authenticity, the authority, the power of its prayer and, moreover, is what makes prayer itself "political and influential."[92] Metz repeatedly calls for a Church with the poor, for a transformation whereby the "protectionist 'Church for the people' . . . becomes a real 'Church of the people.'"[93] That call is clearly inspired by his encounter with the base communities in the Third World.[94] As noted above, the poor ecclesial communities of the south are where Metz has encountered not only the painful otherness of poverty and oppression but also the redemptive power and potential of the positive biblical images of the kingdom of God. One suspects that Metz has also experienced the qualitative difference in the celebration of the Eucharist that northern visitors to base communities often describe.[95] The problem that remains, however, is how the inspiration of the southern church can translate into actual practice in the north; indeed, the social-political circumstances are markedly differ-

---

[91] Metz, "The Courage to Pray," 20. See also Metz, *A Passion for God*, 115–6.

[92] Metz, "The Courage to Pray," 20.

[93] Metz, *Faith in History and Society*, 231. For Metz's further reflections on this theme, see the book's entire eighth chapter, "Church and People: The Forgotten Subject of Faith," 136–53.

[94] See Metz, *The Emergent Church*, 82–94; and Metz, *A Passion for God*, 4–5.

[95] Gustavo Gutiérrez offers a theological reflection upon the quality of the eucharistic celebrations in the communities of the poor in South America:

"Here, on the terrain of real life, among the very poorest, is where the eucharistic celebration takes on its full meaning of a sharing in the death and resurrection of Christ. . . . In the fullness of life brought to us by liberation in Jesus Christ, and in the historical power of the poor, we discover the source of the remarkable joy that the poor manifest in their struggle, in their prayerful praxis. No superficial glee, this; no empty 'joy' born of unawareness of the reality of oppression and suffering. This is Easter gladness—joy that passes through death and pain, in intense, profound hope."

Gutiérrez, *The Power of the Poor in History*, 107.

ent.[96] This present study's concern is not only with the relationship between liturgy and its social context but also with the nature and practice of liturgy itself. One gets a sense throughout his writings that the latter has largely been uncharted waters for Metz, yet a potential resource in the tradition to which he has become increasingly attracted.[97] The attraction, nevertheless, has been a wary one, as a brief examination of his treatment of symbol and ritual will now show.

MYSTICISM III: SYMBOLS AND SACRAMENTAL RITUAL

Metz's study of critical theory has led to his awareness of how the instrumental reason pervasive in modern society has resulted in not only an impoverishment in the expressive range and capacities of language but also a restrictiveness or abandonment of a wider range of epistemological capacities. The society based on economic exchange and technical reason provides increasingly fewer sources of imagination. Bourgeois sensibilities become increasingly alienated from "forms of sensitive-intuitive access to reality," such as the visual, aural, and tactile, or else these are banished to the "realm of the private and the irrational."[98] An increasingly widespread reaction on the part of theologians has been the call for "a purely cultic spirituality," one that is "isolated and free from all the conflicts, repressions and challenges of everyday life," and Metz concurs that this "would certainly seem to be an objective need in the middle class."[99]

Such an isolated pursuit of the humanly freeing potential of celebration and openness to mystery, however, is unable to realize what Metz has identified as genuinely religious (Christian) freedom. In a manner similar to his critique of the middle-class subject of religion, Metz identifies in modern theology and practice an "ideal" of the "purely religious parish community," when in reality the parishes merely mirror and uphold bourgeois values: "And so, just as our bourgeois society provides less and less material for dreaming and

---

[96] Other analysts of Metz's theology have noted this same problem. See Colombo, *An Essay on Theology and History,* 209; and Ashley, *Interruptions,* 254, n. 82.

[97] I should note here that by this statement I mean to say that the sacraments and liturgy are uncharted theoretical waters for Metz, who is dedicated to his pastoral work as a presbyter in the Roman Church.

[98] Metz, *The Emergent Church,* 35.

[99] Metz, *Faith in History and Society,* 95; see 68. See also, Metz, *A Passion for God,* 102–3.

poetry, our bourgeois religion itself supplies scarcely anything for mysticism and adoration, for resistance and conversion."[100] The ironic result is that these middle-class parishes prove unable to provide relief (the "opium") from the pressures of the instrumentalist, evolutionary world. These churches which do not challenge likewise do not console, and so Metz does not find it difficult to understand why in Germany and in other First World nations the churches are so empty.

On this point we can make a brief comparison with the analysis of liturgical life in American middle-class parishes reviewed in Chapter 1. While the numbers of Catholics attending Sunday liturgies in the United States is significantly higher than in Europe, nevertheless several of the authors were critical of the lack of an "otherness" of symbols or an "illative sense" in those liturgies. They found too little challenge and transformation in the way the ritual elements were being performed, and ventured hypotheses that this was not unrelated to the paltry evidence of connections being made between the liturgy and active concern for social justice.

Metz does not restrict his analysis of the hobbled condition of symbol and ritual and, thus, liturgy in northern churches to the pervasive influence of instrumental reason and bourgeois values. He also cites, in admittedly broad and summary fashion, shortcomings in the theologically argued positions among Protestants and Catholics since the rise of the Reformation. Protestant theologians' disavowals of "religion" have resulted in a dualism between sense-related experience and grace that is alien to biblical narratives (notably those of Jesus' ministry) as well as principles that arise from belief in the incarnation.

"If Protestantism could ever trust itself to be a religion, how powerful a religion it would be! It is, in fact, surely the only religion in the world which, through the voice of its theologians, proclaims that it in no way wishes to be a religion, that it is 'faith alone,' 'grace alone,'— as if visible religion, festive religion, religion with liturgies based on contact and accompanied by the delight in symbols and myths did not comprise an essential, though always threatened, praise of grace present within the senses."[101]

---

[100] Metz, *The Emergent Church*, 45; see also 88.
[101] Ibid., 52–3.

Metz's concern for robust liturgical practice is not for its own sake but for nurturing the conviction that God's gift of freedom in Christ is offered for the salvation of all aspects of human life. The latter is the point upon which Protestantism has stumbled, isolating redemptive grace not only from liturgical "sense-related" experience but also from "historical-social experience." This excessively "spiritual" view of grace helped to render Protestantism duplicitous in the rise of bourgeois religion, and Metz describes the result as "a graceless form of humanity, strictly oriented to property, competition, and success, with grace overarching the whole."[102] Idealistic theology has played no small supporting role in this process.

Metz identifies a different sort of flaw in the history of the Catholic theology of grace which contributed to that Church's failure to criticize effectively the social-economic consequences of the Enlightenment:

"Just as we find in Protestantism a kind of constitutional suspicion regarding our connectedness to the senses, to the visible and representational dimension of grace—in brief to what is called the incarnational principle—so we find in Catholicism a kind of constitutional suspicion regarding grace as freedom. This is why the sense-related dimension in Catholicism often appears so reified, so distorted by sacramentalism and ritualism, so monolithic and regimented—as if the human being is no longer present there at all in his [sic] spontaneity and freedom."[103]

Metz provides no further commentary here on what he means by "sacramentalism and ritualism," but one can surmise the phenomenon to which he is globally referring. An excessively legalistic, rubrically-oriented, and often magical focus on the physical objects of sacramental action has greatly hindered Catholicism from making connections between sacramental practice and the other sensual and social-historical dimensions of experience. We shall take up this issue of "ritualism" in the next chapter. Metz's primary concern in the essay presently quoted, and one consistent with his other writings, turns out to be not for freedom as spontaneity-in-itself but for social-political freedom, freedom in solidarity, a freedom that needs moments of spontaneous expression. Metz offers the base communities of the Third World church as exemplars in their ability to "bind together

[102] Ibid., 53.
[103] Ibid., 56.

mysticism and politics, religious and societal praxis, and to assimilate into their eucharistic table fellowship the fundamental social conflicts and sufferings surrounding them."[104] He provides no explanation or description of how this is accomplished. One suspects, however, that part of the answer resides in the fact that their religious practices, unlike the "bourgeois Christianity" plaguing both Catholic and Protestant churches to the north, are not "founded on invisibility, on noninterference, on nontouching, on dualism."[105] The solidarity they have forged amidst their suffering will not allow that.

The other crucial factor for realizing the integration of mysticism and politics in the liturgy resides in Metz's fundamental theological category of narrative. As noted above, Metz relates that encounters with the poor in the Third World have brought to life for him the symbols and images of the biblical narratives of the kingdom of God. Although he does not mention the base communities' typical celebration of the word of God by reflecting upon biblical texts in relation to their praxis and experiences, we can note this narrative element as essential to their ability to "assimilate" their "social conflicts and sufferings" into their liturgies.[106] Here the "mystical" practice of liturgy provides evidence for Metz's argument that the "irreducible original experiences" of faith in history necessitate narrative's role in a practical fundamental theology and, thus, in the praxis of mysticism and politics which that theology seeks to "define."[107]

Metz, moreover, makes an explicit connection between narrative and sacrament through a brief excursus on the transformative potential of storytelling.[108] Metz relays a Hasidic tale (found in a work by

[104] Ibid., 63.

[105] Ibid., 54.

[106] For a comprehensive account of this communal proclamation and interpretation of the Word of God in a specific, Central American context, see Ernesto Cardinal, *The Gospel in Solentiname*, trans. Donald D. Walsh (Maryknoll, N.Y.: Orbis Books, 1976).

[107] Metz, *Faith in History and Society*, 206, 77.

[108] Walter Benjamin exercises particular influence upon Metz in this aspect of his theology. Metz draws upon Benjamin's argument for storytelling's ability to exchange and transform experience and quotes selectively from a passage of Benjamin's "Der Erzäler." See Metz, *Faith in History and Society*, 206, 207; and 217, nn. 4, 5. For a translation of Benjamin's essay, see "The Storyteller," *Illuminations*, 83–109.

Martin Buber) in which a rabbi asked his paralyzed elderly grandfather to tell a story about the holy teacher under whom he studied. In telling how his teacher jumped and danced while praying the old man himself gets carried away into those very gestures, only to find himself thereby cured of his paralysis. From this account Metz realizes that if stories can thus function as

"'effective signs,' then this should also point to a 'narrative aspect' of sacraments: The sacramental sign can easily be characterized as a linguistic action in which the unity of the story as an effective word and as a practical effect is expressed in the same process. The aspect of ceremony and ritual may perhaps mean that the sacrament is not clearly recognized as a saving narrative. On closer inspection, however, it is evident firstly that the linguistic formulae used in the administration of the sacraments are typical of what are known as performative expressions, and secondly that they narrate something."[109]

Metz's comments on this point are brief but, nonetheless, astutely suggestive. He gives the example of how the story of Jesus' actions "on the night that he was betrayed" is present in the Eucharistic Prayer and implies that the function of this narrative has not been adequately appreciated in the theology and practice of the liturgy. His tentative opposition of "ceremony and ritual" to "saving narrative" in the liturgy points toward the important and disastrous history of how these two became separated in the Roman Mass and led to often polemically motivated distortions in the relationship between word and sacrament in the churches of both the Reformation and Counter-Reformation. Liturgical and sacramental theologians have indeed availed themselves of hermeneutical and language-performance theories in their efforts to reform liturgical theory and practice—and reform it precisely so that it might have a more transformative effect upon its participants.[110] Metz hopes that such theological efforts will

---

[109] Metz, *Faith in History and Society*, 208.

[110] See especially the work of David N. Power, including *Unsearchable Riches: The Symbolic Nature of Liturgy* (New York: Pueblo, 1984), and *The Eucharistic Mystery: Revitalizing the Tradition* (New York: Crossroad, 1992). See also, Louis-Marie Chauvet, *Symbol and Sacrament: A Sacramental Reinterpretation of Christian Existence,* trans. Patrick Madigan and Madeleine Beaumont (Collegeville: The Liturgical Press, 1995) 130–5.

especially enable people to relate the words and actions of liturgy to the "stories of life and suffering." That is the very challenge that I shall take up in the following chapters. I thus draw this present chapter to its conclusion by identifying several points of contact between Metz's theological categories and themes and the resources of liturgical theology.

CONCLUSION: POINTS FOR DIALOGUE WITH LITURGICAL THEOLOGY

This study initially turned to Metz's political theology in its capacity as a critical theology. Metz's critique of the middle-class subject of religion and of the technological-economic world view that pervades North Atlantic societies provided a systematic analysis of the problems and challenges that liturgical theologians in the United States are identifying in the implementation of the Second Vatican Council's liturgical reform. The chapter then moved to the constructive project in Metz's theology, which he understands as an effort to establish the Christian religion not on the basis of speculative (transcendental) theories about God and humanity but on the basis of a narrative memory of the God of Jesus Christ. In a manner that, in the end, is consistent with his suspicion of non-dialectical systematic thought, Metz's development of his theological categories, as well as his treatment of such themes and topics as christology, anthropology, ecclesiology, eschatology, and prayer, disorient modern theological concepts, offering challenging, if not at times problematic, solutions and suggestions. Joseph Colombo states the situation well: "The protean nature of Metz's reflections and style leaves the reader with a bundle of 'loose ends' which open up a space for further critical reflection."[111] In my selective

---

Among the most important philosophical works in language performance theory to have influenced liturgical theologians are J. L. Austin, *How to Do Things with Words* (Cambridge, Mass.: Harvard University Press, 1962), and John R. Searle, *Speech Acts: An Essay in the Philosophy of Language* (Cambridge, Mass.: Cambridge University Press, 1969). For an overview of theory and its application to the Church's sacramental worship, see Joseph J. Schaller, "Performative Language Theory: An Exercise in the Analysis of Ritual," *Worship* 62 (September 1988) 415–32.

[111] Colombo adds, "In part, this arises from [Metz's] penchant for 'assertions' with little or no explanatory warrant. . . ." *An Essay on Theology and History*, 208. See also, Ashley, *Interruptions*, 192, 197.

rehearsal of Metz's work I have already noted several such instances with a view to pursuing them in the field of liturgical theology. In this concluding section I shall now take special note of two topics of general concern to both Metz and liturgical theology, action and tradition, and then move on to the specific theological category of memory.

First, there is the singular importance that Metz assigns to action or praxis in his effort to establish political theology as a practical fundamental theology. The precise theological method Metz intends, including the problem of the relationship between theory and praxis, is a question open to debate and beyond the scope of the present study.[112] Nonetheless, Metz is clear in his insistence that the Christian faith is only authentically realized in a praxis of politics and mysticism and that theology's task, therefore, is to narrate, reflect upon, argue for, and define the practices that constitute the life of following Christ at the present moment in history. Metz considers himself to be providing an urgently needed corrective to the discipline of theology. In light of this, Metz questions the extent to which theology has become the function of Church officials and academicians to the detriment of hearing and representing the "new religious experiences" of the people.[113] In a parallel or similar fashion, liturgical theologians insist that academic theology is practiced from a position at least once removed from the primary theological activity of the Church, namely, the actual performance of the liturgy. The scholarly study of liturgy is at the service of the Church's practices for the worship of God and the salvation of people.[114]

[112] See Lamb, *Solidarity with Victims*, 82–8; Colombo, *An Essay on Theology and History*, 208; and Don S. Browning, *A Fundamental Practical Theology: Descriptive and Strategic Proposals* (Minneapolis: Fortress Press, 1991) 68. James Matthew Ashley has pursued the question of Metz's methodology in depth by not only identifying "trajectories" in Metz's theology but also arguing from them to a "systematic coherence" in what he calls Metz's mature work. See *Interruptions*, 59–167, especially 60, 94–5, 99–100, 132–5.

[113] Metz, *Faith in History and Society*, 148.

[114] Alexander Schmemann, as we shall see in the next chapter, passionately argued that the performance of liturgy is the Church's fundamental theological act. See also Teresa Berger, *Theology in Hymns? A Study of the Relation of Doxology and Theology According to a Collection of Hymns for the Use of the People Called Methodists*, trans. Timothy E. Kimbrough (Nashville: Abingdon Press, 1995) 31–57; Aidan Kavanagh, *On Liturgical Theology* (New York: Pueblo, 1984) 73–95; and David W. Fagerberg, *What Is Liturgical Theology? A Study in Method* (Collegeville: The Liturgical Press, 1992) 180–227.

Metz, moreover, is highly critical of the extent to which the Christian religion has become for middle-class subjects a "purely believed in faith" or "mere contemplation." There is a certain ambiguity about these phrases or images that may serve Metz better than he himself realizes. Metz's basic intention by them is to convey the attitude whereby religious faith is seen as only concerned with credal confession, prayer, and ceremony, to the exclusion of their having any impact on people's lives in society—or vice versa. Metz is scrutinizing anew the unfortunate contrast of prayer and action that has historically dogged the practice of Christian faith. He argues that prayer should be a freeing source for liberative action.[115] Liturgical theologians have been hard about the work of exposing and correcting the extent to which the ancient sense of the liturgy itself as an action of the people became lost in the Church.[116] The failure on the part of Christians to see an intrinsic link between worship and social-ethical practice cannot be unrelated to their failure to realize themselves as participants in a communal action when assembled for worship. This, nonetheless, raises the further question of how the work of the liturgical assembly *(leitourgia)* is indeed related to the people's work in the world. The next chapter will explore critically Alexander Schmemann's significant contribution to this question.

The second general concern for Metz which invites a constructive dialogue with liturgical theology is the authority of tradition. Metz's appreciation for tradition is a positive counterpart to his heightened critical awareness of the negative social-historical consequences of the Enlightenment: the "post-historistic" priorities of instrumental reason, the equation of social value with the market value of exchange, and the relativizing of tradition even when invoked in the private

[115] See Metz, *Faith in History and Society*, 95. Don E. Saliers and Peter E. Fink discuss the tensive relationship in Christianity between prayer and action in their contributions to *Liturgy and the Moral Self: Humanity at Full Stretch Before God*, ed. E. Byron Anderson and Bruce T. Morrill (Collegeville: The Liturgical Press, 1998) 30–2, 127–38.

[116] Aimé Georges Martimort played a leading role in the recovery of the theological significance of the liturgical assembly. See A. G. Martimort, "The Assembly," *Principles of the Liturgy*, vol. 1 of *The Church at Prayer*, trans. Matthew J. O'Connell, ed. A. G. Martimort (Collegeville: The Liturgical Press, 1987) 89–111. See also, in the same volume, Irénée Henri Dalmais, "The Liturgy as a Celebration," 233–48.

sphere. Metz astutely observes in the First World church two diverging patterns of response to late modernity. One is a liberal, uncritical adaptation of the message and symbols of Christianity to the "modern processes in the world," reducing the faith to a "symbolic paraphrase" of what is already happening in society. The other, borne of anxiety in the face of late modernity, is a "pure traditionalism" which seeks a sense of stability in a rigid retrieval of past forms of religious practice and thereby threatens the Church with sectarian isolation.[117]

Whereas Enlightenment came to oppose human freedom to religious and other cultural traditions, Metz calls for a critical and constructive retrieval of tradition in the interest of the human history of suffering.[118] Political theology does not deny the need for the criticism of myth and ideology but, rather, it denies that the goal of criticism should be their elimination. The theological critique of religious symbols, myths, narratives, and rituals is directed not at these traditions in themselves but at the unjustifiable assumption that the knowledge and practice of these traditions is politically and socially innocent: "It is not symbols, mysticism, the collective memory and its images that corrupt religion and deprive the people of their independence, but the way in which these are exploited for alien interests and can be used against the religious identity of the people."[119] Metz has put his finger

---

[117] Metz, *Faith in History and Society*, 97. See also Metz, *A Passion for God*, 49, 53. This problem shall receive further discussion in the following chapter.

[118] See Metz, *Faith in History and Society*, 74–6; Chopp, *The Praxis of Suffering*, 81.

[119] Metz, *Faith in History and Society*, 150. One of the modern, rationalistic biases which ritual theorists have had to identify and correct is the extent to which social theorists, across a wide range of disciplines, have considered ritual and myth as merely reflecting and reinforcing social structure. Bruce Lincoln argues that academic efforts at a conclusive, comprehensive definition of society have reduced the societal to the rational, often reflecting taxonomies of power and knowledge within the "disciplines" of the academy itself. What the academy has neglected is the extent to which *sentiment* plays a powerful role in the dynamic, fluid entities called societies. As a corrective to the excessively rationalist view, and on the basis of numerous comparative studies of social practices, Lincoln argues that performances of discourse—myth, ritual, and classification—do not merely reflect the structures of a given society but *make* those structures by either reinforcing, modifying, or contributing to a radical change in the structures of power. Members of a given society use various performative forms of discourse in order to negotiate their own positions of power and to maintain or change the status quo. Lincoln's descriptions and

on the ambiguity and vulnerability of religious symbolism. In order for the "mystical" elements of the Christian practice of faith to enable liberative action in history and society they must constantly be evaluated in light of their own social histories and present social locations.[120] Metz follows a similar tact in understanding dogmas to be "formulations of the collective memory" of the Church in history that have the "dangerous" potential of challenging "a middle-class or totalitarian idea of progress."[121] The rehearsal in this present chapter of Metz's treatment of such dogmatic traditions as christology and eschatology provide demonstrations of Metz's critical retrieval of tradition for the purpose of political praxis.

Metz's concern for tradition resonates with the agenda of liturgical theologians, a great part of whose work, from the beginnings of the liturgical movement, has been to retrieve and study specific liturgical traditions as they were practiced and reflected upon at certain times and places in history.[122] The social and political contexts of those liturgical traditions, as well as how they related to the doctrinal teachings, debates, or even controversies of a given period, all provide insight for the present theory and practice of liturgy. The critical retrieval of traditions contributes to the ongoing reform and revision of liturgy so

---

analyses of how both governing bodies and revolutionary movements have used myth and ritual for ideological purposes is particularly pertinent to Metz's point here. See Bruce Lincoln, *Discourse and the Construction of Society: Comparative Studies of Myth, Ritual, and Classification* (New York: Oxford University Press, 1989).

[120] Edward Schillebeeckx's study of the history of presbyteral ministry is an example of the type of theological scholarship for which Metz calls here. Schillebeeckx insists that the sociological (historical) and theological (grace-revealing) aspects of actual forms and structures of ministry at given times and places are inextricably interrelated. Given this reality, Schillebeeckx argues, one must study the patterns and criteria for ministry from numerous historical periods in order to evaluate the present state of affairs and propose new courses for action. See Edward Schillebeeckx, *The Church with a Human Face: A New and Expanded Theology of Ministry*, trans. John Bowden (New York: Crossroad, 1985) 1–12.

[121] Metz, *Faith in History and Society*, 202–3.

[122] This approach is exemplified in the work of Robert Taft, historian and theologian of liturgy. See his essay "The Structural Analysis of Liturgical Units: An Essay in Methodology," *Worship* 52 (1978) 314–29.

that the worship of God might coincide with a more effective transformation (sanctification) of people in the world today. This work is
an execution of the mandate set forth by the Second Vatican Council,
as I noted in Chapter 1, that "the rites be revised carefully in the light
of sound tradition, and that they be given new vigor to meet present-
day circumstances and needs."[123]

Through their ongoing efforts to understand the relationship between *lex orandi* and *lex credendi* (to be addressed in Chapter 3), liturgical theologians share with Metz an appreciation for tradition as a
dynamic source for faith that can be reduced to neither "the intellectual model of consent to certain articles of faith nor the existential
model of a decision made in man's [*sic*] existence."[124] Rejection of
those two positions contributes to Metz's definition of the faith as a
collective memory of promises made and hopes yet to be fulfilled. At
the end of the introductory paragraph of his excursus on "Dogma as a
dangerous memory," in which he thus presents faith in terms of "the
figure of eschatological memory," Metz appends the following footnote: "It would be interesting to investigate how it was possible for
the memory to change so much in sacramental theology and, to the
detriment of the memory and the sacrament, to be isolated and fre-
quently given a wrong ritualistic interpretation, devoid of the subject."[125] This parenthetic introduction of the sacramental-liturgical
form of memory—on the heel of his rejection of the extreme positions
of identifying faith with intellectual assent or personal, existential decision—indicates Metz's awareness of the eucharistic liturgy as the
premiere ecclesial tradition for both expressing and empowering faith
as a practical imitation of Christ in solidarity with the living and the
dead. Only gradually, however, did Metz make this ritual location of
Christian memory explicit.

In 1990 Klemens Richter, Metz's colleague at the University of
Münster, observed both that Metz had not related the central category
of memory in his political theology to its liturgical locus and, yet, that

[123] *Sacrosanctum concilium*, no. 4; see also no. 50.

[124] Metz, *Faith in History and Society*, 200. In the latter alternative for defining
faith Metz seems to be alluding to the theology of Karl Rahner. See, for example, Karl Rahner, "Thoughts on the Possibility of Belief Today," *Theological
Investigations*, vol. 5, trans. Karl H. Kruger (New York: Seabury Press, 1966)
3–22.

[125] Metz, *Faith in History and Society*, 204.

Metz's formulation of the faith as dangerous memory was "ultimately founded on liturgical celebration."[126] Indeed, Metz's formal development of the category of memory in *Faith in History and Society* traces the Platonic notion of *anamnesis* in the history of Western philosophy, faulting its metaphysical inability to allow historical events and historical consciousness their proper integrity and authority.[127] Metz associates the term exclusively with Plato's epistemology, wherein rational knowledge is the recollection of previously known divine truths, and briefly traces this Platonic notion in the history of Western philosophy. Metz characterizes the "Christian tradition" as introducing a historical (memorative and narrative) *memoria* in conjunction with the Platonic view, citing Augustine's *Confessions* as the exercise in which "memory acquired the status of a hermeneutical category, able to interpret history in the presence of God."[128] The chapter is unclear both in its details and general argument. As Colombo reports, one struggles to perceive "to what degree Metz's formal reflections on memory are constituted and conditioned by his material retrieval of Christian faith through *memoria Jesu Christi* as a *theological* category."[129]

Metz must have seen the problem himself, for by the beginning of the early 1990s he came to focus more intently on the Jewish tradition as the crucial source or "spirit" *(Geist)* of a genuinely Christian theology of memory. Metz argues that from an early period Christian theology became methodologically split in its use of the Jewish-biblical

[126] "We will not at this point pursue the question why Metz, the systematic theologian, despite all his impressive admonitions to locate this *memoria* at the center of Christian faith and action, does not get around to speaking about the liturgy, which effects this *memoria* in celebration, and which is the foremost locus of memory of God's dealings with God's people. But his central thesis, according to which 'the Church must understand and justify itself as the public witness and bearer of the tradition of a dangerous memory of freedom in the "systems" of our emancipative society,' is ultimately founded on liturgical celebration." Klemens Richter, "Liturgical Reform as the Means for Church Renewal," *The Meaning of the Liturgy*, ed. Angelus A. Häussling, trans. Linda M. Maloney (Collegeville: The Liturgical Press, 1994) 119–20. Richter's essay was originally given as a conference paper in 1990.

[127] See Metz, *Faith in History and Society*, 184–99. Metz had already raised this criticism in his earlier work. See *Theology of the World*, 88, 100.

[128] Metz, *Faith in History and Society*, 188.

[129] Colombo, *An Essay on Theology and History*, 190.

and Greek-Hellenistic traditions, relying on the former as the source of faith but too exclusively on the latter for philosophical reason characterized by "an ahistorical and subjectless metaphysics of ideas and of nature."[130] Such philosophy of memory lends itself to a scientific objectification of the past and an explanation for the success of those who are victorious in the present, that is, a form of memory utterly compatible with the modern evolutionary world view.

The significant advance in Metz's more recent thought, and a liturgical one at that, has been his coining of a German neologism to articulate this biblical tradition of memory: *Eingedenken*, which Matthew Ashley translates as "remembrancing," an English gerund that conveys the verbal form that Metz intends.[131] As Ashley explains, Metz constructs this word on the basis of the German adverb *eingedenk*, which means "in remembrance of," the very phrase used in the institution narrative of the Church's Eucharistic Prayer, "Do this in remembrance of me."[132] Metz argues that this cultic action of the Church constitutes the key way in which Christianity has preserved its distinctive form of memory.[133] Christian theology now needs to recognize this intrinsically historical way of remembering ("remembrancing") as "the fundamental anamnestic structure of mind and spirit" or a "remembrance-structure" that Christians can bring to the social, political arena.[134] Metz emphasizes the Jewish origins of this type of remembering, which entails a sense of absence, refusing to forget the suffering and dead. He also notes that from its origins the eucharistic act of remembrance was meant to be celebrated in festive expectation of Christ's return, an anticipatory awareness long dormant in much of the First World church.[135] It is precisely on this point of the function of remembrance in the Jewish and Christian ritual traditions that recent

---

[130] Metz, *A Passion for God*, 64; see also 130. Ashley tracks Metz's recognition of the inadequacy of Western philosophy to the thought demanded by Christian faith across Metz's career. See Ashley, *Interruptions*, 71, 90, 126–7.

[131] Metz, *A Passion for God*, 181, n. 10.

[132] Ashley, *Interruptions*, 161.

[133] See Metz, *A Passion for God*, 131. See also, Johann Baptist Metz, "Unity and Diversity: Problems and Prospects for Inculturation," trans. Francis McDonagh, *Faith and the Future*, 63; and Johann Baptist Metz, "Freedom in Solidarity: The Rescue of Reason," trans. John Bowden, *Faith and the Future*, 77.

[134] Metz, *A Passion for God*, 64, 131.

[135] Ibid., 85.

biblical and liturgical scholarship can augment the force of Metz's argument for the centrality of this form of memory to the practice of faith in society. Liturgical scholarship, in turn, can find in Metz both profound motivation for pursuing this line of theology and insights into the practical implications it bears.

We may close this chapter, then, by noting a few more explicit insights and challenges that arise from thinking liturgically in relation to Metz's concept of the dangerous memory.

(1) By describing the *memoria passionis, mortis et resurrectionis Jesu Christi* as that which Christians "accomplish,"[136] as well as arguing for an anamnestic reason inherent to Christianity, Metz points toward the eucharistic memorial as an action which can neither be reduced to psychological recollection nor isolated from the wider question of Christian praxis. Issues raised in Chapter 3 will lead into a detailed study of these specific aspects of eucharistic *anamnesis* in Chapter 4.

(2) Metz's argument for the essentially practical nature of christology as the *imitatio Christi* finds support in the dominical command to do the meal-ritual of bread and wine *eis ten emen anamnesin* (1 Cor 11:24, 25; Luke 22:19b). How the logic internal to the eucharistic liturgy prohibits the keeping of this command of imitation from being "mere contemplation" will be explored in the ensuing chapters.

(3) The (always broken) accomplishment of Christian faith has an essential need for the Eucharist due to the fact that the faith is based upon the remembrance not only of an event that is "historical" like other events in history—Jesus' death—but also an event that does "not fall to the same degree under the same concept of remembrance"—Jesus' resurrection.[137] While Metz rightly notes that narrative, as opposed to argument, is the only way to communicate "the totally new experience of the resurrection,"[138] the theology of the liturgy also holds to the unique and ecclesially essential role of the eucharistic ritual as the medium for experiencing this tensive, anticipatory memory at the heart of Christian faith. The elucidation of precisely this function of the eucharistic liturgy is one of the hallmarks of Schmemann's work, which we shall explore in detail in the

---

[136] Metz, *Faith in History and Society*, 90.

[137] Edward Schillebeeckx, *Christ: The Experience of Jesus as Lord*, trans. John Bowden (New York: Crossroad, 1981) 893, n. 100. For Schillebeeckx's critique of Metz see 751–6.

[138] Metz, *Faith in History and Society*, 206.

next chapter. In Chapter 4 we shall study the extent to which *anamnesis* pervades several key ecclesial practices that carry out the tradition of the faith. The eucharistic liturgy will be found, nonetheless, to hold pride of place among these practices.

(4) Metz's reflections on the problem of time, in the context of apocalyptic eschatology, invite comparison and contrast to the extensive work of liturgical theologians concerning the liturgy's relationship to time. Our study of Schmemann's theology will afford such an investigation, as his work on the question of time and the liturgy is both representative of the topic within the discipline and a significant contribution thereto.

(5) Metz's insistence on an "apocalyptic sting" in Christian faith, moreover, raises a worthy and formidable caution to the theory and practice of the Eucharist. One of Metz's fragments on "Hope as Immanent Expectation" warrants full citation in this regard:

"It is not only necessary to be careful about the overworked specifically Christian element, the Christian identity that, at every opportunity, insists on the salvation that has already been given in Christ. There may also be a special kind of weariness with regard to this identity, with the result that all the safety signals are put out because the danger of old age and the dictatorship of what has already been experienced is preferred to the way of hope and expectation. As Teilhard de Chardin observed, 'We go on asserting that we are awake and are waiting for the master. But, if we were honest, we would have to admit that we expect nothing at all.'"[139]

It could be argued that an overworked identity—for example, in certain notions of real presence or interpretations of the role of the priest in Christian liturgy—has been operative for centuries in the Roman Catholic theology of the Eucharist. The influence of transcendental-idealist and personalist theologies in many of the new theoretical approaches to the Eucharist since the 1950s has contributed at times, albeit in new and different ways, to this problem of overworked identity. Certain sacramental and liturgical theologians, increasingly influenced by the critical agendas of political and liberation theologies, have begun to identify and address ways in which identification of salvation in the Eucharist can lull individuals and churches into a

---

[139] Ibid., 179.

complacency with regard to social problems or, perhaps, a sense of their irrelevance to faith. The following chapters will draw upon these recent critical developments in liturgical theology with a view to contributing to the recovery of eschatology in the theology of the Eucharist, an eschatology that takes seriously Metz's insistence on a dialectic between consolation and catastrophe. I believe, however, that Metz's emphasis upon the latter, which he admittedly does as a corrective to modern theology, awaits, in turn, its own correction. An "identification of suffering with hope in Jesus Christ" can be augmented in the liturgy such that God does not end up being "wholly *Deus Absconditus*,"[140] as seems to be the case at times in Metz's theology. I consider this to be a charge to liturgical theology, one that at this moment in history it would dodge not only to its own peril but to that of the Church in the late-modern world.

[140] Chopp, *The Praxis of Suffering*, 75.

Chapter 3

Alexander Schmemann's Liturgical Theology: Joyous, Thankful Remembrance of the Kingdom of God

INTRODUCTION

The idea of comparing the work of Johann Baptist Metz and Alexander Schmemann, indeed, of joining them in a constructive dialogue and collaborative effort, might seem at first blush to be a strange match of bedfellows. In many ways that impression would be understandable. One is a Roman Catholic theologian, long and deeply located in his native Germany, who has constructed a somewhat idiosyncratic theology labeled, throughout the marked turns in its development, "political."[1] The other is a Russian Orthodox theologian, whose life's journey took him from Estonia to Paris to New York, and whose life's work was the focused, consistent pursuit to define liturgical theology and establish its fundamental principles.[2] A close reading of the corpus of each man's writings, however, reveals remarkable similarities or parallels in both style and content.[3] This fact, I would

---

[1] The most comprehensive study of Metz's theology, examining stages in its development and the elements of continuity and discontinuity therein, is J. Matthew Ashley, *Interruptions: Mysticism, Politics, and Theology in the Work of Johann Baptist Metz* (Notre Dame, Ind.: University of Notre Dame Press, 1998). For Ashley's discussion of Metz's Catholicism and Germanness as key elements influencing his thought see 30–2. For one of Metz's own treatments of the German context out of which he writes, see Johann Baptist Metz, *A Passion for God: The Mystical-Political Dimension of Christianity*, trans. J. Matthew Ashley (New York: Paulist Press, 1998) 127–32.

[2] For a brief account of Schmemann's life in relation to his theological and presbyteral career, see John Meyendorff, "A Life Worth Living," *Liturgy and Tradition: Theological Reflections of Alexander Schmemann*, ed. Thomas Fisch (Crestwood, N.Y.: St. Vladimir's Seminary Press, 1992) 143–54.

[3] Comparisons—as well as contrasts—in the content of Metz's and Schmemann's work will emerge in the main body of this chapter. As for stylistic

propose, testifies to the dedicated and passionate concern for the Church (in its most genuinely catholic sense) and for the late modern world with which each author took up the vocation of theologian. Notable, moreover, is the fact that both theologians' careers came into full stride, albeit along different paths, in the crucible of the 1960s. At that time each wrestled with the then-current issue of secularism, but from significantly different perspectives.[4]

In the earliest of his collected essays Metz welcomed secularism as the ultimate social-historical consequence of belief in the incarnation. He disparaged the practice of contemplation,[5] made little mention of word (Scripture) and even less of sacrament, and redefined asceticism as a risk-filled acceptance of the world and its potential, the Christian life as an anonymous encounter with God in creation and history.[6]

---

similarities, a few can be mentioned here. A polemical stance characterizes each one's writings, at times giving themselves over to extreme statements that seem to contradict positions they take elsewhere. Zealous for ecclesial reform, each has a penchant for hyperbole, with the apparent intention of shocking the reader. The pattern is often one of taking away (severely criticizing or even discounting) a theological concept or religious practice only to bring it back eventually in a form amenable to a larger theological argument that the author has made. In this regard their work resembles a pattern consistent in Karl Barth's *Church Dogmatics* (I am indebted to Professor James Gustafson, who in leading a seminar through a close reading of the *Church Dogmatics* highlighted Barth's tendency to "take away something only to slip it back in"). These qualities in their writing, I believe, have contributed to both Metz and Schmemann often being misunderstood in terms of their fundamental projects. Finally, like Metz, Schmemann often repeats ideas and illustrative examples in various articles or books and, moreover, similar to but not quite as extreme as Metz, Schmemann tended to write in the form of articles or relatively autonomous essays collected into books.

[4] For a review and appraisal of the theme of secularization in the theology of the 1960s, see Gregory Baum, *Religion and Alienation: A Theological Reading of Sociology* (New York: Paulist Press, 1975) 140–61.

[5] See Johann Baptist Metz, *Theology of the World,* trans. William Glen-Doepel (New York: Seabury Press, 1969) 94, 98.

[6] "In the hominized world, which ultimately Christian faith itself will have made historically possible, man [sic] moves in an incomparable way into the center of the world. This anthropocentricity does not mean that man's experience of God is radically obscured, but that ultimately a greater immediacy is given to the experience of the numinous: we encounter God as the transcendent

From that initial christening of modernity Metz gradually developed in the course of the 1960s a critical assessment of the Enlightenment which, based on his study of critical theory, solidified into the "political theology of the subject" analyzed in the preceding chapter of this work. As Metz's assessment of technological society became increasingly negative, his appreciation for religious (Christian) tradition as a liberating source of resistance to the various deficiencies of modernity grew to the point, as we saw in Chapter 2, of his defining Christian faith as a praxis of mysticism and politics. In so doing Metz's practical fundamental theology remains a call for a type of Christian subject, theology, and church that is yet to be widely realized and, moreover, that faces a formidable obstacle in the middle-class religion that Metz so perceptively analyzed. Precisely in this challenging situation, however, Metz recognizes the opportunity for Christian tradition to discover a new, reinvigorated role that is at once dangerous to the prevailing social systems and redemptive to the subjects who would undertake it. Thus, at this latter point in his career the political theologian Metz desires that theologians and ecclesial leaders tap into the practical force of the Church's traditions—including liturgy—in such a way as to recover their transformative power for society.

The liturgical theologian Schmemann, on the other hand, perceived early in his life and work that the ancient traditional practices of the Church's liturgy included among their fundamental purposes and goals the transformation of all who participated therein and a charge for all to witness to God's redemptive will for the world.[7] In Paris

---

mystery of the unity and richness of human life, which is constantly lost in the pluralism of its areas of experience; as the uncontrollable future of human freedom impinging on the world itself; finally, as the God whose nearness seeks to reveal itself in our encounter with our brother. Thus faith has a genuine future in the hominized world—less obvious, it is true, less apparent, but more inescapable than ever." Ibid., 76–7.

[7] For reviews—both highly appreciative—of the major influences upon and original contributions of Schmemann's liturgical theology see Meyendorff, "A Life Worth Living"; Thomas Fisch, "Introduction: Schmemann's Theological Contribution to the Liturgical Renewal of the Churches," *Liturgy and Tradition: Theological Reflections of Alexander Schmemann,* ed. Thomas Fisch (Crestwood, N.Y.: St. Vladimir's Seminary Press, 1990) 1–10. For a clear and insightful exposition of Schmemann's theology see David W. Fagerberg, *What Is Liturgical Theology? A Study in Methodology* (Collegeville: The Liturgical Press, 1992) 143–79.

Schmemann learned extensively from the outstanding historical and theological work of Jean Daniélou and Louis Bouyer, as well as Irénée Henri Dalmais and Cipriano Vagaggini, that the liturgy has a unique and irreducible theological dimension (summarized in the concept of the paschal mystery and a philosophy of time). Schmemann judged that the liturgical principles which those Western scholars had discovered among the early liturgical families and patristic authors were still operative in the Eastern Orthodox liturgy which, despite many accretions in its form and distortions in its practice, carried the tradition more faithfully and continuously than that of any other church. Schmemann made it his life's work to clarify the theology inherent in the liturgy itself as fundamentally the epiphany (manifestation) of the inextricable relationship between the Church, the kingdom of God, and the world.

While Metz's passionate critique of modern society and constructive effort at political theology included an ever-burgeoning role for tradition (under his broad concept of "mysticism"), Schmemann's work on the foundations and structures of liturgical tradition was not accompanied by a complementary increase in appreciation for the developments in liberation and political theologies. Just the opposite was the case. Schmemann moved from involvements (albeit some very brief) in projects of the World Council of Churches to association in what John Meyendorff describes as "more conservative Christian circles," including participation in the "Hartford Appeal."[8]

The preface to the English edition of his last book, finished within a month of his death in 1983, demonstrates the gravely unfortunate opinion Schmemann held of theologies of liberation. Lest any element of this vitriolic statement be construed out of context, the paragraph requires citation in full:

"Meanwhile, it can be said without exaggeration that we live in a frightening and spiritually dangerous age. It is frightening not just because of its hatred, division and bloodshed. It is frightening above all because it is characterized by a mounting rebellion against God and his [sic] kingdom. Not God, but man [sic] has become the measure of all things. Not faith, but ideology and utopian escapism are determining the spiritual state of the world. At a certain point, western Christianity accepted this point of view: almost at once one or another

---

[8] Meyendorff, "A Life Worth Living," 10.

'theology of liberation' was born. Issues relating to economics, politics and psychology have replaced a Christian vision of the world at the service of God. Theologians, clergy and other professional 'religious' run busily around the world defending—from God?—this or that 'right,' however perverse, and all this in the name of peace, unity and brotherhood [sic]. Yet in fact, the peace, unity and brotherhood that they invoke are not the peace, unity and brotherhood that has been brought to us by our Lord Jesus Christ."[9]

In light (or, perhaps, the darkness) of such a statement the reader unacquainted with the entire corpus of Schmemann's work might wonder how the present writer can turn to it without showing grave disrespect for Metz and the wider circle of his colleagues. Beyond Schmemann's rhetoric against liberation theologies, his separation of "hatred, division and bloodshed" from "rebellion against God," entailing the logically consequent denigration of the former, is a fundamental theological error for the student of political theology. This protest having been registered, however, I believe that Schmemann's singular work on the "crisis" (his recurrent term) of theology, liturgy, and spirituality answers in large part the concern for tradition to which Metz has led this present project. We turn, therefore, to Metz's own summary statement of the contemporary "crisis" of Christianity before letting Schmemann's treatment of the theme, in turn, lead into the heart of his liturgical theology.

THE CONTEMPORARY CHRISTIAN CRISIS

At three points in *Faith in History and Society* Metz summarizes the present crisis of Christianity in a nearly identical formula: "The crisis in Christianity is not really a crisis of its message and the content of faith, but rather a crisis of its subjects and institutions, in that these are too remote from the practical meaning of the Christian message."[10] In the first half of the statement Metz seems to be referring to a common reaction to the phenomenon of secularization, namely, that the

---

[9] Alexander Schmemann, *The Eucharist: Sacrament of the Kingdom of God*, trans. Paul Kachur (Crestwood, N.Y.: St. Vladimir's Seminary Press, 1987) 9–10.

[10] Johann Baptist Metz, *Faith in History and Society: Toward a Practical Fundamental Theology*, trans. David Smith (New York: Seabury Press, 1980) 169. See also ix–x and 165. Metz has continued to reiterate this argument in his later writings. See *A Passion for God*, 36, 102.

content of Christian Scripture and doctrine (dogma) is so inconsistent with modern reason and social systems as to require its either being adapted to modernity or utterly isolated therefrom. Given the fact that Metz tended toward the former option in his earlier work, the present statement can easily be considered a confessional or credal one for Metz's effort to establish political theology as a fundamental theology. That effort required Metz to consider carefully the history of Roman Catholic theology's reaction to the Enlightenment, which he lays out at the beginning of the text.[11]

One of the keys for Metz's historical analysis is his recognition of how Neo-Scholasticism, feeling threatened by modern philosophy and the masters of suspicion, itself isolated the content of faith not only from the modern world but from the rigid, formalistic apologetics behind which it functioned. Claiming recourse to the practice of the earliest Christians, Metz defines apologetics, the defense and justification of the faith in terms of the current challenges and social context, as integral to fundamental and dogmatic theology. The contemporary Christian crisis, therefore, resides in the institution of theology which, due to its extremely transcendental turn, is "too remote" from the practical content of faith and thereby unable to recognize and address the crises of the contemporary religious subject and ecclesial institutions (bureaucratic structures and parochial practices). As we have seen, Metz wants theology to convey the transformative, practical meaning of the content of faith so as to encourage Christians in practicing lives of kenotic service in the world as followers of Christ.

Although from an obviously different ecclesial and social-political perspective, Schmemann possessed an insight, similar to that of Metz, that the situation of Christianity in North Atlantic societies in the 1960s and 1970s was in a state of fundamental crisis. For reasons that will become clear as this study proceeds, Schmemann considered the Church's liturgy to be the key to the Church's self-

---

[11] See Metz, *Faith in History and Society*, 14–31. For a more extensive study of the history and current approaches to fundamental theology and apologetics, see Francis Schüssler Fiorenza, *Foundational Theology: Jesus and the Church* (New York: Crossroad, 1984). Fiorenza provides an abbreviated version of his work—including a paragraph on Metz—in "Fundamental Theology," *The New Dictionary of Theology*, ed. Joseph A. Komonchak and others (Wilmington, Del.: Michael Glazier, 1987) 408–11.

understanding and its mission in the world. What he observed both in Russian Orthodoxy and Roman Catholicism were efforts on the part of liturgists at tinkering, as it were, with various isolated elements of the rituals without the requisite grasp of the theology of the liturgy itself. Lacking the latter, these reformers often worked on the premise that the liturgies needed to be made more relevant or modern or, at the other extreme, more conservative of what were considered normative—because traditional, i.e., older—forms. After several years of publishing articles and a number of books Schmemann found himself regularly misunderstood as belonging to the latter camp. This was a cause of great frustration for him, since he considered himself, and not his Roman Catholic peers,[12] to be carrying out the spirit and principles of the earlier great scholars of the Liturgical Movement.

A particularly poignant and programmatic statement, one in which Schmemann articulates both what he rejects and what he seeks for liturgical theology, is the following:

"It must be clear by now that the tragedy which I denounce and deplore consists not in any particular 'defect' of the liturgy—and God knows that there have been many such defects at all times—but in something much deeper: the *divorce between liturgy, theology, and piety,* a divorce which characterizes the post-patristic period of the history of our Church and which has altered—not the faith and not too much the liturgy—theology and piety. In other terms, the crisis which I try to analyze is the crisis not of liturgy but of its *understanding*—be it in the 'key' of post-patristic theology or in that of rather recent, but assumed to be traditional, liturgical piety. And precisely because the

---

[12] In what one might consider excessive mockery of Pope John XXIII and the Second Vatican Council, Schmemann dubbed such reform-minded liturgists "the *aggiornamento* generation." As my study of *Sacrosanctum concilium* in Chapter 1 demonstrated, the council mandated a liturgical reform attentive to the modern world but based upon early sources of the liturgical traditions. In any event, Schmemann's derogatory phrase does capture the conflicted and troubled history of the reception of the council's teaching—from the start up to this day—by the hierarchy, theologians, and laity. See Alexander Schmemann, "Liturgical Theology: Remarks on Method," *Liturgy and Tradition: Theological Reflections of Alexander Schmemann,* ed. Thomas Fisch (Crestwood, N.Y.: St. Vladimir's Seminary Press, 1990) 139.

roots of the crisis are theological and spiritual rather than liturgical, no liturgical reform can by itself and in itself solve it."[13]

The structural parallel between Schmemann's and Metz's descriptions of the contemporary Christian crisis is quite remarkable. While Metz frames the problem in terms of message, subjects, and institutions, of how the latter two are "too remote" from the first, Schmemann thinks in terms of liturgy, piety, and theology, of the "divorce" of the latter two from the first. The contents intended by the authors for each of their three terms hold much in common as well. First, Schmemann's concern about *piety* is indeed a concern about the actual practices and attitudes of the religious *subject*. While he does indeed define the crisis of the subject and its piety as "spiritual," we shall see (1) that Schmemann does not isolate this concept from the subject's social and practical aspects, and (2) that he can nonetheless benefit from Metz's concerted attention to the latter. Second, the *theology-institution* pairing is likewise pronounced, in that both authors, again, with mutually-informative differences of focus, view theology as an institution that has lost a crucial sense of its mission and its relation to other, and equally problematic, ecclesial institutions.

The third pairing, *message-liturgy*, indicates the fundamental way in which each theologian perceives the *content of faith* to be formulated, conveyed, and shared. In Metz's crisis-formula the words "message" and "content of faith" are cognates, and the rub lies in the failure of middle-class Christians to recognize the practical (mystical and political) import of that content. In Schmemann's statement "faith" and "liturgy" comprise the unaltered and (apparently) unalterable source of Christianity. In his text on the Eucharist Schmemann demonstrates the extent to which he understands liturgical celebration and the content of faith to be, in Metz's terms, of practical import. Criticizing members of Russian Orthodoxy, Schmemann perceives

"the startling indifference to the content of faith, the complete lack of interest in what *faith believes,* on the part of the overwhelming majority of people who call themselves believers and who are most sincerely

[13] Alexander Schmemann, "Liturgical Theology, Theology of Liturgy, and Liturgical Reform," *Liturgy and Tradition: Theological Reflections of Alexander Schmemann,* ed. Thomas Fisch (Crestwood, N.Y.: St. Vladimir's Seminary Press, 1990) 41.

devoted to the Church. . . . The content of faith, the truth to which it is directed, holds no interest for ['religious man' *(sic)*] because it is not necessary for his 'religiosity,' for that religious feeling that gradually substituted itself for faith and dissolved faith in itself."[14]

For both authors, as is the case for any sound Christian theologian, the notion of "faith" cannot be reduced to words or actions yet, nonetheless, must be humanly realized through the definite content of words and actions. Metz, as we have seen, approaches tradition (the content of faith) in terms of texts (dogmas, especially as formulaic statements, and "narratives")[15] complemented by a growing appreciation for the role of symbol and sacrament. For Schmemann, on the other hand, the primary locus of tradition is the Church's liturgy, which entails an integral relationship of word and sacrament and manifests the Church's world view and mission.[16] On the bottom line, both theologians want their respective identifications of the present crisis of Christianity to be addressed on the basis of the content of

[14] Schmemann, *The Eucharist*, 146.

[15] For Metz's excursus on dogma, see *Faith in History and Society*, 200–4. I have noted Metz's formulaic use of christological and eschatological dogma and doctrine in Chapter 2. Metz's exposition on his theological category of narrative is found in *Faith in History and Society*, 205–27. Of note are his argument for narrative as the "medium" of salvation and history (210–3) and his tribute to Karl Rahner as an exercise in what Metz considers to be theological biography (see 219–27).

[16] "All church theology, all tradition, grows precisely out of the 'assembly as the Church,' out of this sacrament of proclamation of the good news. Here we see why in it is comprehended the living, and not abstract, meaning of the classic Orthodox affirmation that only the Church is given custody of the scriptures and their interpretation. For tradition is not another source of the faith, 'complementary' to the scriptures. It is the very source: the living word of god, always heard and received by the Church. Tradition is the interpretation of the word of God as the course of life itself, and not of any 'constructions' or 'deductions.'" Schmemann, *The Eucharist*, 78; see also 66. For a Scripture scholar's treatment of the theological relationship between word of God, sacrament, and tradition, see Part I of Sandra M. Schneiders, *The Revelatory Text: Interpreting the New Testament as Sacred Scripture* (San Francisco: Harper Collins, 1991) 9–93. Liturgical theologian Kevin W. Irwin gives rewarding attention to the topic at points throughout his *Context and Text: Method in Liturgical Theology* (Collegeville: The Liturgical Press, 1994) esp. 85–127.

faith. In this sense each can be seen as engaged in a type of fundamental theology.

In order to get at Schmemann's fundamental theses for liturgical theology it is necessary to follow his oft repeated pattern of articulating what is so drastically wrong with the spirituality (or piety) of the contemporary Orthodox faithful and with the theology performed in the academy (mainly seminaries). Although Schmemann's project is rightfully situated in the context of a specific Church's theory and practices, his critical analysis and constructive proposals can readily be related or applied to wider circles of contemporary northern Christianity.

As should be evident from this rehearsal thus far, Schmemann is consistently critical throughout the corpus of his writings of the widespread efforts in the Western (most often, Roman) Church to adapt liturgy to the proclivities, tastes, and sensibilities of modern people.[17] While the fundamental reason for that condemnation is Schmemann's sound principle that the theology inherent in the liturgy should direct all aspects of its practice, he also emphatically insists that certain features of modern society and its subjects are far from worthy of Christian reinforcement. In rhetoric that resonates with that of Metz, Schmemann regularly notes and condemns the individualism and privatism that characterize modern (Metz would say, middle-class) religion. One especially satisfying example may suffice.

In introducing his analysis of how religion is not constitutive of but, rather, added to the identity of the modern subject, Metz describes the latter as "the creator of that form of religion which is used, as it were, to decorate and set the scene, freely and in private, for middle-class festivals and which has for a long time been current even in normal Christianity."[18] In a manner that not only Metz but Horkheimer and Adorno would appreciate, Schmemann perceives in modern Christianity "a serious crisis in the very idea of a feast."[19] The problem is that a feast is fundamentally about joy, a shared human capacity crucial to the viability of society but which modernity, in its all-encompassing public (technological and market-centered) "seriousness," has reduced to mere "fun" and "relaxation" and relegated to

[17] *The Awakening Church* project, reported in Chapter 1, provides further evidence for this issue of significant concern to Schmemann.

[18] Metz, *Faith in History and Society*, 33.

[19] Alexander Schmemann, *For the Life of the World: Sacraments and Orthodoxy*, 2d ed. (Crestwood, N.Y.: St. Vladimir's Seminary Press, 1973) 53.

the individual's "time off." Since Christians uncritically accepted their individual places in this culture "the 'Christian year'—the sequence of liturgical commemorations and celebrations—ceased to be the generator of power, and is now looked upon as a more or less antiquated decoration of religion . . . it is neither a root of Christian life and action, nor a 'goal' toward which they are oriented."[20] Neither author is seeking a romantic return to one or another era or locale in Christendom, for that would only reinforce religion's social role as a quaint decoration. Rather, both perceive in modern Christians' participation in the diminishment of the authority of religious tradition a grievous loss not only for Christianity but wider society (in Schmemann's terms, "the world") itself.

If the spirituality or piety of contemporary (Orthodox) Christians is alienated from its genuine liturgical source, theology is no better off. Performed by academicians pursuing "esoteric controversies" by means of "highly technical language," theology is of little interest to not only the laity but also the clergy and hierarchical leadership of the Orthodox Church.[21] Schmemann calls such theology "scholastic" or "school" theology, by which he does not intend a particular school or period but, rather, a general manner of doing theology as an academic discipline "virtually isolated from the Church's life" and, most importantly, without an "organic connection" to the liturgy as its source.[22] Schmemann calls this the "Western captivity" of Orthodox theology and argues that it amounts to nothing less than the abandonment of the Church's tradition. Tradition he identifies with the patristic figures of the second and third centuries, for whom theology entailed the dynamic relationship between the Church's liturgy and spirituality—its *lex orandi*—and the articulation of the Church's belief—its *lex credendi*. (Just how Schmemann understands that relationship will be elaborated later.) Post-patristic theology, on the other hand, is marked by its abstractness, its use of texts as the exclusive *loci theologici,* and excessively legalistic and hierarchical views of the Church. Not only

[20] Ibid.

[21] Alexander Schmemann, "Theology and Eucharist," *Liturgy and Tradition: Theological Reflections of Alexander Schmemann,* ed. Thomas Fisch (Crestwood, N.Y.: St. Vladimir's Seminary Press, 1990) 71.

[22] Alexander Schmemann, "Liturgy and Theology," *Liturgy and Tradition: Theological Reflections of Alexander Schmemann,* ed. Thomas Fisch (Crestwood, N.Y.: St. Vladimir's Seminary Press, 1990) 71, 64.

impoverished in itself, theology's isolation has amounted to a veritable tragedy for the Church. Unreflective pragmatism, uninformed historical opinions, inappropriate liturgical accretions, and excessive reliance on ecclesial bureaucracy (here Metz would smile) have long been the norm when, in fact, the Church has needed the theoretical perspective of theology to provide "purifying self-criticism" and a "conscience" for the Church in its effort faithfully to interpret and implement tradition.[23]

At the present moment in Church history Schmemann identifies two predominant approaches to theology, both of which move away from scholastic isolation but, nonetheless, fail to fulfill theology's proper mission for the sake of both the Church and the world.[24] Schmemann's typology bears a notable resemblance to the two patterns of Christianity Metz recognizes in late modern Christianity: the one a "symbolic paraphrase" of societal processes, the other a rigid

---

[23] Ibid., 71. Schmemann's *apologia* for the irreducible importance of theology as theory in relation to the practical agendas of the Church is a point that would seem to be particularly agreeable with the thought of Walter Lowe. Lowe's careful and appreciative review of Metz's project leads him nonetheless to criticize Metz gently for leaving "unexplored the extent to which theoretical reason (and most particularly the transcendental reason [Metz] so distrusts) can move in the direction of praxis—and even in the direction of that crucial, broken but perceptive thinking represented by the memory of suffering." Lowe thereby sets the agenda for his own work. See Walter Lowe, *Theology and Difference: The Wound of Reason* (Bloomington: Indiana University Press, 1993) 10–11. Lowe, however, while sharing with Schmemann the principle that the practices of the Church and Christians in society need the theoretical criticism theology can provide, nonetheless pursues a radically different epistemology. Whereas Schmemann, as we shall see below (and with proper citations), seeks a "center" for theology in the liturgical "experience of the joy of the Kingdom," Lowe argues for the wounded and wounding character of a (transcendental) reason that honors interruptive and fragmenting experiences of suffering.

[24] "Theology is and always has been aimed at the world. Theology is not exclusively for the inner consumption of the Church. There has always been an effort, on the Christian side, to explain the Gospel in terms of a given culture, of a given world commonwealth." Alexander Schmemann, "Liturgy and Eschatology," *Liturgy and Tradition: Theological Reflections of Alexander Schmemann*, ed. Thomas Fisch (Crestwood, N.Y.: St. Vladimir's Seminary Press, 1990) 90.

"pure traditionalism."[25] Metz, of course, offers a third way: political theology. The latter Schmemann subsumes under his first type, theology in which the world sets the agenda for the Church, with theology thereby pursuing "various trends."[26] Schmemann relegates the societal concern for "justice and politics" to this pejorative level of trend, as he does "therapeutic" attention to the individual, and judges both to be reductions of Christianity to Hegelian-type transformations of history. The other general type of contemporary theology Schmemann identifies with a radical isolation of Christianity from the world. Under this admittedly broad category he includes all who pursue "a spirituality of escape, a highly personal spirituality," those who give priority to spiritual practices eclectically drawing on various religions, as well as those with an "almost apocalyptic hatred for the world."[27] Schmemann admits that many of these theologies hold some measure of validity in light of the New Testament's paradoxical attitude toward the world (steeped in his Orthodoxy, he cites the Johannine tradition). The notion of paradox, I would propose, is a key to Schmemann's corrective response. Paradox and antinomy pervade his (liturgical) theology.

Insofar as Schmemann wants theology to be integrated with spirituality—and both with the Church's liturgy—we must take a brief but closer look at what he opposes in order to grasp better what he proposes. Schmemann's positive agenda is with Russian Orthodoxy, but his work is ecumenically pertinent for at least two reasons: first, because he, considering Orthodoxy to bear the genuine rudiments of theology and liturgical practice, held it to be so; second, because he seems to have become increasingly aware of the broader relevance of his analysis of the Orthodox crisis. Felicitous to this present study, moreover, is the fact that at the end of his life Schmemann wrote about the crisis in terms of *faith* as the standard by which to judge practices of theology, spirituality, and liturgy. The analysis, as we have already begun to see, echoes Metz's concern to define faith as a praxis informed by the definite message of the Gospel and to contrast

[25] Metz, *Faith in History and Society*, 97. This Metzian typology, as well as his argument for a proper retrieval of tradition, are discussed in the concluding section of this book's second chapter.

[26] Schmemann, "Liturgy and Eschatology," 91.

[27] Ibid., 92–3.

such practical belief with a religion of "mere contemplation" or "purely-believed in faith."[28]

Schmemann finds the Church pervaded by a piety of "religious feeling" which, in a chapter of *The Eucharist* already noted above, he sharply contrasts with faith:

"Faith is always and above all a meeting with the Other, conversion to the Other, the reception of him as 'the way, the truth and the life,' love for him and the desire for total unity with him, such that 'it is no longer I who live, but Christ who lives in me' (Ga 2:20). . . . Meanwhile, 'religious feeling,' which in our day again dominates in religion, is so distinct from faith because it lives and is nourished by itself, i.e., through the gratification that it gives and which, in the final analysis, is subordinated to personal tastes and emotional experiences, subjective and individual 'spiritual needs.'"[29]

From this initial contrast Schmemann unfolds three others between faith and religious feeling. (1) Whereas faith necessitates struggle within the subject, religious feeling, insofar as it is oriented toward relieving life's burdens, renders the subject passive. (2) While committed to the subjectivity of each individual, faith is anything but individualistic and requires confession, articulation, and conversion. Religious feeling is thoroughly individualistic and is suspicious of efforts at expressing or comprehending what it "simply" knows. (3) Faith seeks an integration of people's whole lives—their reason, will, desires—while religious feeling ruptures religion from life and, moreover, establishes ideas, even complete world views, that are foreign if not contradictory to Christianity.

Schmemann astutely observes the insidiousness with which religious feeling has so replaced faith as to claim to be the latter. Its "Orthodox variant" is "an outward 'churchliness' of religious feeling," the hallmark of which is "a uterine attachment to rituals, customs, traditions," which fosters an inordinate conservatism "bewitched by the form, 'form-in-itself,' its immutability, sacredness, beauty."[30] Thus

---

[28] See Chapter 2, p. 64.

[29] Schmemann, *The Eucharist*, 144.

[30] Ibid., 145. Prescinding from any judgment of Schmemann's intentions, nevertheless, one cannot help but note a certain misogynistic tone ("uterine," "bewitched") here in his criticism of Orthodox piety.

nourished by the elements of ritual in themselves Orthodox piety "fails to relate the form to its content—the faith incarnate in it, revealed and granted through it"—indeed, is "troubled and irritated by any attempt to comprehend the form, to seek the truth incarnate in it and manifested by it."[31] The conviction that Christian faith and truth are made "incarnate" in the liturgy is an axiom, if not the fundamental principle, of Schmemann's liturgical theology. Piety and theology, obsessed with experiences (ritualistic or emotional or therapeutic or political), are nonetheless alienated from *experience*, "the living experience of the Church,"[32] by which Schmemann means the liturgy, the "rule of faith" experienced within the "rule of prayer."

CHRISTIAN LITURGY:
ITS BASIS, CONTENT, AND FUNCTION

Like Metz, Schmemann developed his theology with an awareness of the wider contemporary currents flowing around him. Like Metz, as well, Schmemann placed himself on a rock, standing in firm resistance to both the currents of an abstract theological turn to (subjective) experience and actual (bourgeois) subjects' practical reductions of Christianity to ritualistic and/or personalistic religious experiences.

---

[31] Ibid. Schmemann describes here a phenomenon not by any means unknown in contemporary Roman Catholicism. The extreme is a pining for (and now, once again, a limited but officially sanctioned practice of) the so-called Tridentine Mass. Even that title for the Latin Mass that originated in the sixteenth century demonstrates a lack of historical knowledge. Its proper title is the Mass of Pius V which, promulgated in 1570, implemented (more or less) the practical mandates that emerged along with the doctrinal decisions of the Council of Trent. As Robert Cabié demonstrates through historical and textual analysis, the Order of Mass of St. Pius V was a product of medieval liturgical developments and, despite a reforming spirit that wished to be faithful to patristic norms, realized only uneven measures of critical revision. In conclusion to his study of the medieval and Tridentine origins of the 1570 Order of Mass Cabié comments on what Schmemann would call the "pseudo-conservatism" found among contemporary Church members: "Pius V was a courageous innovator, and it is an almost unbelievable paradox that some should today be invoking his patronage to oppose a reform inspired by the same spirit as continued and brought to bear at the Second Vatican Council." Robert Cabié, *The Eucharist*, vol. 2 of *The Church at Prayer*, trans. Matthew O'Connell, ed. Aimé Martimort (Collegeville: The Liturgical Press, 1986) 176.

[32] Schmemann, *The Eucharist*, 144.

For both theologians the rock is a faith borne of experience, such experience, however, being not a synchronic valorization of the present but, rather, a critical and constructive recovery of the Christian tradition. For Metz the experience of tradition is a praxis of mysticism and politics attentive to the practical content of the Christian message or Gospel. For Schmemann the tradition fundamentally is the liturgy. At this point, however, one might protest to Schmemann that he has provided more than enough indication of the current crisis-ridden state of the liturgy. How, one might ask, can the liturgy be the essential experience of Christians? Schmemann's answer is an unflinching acknowledgment of the problem and an insistence that the question establishes the positive task of liturgical theology.

The starting point is to define what is meant by the term "liturgy." Schmemann explains that "the Church's *leitourgia*" is

"an all-embracing vision of life, a power meant to judge, inform and transform the whole of existence, a 'philosophy of life' shaping and challenging all our ideas, attitudes and actions, . . . an *icon* of that new life which is to challenge and renew the 'old life' in us and around us."[33]

This is a functional definition of liturgy, and necessarily so, since for Schmemann "the very function of worship" is to practice a knowledge of the integral "*continuity* between 'religion' and 'life'" through the liturgy's "power of transformation, judgment, and change."[34] What this all means, nonetheless, can only be grasped through consideration of what Schmemann calls the basis and content of Christian worship.

The basis of Christian worship Schmemann identifies with the incarnation, the content with the Cross and the resurrection.

"Through these events the new life in Christ, the Incarnate Lord, is 'hid with Christ in God,' and made into a life 'not of this world.' The world which rejected Christ must itself die in man [*sic*] if it is to become again means of communion, means of participation in the life which shone forth from the grave, in the Kingdom which is not 'of this world,' and which in terms of this world is still to come."[35]

---

[33] Schmemann, "Liturgy and Theology," 51–2.
[34] Schmemann, *For the Life of the World*, 133.
[35] Ibid., 122.

With a statement such as this, one begins to grasp the extent to which Schmemann's liturgical theology entails consideration of the fundamental tenets of Christian faith, clearly drawn from the Orthodox appropriation of Scripture and the patristic sources of tradition, and allows no shortcuts in theory or stopgaps in practice. The statement, effectively a summary of what Roman Catholic theologians subsume under the concept of the *paschal mystery*,[36] includes all the key elements in Schmemann's theology and sets the itinerary for an exposition thereof. The basis of Christian worship, namely, the doctrine of the incarnation, expounds a world that was created to be a means of communion or participation in life, which is God-the-Logos, Jesus the Christ. This life is hidden in the world due to sin. Thus the content of worship is the revelation of life in the risen Christ as the kingdom of God, realized presently in the Church through the eucharistic liturgy and anticipated amidst a world wherein time is yet to be fulfilled. Schmemann thereby regularly summarizes genuine Christian liturgy as cosmological (the world as sacramental), eschatological (the kingdom which is to come), and ecclesiological (the Church as manifestation and witness of the kingdom in this world). Liturgy's transformative potential for the Church and Christians in society lies herein.

In a synthesis of patristic teaching and its particular revival in mid-twentieth-century Paris, Schmemann posits the world as essentially sacramental:

"The term 'sacramental' means here that the basic and primordial intuition which not only expresses itself in worship, but of which the entire worship is indeed the 'phenomenon'—both effect and experience—is that the world, be it in its totality as cosmos, or in its life and becoming as time and history, is an *epiphany* of God, a means of His [*sic*] revelation, presence, and power."[37]

[36] For a concise, representative Roman Catholic treatment of the liturgical concept of "paschal mystery" see I. H. Dalmais, "Theology of the Liturgical Celebration," *Principles of the Liturgy,* vol. 1 of *The Church at Prayer,* trans. Matthew O'Connell, ed. A. G. Martimort (Collegeville: The Liturgical Press, 1987) 262–6. For a more recent and sustained treatment of the concept within a comprehensive liturgical theology, see Irwin, *Context and Text,* 24–5, 49, 144, 275–8, 178–9, 298–9, 312, 315–7, 330–1, 345.

[37] Schmemann, *For the Life of the World,* 120. The reader acquainted with the early work of Edward Schillebeeckx will readily recognize here—and in what

Only through the great variety of the world's matter and energy and the events of individual and social histories is humanity able to know God, that is, to have communion with God, and thus to know themselves as participants in the creative life of God in the world. This communion is true knowledge of God and the world. Thus, knowledge entails both understanding and participation. Such knowledge is both the purpose of worship and the solution to theology's "ultimate problem," the epistemological problem, namely, "the possibility and nature of the knowledge of God."[38] This argument is the basis for Schmemann's insistence that one cannot do theology—pursue the *lex credendi*—without practicing the liturgy—participating in the *lex orandi*. Anthropologically this means that humans are essentially worshiping beings. Worship is the essential work *(leitourgia)* of humanity in that it highlights and informs all human activity as the pursuit of communion with God through communion with the good world God has created.

The "primordial intuition" to worship is evident throughout human cultures, Schmemann argues. Christian theologians need not, therefore, be threatened by the theses about cultic ritual that have emerged from the methodologies proper to the discipline of comparative religions, *Religionswissenschaft*. The theologian ought to recognize that Christian liturgy is the quintessence of the phenomenon of worship on the basis of belief in the incarnation, the Logos made flesh.

---

follows—marked parallels between Schmemann's and the Flemish Dominican's basic sacramental theology. While both incorporate the recovery of patristic thought in conjunction with insights from contemporary phenomenology (which Schillebeeckx studied not only with the Dominican faculty in Paris but also at the University of Louvain), Schillebeeckx also contributed mightily to the renewed authentic reading of Thomas Aquinas—of whom Schmemann seems always to have taken a jaundiced view. See Edward Schillebeeckx, *Christ the Sacrament of the Encounter with God* (New York: Sheed and Ward, 1963) 1–80. For background information on Schillebeeckx's work see "Edward Schillebeeckx: An Orientation to His Thought," *The Schillebeeckx Reader,* ed. Robert J. Schreiter (New York: Crossroad, 1984) 1–24; William J. Hill, "Human Happiness as God's Honor: Background to a Theology in Transition," *The Praxis of Christian Experience: An Introduction to the Theology of Edward Schillebeeckx,* ed. Robert J. Schreiter and Mary Catherine Hilkert (San Francisco: Harper and Row, 1989) 1–17; and Philip Kennedy, *Schillebeeckx* (Collegeville: The Liturgical Press, 1993).

[38] Schmemann, *For the Life of the World,* 140.

"It is indeed extremely important for us to remember that the unique-
ness, the *newness* of Christian worship is not that it has no *continuity*
with worshop [*sic*] 'in general,' as some overly zealous apologists
tried to prove at the time when *Religionswissenschaf* [*sic*] simply reduced Christianity and its worship to pagan mystery-cults, but that in
Christ the very continuity is fulfilled, receives its ultimate and truly
new significance so as to truly bring [*sic*] all 'natural' worship to an
end. Christ is the fulfillment of worship as adoration and prayer,
thanksgiving and sacrifice, communion and knowledge, because He
is the ultimate 'epiphany' of man [*sic*] as worshiping being, the fulness of God's manifestation and presence by means of the world. He
is the true and full Sacrament because He is the fulfillment of the
world's essential 'sacramentality.'"[39]

Elsewhere in his writings Schmemann approaches Christian worship and
the role of Christ therein from their historical origins in Judaism. That
earliest Christian worship was not the product of the pagan mystery-
cults is of great importance to Schmemann's liturgical theology.[40] There
is indeed a continuity between Jewish and all other human worship, to
the extent that the Jewish cult of temple, priesthood, and sacrifice was
"a 'cult' and a 'religion' in the deepest sense of these words, in the
sense of mediation, of a connecting, of a system of contacts and relationships with the 'holy,' with 'God.'"[41] Of unique and irreducible
importance to the history of the chosen people, however, is God's revelation of the world, to use Schmemann's favorite term, as "fallen."[42]
Although he seldom explicitly states so to the extent that this present

[39] Ibid., 122.
[40] The theologian who most creatively constructed a theory of early Christian worship on the premise of its primary indebtedness to the mystery-cults
was Dom Odo Casel. For expositions of Casel's work and reviews of the
major figures who subsequently critiqued him, see Irwin, *Context and Text*,
21–4; and Dalmais, "Theology of the Liturgical Celebration," 267–71.
[41] Alexander Schmemann, *Introduction to Liturgical Theology*, trans.
Asheleigh E. Moorhouse (Crestwood, N.Y.: St. Vladimir's Seminary Press,
1966, 1986) 100. Here Schmemann relies directly and explicitly on the work of
the great French Dominican theologian Yves Congar.
[42] See Schmemann, "Liturgy and Eschatology," 98–9. Evident here again is
the extent to which Schmemann's theology is steeped in patristic tradition. One
must at least note, however, that—consistent with that heritage—Schmemann
performs a Christian appropriation of the Jewish Scriptures and religion,

writer wishes he would, one gets the sense that for Schmemann Judaism's awareness (knowledge) of humanity's sinfulness or alienation from God heightens the desire for union with God and, thus, deepens the quality of its cultic activity—and reflection thereon.[43] This is, however, to shift the focus from the cosmological basis of Jewish worship to its eschatological content. The evidence and continuity of the latter at Christianity's origins, whose long suppression in ecclesial history Schmemann joins Metz in excoriating, is the reason for Schmemann's emphatic rejection of the mystery-cult thesis of early Christian liturgy.

THE LITURGY OF TIME:
TIME MADE "ESCHATOLOGICALLY TRANSPARENT"

For Schmemann the hope for the Church and the world amidst their current crises lies in the Church's liturgy, and the hope that the liturgy can indeed be salvific lies in the structure and content, the shape (with a bow to Dix), of the earliest Christian practices. One of Schmemann's major contributions to liturgical theology, and one which can now contribute to the important Metzian project of political theology, is his theory of the early Church's "liturgy of time" and, more specifically, of Christianity's reliance on what Schmemann terms Hebrew messianism and apocalypticism.[44] Sacramental and liturgical

---

formulating them in categories which Jewish believers might not appreciate readily (if at all, in some cases). Given the significant weight that numerous liturgical theologians, whose company I seek to join, have come to place on the Jewish influence upon the "shape" of early Christian liturgy (to join Schmemann in his tribute to Dom Gregory Dix), this issue necessarily remains an important one which one must at minimum flag in a footnote.

[43] Schmemann does not write directly in terms of the people's sinfulness but, rather, in terms of their need for salvation, redemption, and faithfulness to the covenant relationship with God. Schmemann discusses this topic in the context of his explication of the "Liturgy of time" which Christianity inherited from Judaism (see the next two sections of this chapter). Belief in God's salvation of the people in history, along with the eschatological expectation of the people's final redemption (deliverance from sin or unfaithfulness), are what distinguish Judaism's cultic "sanctification of time" from other religions' cultic and mythic sacralizations of nature or seasons. See Schmemann, *Introduction to Liturgical Theology*, 69–75.

[44] In this area of his work Schmemann builds on the scholarship of Jean Daniélou, citing most often his "La Théologie du dimanche," *Le Jour du*

theology for Schmemann is not simply a matter of focusing upon the symbols, words, and gestures of the liturgy—paramountly the Eucharist (although it does, of course, include all that). Rather, Schmemann recognizes that the weekly pattern of Christian worship itself, and, in a supplementary and derivative way, the daily and yearly cycles, are an integral part of the Church's *lex orandi* and, thereby, a source of its belief and its mission in the world.

Schmemann recognizes a long-lost link between the Eucharist and time in the early Church's celebration of the Lord's Day as "the day of Jesus' resurrection from the dead, the manifestation of the new life, . . . the day of the Eucharist."[45] The key to grasping the significance of the Lord's Day lies in its original relationship to, but distinction from, the Jewish Sabbath. That primordial relationship dissolved within the first few centuries of Christianity into an identification of the two—the Lord's Day as the Sabbath moved one space over on the weekly calendar. Constantine sealed this move by officially sanctioning the "day of the sun" as an obligatory day of rest. Schmemann, however, argues:

"For the early Church the Lord's Day was not a substitute for the sabbath; it was not (so to speak) its Christian equivalent. On the contrary the real nature and significance of this new day was defined in relation to the sabbath and to the concept of time connected with it."[46]

As the day of the Creator's rest, the Sabbath is of cosmological significance, affirming the goodness of the natural world and its cycles of time. The Sabbath, however, has not only cosmological but also eschatological import, for the Jews are a people "of messianic hopes" grounded in the covenant and its law. The time of the weekly cycle is

---

Seigneur, Congrès du Centre de Pastorale Liturgique, Lyons, 17–22 septembre 1947 (Paris: Robert Laffont, 1948). See also Jean Daniélou, *The Bible and the Liturgy* (Notre Dame, Ind.: University of Notre Dame Press, 1956). For further bibliography, as well as a parallel but less theologically developed treatment of the theology of time and Sunday, see Pierre Journel, "Sunday and the Week," *The Liturgy and Time,* Irénée Henri Dalmais, Pierre Journel, and Aimé Georges Martimort, vol. 4 of *The Church at Prayer,* ed. A. G. Martimort, trans. Matthew J. O'Connell (Collegeville: The Liturgical Press, 1986) 9–29.

[45] Schmemann, *Introduction to Liturgical Theology,* 75.
[46] Ibid., 76.

not only one of shared blessings in the created order but of struggle in sinfully disordered history. Such was the extent of evil's reign that, as recorded in the books of the Maccabees, faithfulness to the Sabbath and, thus, to the God of Israel was something for which men and women had to be willing to die. Amidst such experiences of oppression arose Hebrew messianism and apocalypticism and the expectation of an utterly new day, the "eighth day" in the book of Enoch, the first day after God's creation, "the beginning of the New Aeon not to be reckoned in time . . . the beginning of the world that has been saved and restored."[47]

It was in the context of this increasingly universal eschatology that the earliest believers understood what God had done in Jesus. They thereby identified the day of his resurrection as the Day of the Lord, celebrated not on the Sabbath but on the first day of the week as the first and the eighth day, the day of messianic fulfillment. As late as the fourth century Basil the Great referred to Sunday, the day of Jesus' resurrection and now the day of the Church's Eucharist, as "the eighth day," giving evidence that "the symbolism of Hebrew apocalypticism was adopted by Christans [sic] and became one of the theological 'keys' to their liturgical consciousness."[48] Augustine employed the concept as well to articulate the belief that the good but fallen life of God's creation had not been destroyed in Christ's death and resurrection but, rather, redeemed and made eternal. Basil likewise taught that the Lord's Day is without evening or end and, relying on "the psalmist," posited this eighth day as outside of time and opposed to the week and its regular sequence of days. Following Jean Daniélou, Schmemann highlights Basil's point in all this, namely, that the eighth day is utterly complete and whole, not part of a multiplicity of days and events but the finality and completion of time—whether one calls it a day or an age or an aeon.

Such an identification of the *eschaton,* as the finality and completion of time, with the (eucharistic) Lord's Day quickly raises the question of whether and how this day-outside-of-time has any relationship to time and, thus, to this world. Schmemann's answer to this question includes his critique or rejection of what he identifies as two contemporary, disparate misconceptions about eschatology in the first few

[47] Ibid., 78.
[48] Ibid.

Christian centuries. One type is the notion that the earliest believers utterly disregarded the world as they fixed an exclusive gaze on the Lord's Second Coming.[49] Schmemann, however, reports a "uniform witness" in early Christian churches to the "first-eighth day" as the "day of the Eucharist," citing Pliny's testimony (Epistle 10:96) to their gathering on a *statu die*, an "established day," for the Eucharist's celebration. From this fact the following may be concluded: "The eschatology of the new Christian cult does not mean the renunciation of time. There would have been no need for a fixed day *(statu die)* in a 'wholly world-renouncing' cult, it could be celebrated on any day and at any hour."[50] Such practice would amount to a refusal to identify the God of redemption with the God of creation and would betray a false knowledge about fundamental reality.[51] The simplistic notion of a Christian rejection of time and the world denies the complexity of the reality disclosed by the gospel and manifested in the liturgy, which reality, as we shall see further on, is characterized by antinomy and paradox.

On the other hand, a likewise problematic misconception, one which has plagued ritually-oriented churches, is an understanding of the Lord's Day as special but nonetheless situated with the others in

[49] Elsewhere Schmemann reports and applauds "historians who have delivered themselves from a one-sided and false understanding of the 'eschatology' of early Christianity as complete indifference to the world." Ibid., 182.

[50] Ibid., 79–80.

[51] Here Schmemann's work resonates with that of Irenaeus of Lyons, who in his *Against Heresies* argues against the Marcionites and other "Gnostics" who considered all of material reality intrinsically evil—the product of a creator-god other than the God and Father of Jesus Christ. Arguing on the basis of how the president of the liturgical assembly blesses God in the Eucharistic Prayer, Irenaeus demonstrates the inconsistency of his opponents' logic:

"For some, by maintaining that the Father is different from the Creator, when they offer to Him what belongs to our created world, they portray Him as covetous of another's property and desirous of what is not His own. Those, again, who maintain that the things around us originated from downfall, ignorance, and passion, while offering to Him the fruits of ignorance, passion, and downfall, sin against their Father."

Irenaeus of Lyons, *Against Heresies, Book IV.18.4,* quoted in Daniel J. Sheerin, *The Eucharist,* Message of the Fathers of the Church 7, ed. Thomas Halton (Wilmington, Del.: Michael Glazier, 1986) 249.

the context of the week. Schmemann identifies this type most point-edly with the Constantinian reduction of the Lord's Day to a Sabbath, a day of repose in "a natural cycle of work and rest."[52] The distinction and location of the eucharistic Day of the Lord as a day of rest, neatly complementing—on the same plane of reality—the other days of labor, is a simplistic notion of time inadequate to the complex and an-tinomical reality that Christ's paschal mystery has brought about amidst the world. Such a reduction of the Lord's Day is gravely detri-mental to the practice of Christian faith, for it abandons the eschatol-ogy essential to both Judaism and Christianity and results, at best, in a merely cosmological sacramentality.

I use the qualification "at best" because a careful reading of the cor-pus of Schmemann's writings produces an acute, at times frustrating, awareness of the complexity and evasiveness of his general sacramen-tal theory. Recall his assertion that Christianity affirms the sacramen-tality of creation and history. This, to my understanding, is his cosmological sense of sacramental liturgy (later, in light of Metz's criticism of modern theology, we must attend to what Schmemann seems to mean by "history"). This cosmological sense should, at its best, result in believers making connections between (1) their cultic objects and gestures and (2) all created things and human actions as revelatory of God. To put this in traditional terms, liturgy's purpose is for the worship of God and the salvation of people; divine worship and human salvation together constitute the glorification of God.[53]

[52] Schmemann, *Introduction to Liturgical Theology*, 80.

[53] Belief in the inextricable relationship between the glorification of God and the salvation of people finds its origins in the New Testament, was widely evident among the patristic authors (perhaps most famously in Irenaeus' pithy statement), and was integral to Thomas Aquinas' theology of grace and the sacraments. Schillebeeckx masterfully recovered the principle and its sources for a world wide audience in his *Christ the Sacrament of the En-counter with God*. Jesus, in his life and actions, is the manifestation of the di-vine love for humanity and humanity's love for God. The Spirit of the risen Christ bestows grace and the capacity for religious worship: "Therefore the sacraments are the visible realization on earth of Christ's mystery of saving worship" (Schillebeeckx, *Christ the Sacrament of the Encounter with God*, 45). Schillebeeckx honored the work of his teachers in France—and thereby the scholarly Liturgical Movement—by so effectively presenting the patristic and medieval sources (see Dalmais, "Theology of the Liturgical Celebration,"

Nonetheless, the cosmological aspect of liturgy can only thus function, can only be at its best, if both human sin is acknowledged and God is identified as the God of Israel, the people's Savior who has acted definitively in Jesus the Christ. This, however, demonstrates that in Christian ritual the cosmological cannot function without the eschatological: People can never realize the connection between God and creation without the eschatological word of salvation, the Gospel.

The problem, as Schmemann passionately pursued it throughout his work, is not completely solved, however, by the Christian liturgy's structure of word and sacrament, that is, by joining cultic objects and actions with texts and prayers that proclaim the reality of sin and redemption. The entire liturgical action must necessarily be situated in the context of the liturgy of time, the awareness that the purpose of the Lord's Day is to make all time "eschatologically transparent."[54] It is this eschatological transparency that the Constantinian "day of the sun," as well as the complex evolution and ecclesial influence of monasticism and its calendar,[55] greatly obscured. This distortion of Christian

---

245–8, for a representative piece of the older generation's work on this topic). In continuity with the best of the Liturgical Movement, moreover, Schillebeeckx argued for the mutual need of the Church's sacramental liturgical reform and an increasingly active Christian love in the world, a "real love for our fellow men [and women] . . . a solidarity in human experience" (Schillebeeckx, *Christ the Sacrament of the Encounter with God*, 208). Over the subsequent two decades Schillebeeckx's study of Scripture scholarship, history, hermeneutics, and critical theory—along with consistent pastoral involvement in the Netherlands—all contributed to an increasing argument for the ethical and political dimensions of that love for humanity. Schillebeeckx performed his most thorough and convincing theoretical exposition of that topic in the third and fourth parts of his *Christ: The Experience of Jesus as Lord*, trans. John Bowden (New York: Crossroad, 1981) 629–839.

Don E. Saliers argues from the liturgy's dual focus of divine glorification and human sanctification for the necessity of the worshiping community's ongoing concern for moral and ethical transformation in "Liturgy and Ethics: Some New Beginnings," *Journal of Religious Ethics* 7 (Fall 1979) 173–89. Reprinted in E. Byron Anderson and Bruce T. Morrill, eds., *Liturgy and the Moral Self: Humanity at Full Stretch Before God* (Collegeville: The Liturgical Press, 1998) 15–35.

[54] Schmemann, *Introduction to Liturgical Theology*, 71.

[55] In *Introduction to Liturgical Theology* Schmemann devotes a rewarding amount of energy and attention to the emergence, distinctive features, and subsequent impact of monasticism upon the Byzantine liturgy. This comprises

sacramentality Schmemann regularly summarizes as the introduction of the notions of *sacred* and *profane* into the Christian liturgy and, thereby, into Christian life. Therein lies the separation of liturgical action from the rest of a Christian's purposeful activity (practices).

The division of life into sacred and profane sectors is a fundamental flaw in Christian piety or liturgical consciousness. Liturgical theologians and ecclesial leaders can modify or reform aspects or entire economies of rites on the basis of the soundest scholarship. However, as long as both clergy and laity perceive the resultant rituals as functioning in a sacred sector over against the profane realms of not only the rest of the "world" but the rest of the *Church's* activity, their performance cannot but fail to realize the humanly transformative (sanctifying or salvific) purpose of *Christian* cultic action.

For Schmemann the problem with the language or mentality of "the sacred" is that it limits *leitourgia*, the work of worship and sanctification, to isolated religious practices. People contemplate extra-temporal realities (for Orthodoxy, they dramatically reenact salvific events of the past) which have no impact on the profane commerce of humanity in the world today. The development of an increasingly elaborate Church calendar in Byzantium (and, of course, the West as well) exacerbated what had already happened to the Lord's Day. Numerous Christian feast days emerged as breaks from the profane work-a-day world. As such, they became occasions for "mysteriological" commemorations, ritual experiences of past sacred events, from which one returned (refreshed, perhaps) to grapple with the harsh realities of the world on its own terms. Schmemann's metaphor for this long-running phenomenon is one in which "separate bits" of the world's time are converted "into 'sacred time' to mark the contrast with time that is profane."[56]

Schmemann argues, on the contrary, that the eschatological consciousness of the early Church did not conceptualize the world in categories of sacred and profane but, rather, old and new, fallen and saved, dying and regenerated. A fundamental "antinomy" characterizes this eschatological construction of reality:

---

another of the outstanding contributions he has made to the discipline of liturgical theology—an explication of how the Byzantine liturgy is a "synthesis" of "secular" and "monastic" cultic-religious practices. For his comprehensive conclusion and analysis of that historical process see ibid., 201–12.

[56] Ibid., 183.

"In the early eschatological theology of time, time as such, i.e. the time of 'this world,' could not become 'sacred,' since the 'form of this world was passing away.' It could not become the Kingdom; it was ultimately condemned, and 'lay in evil.' The Lord's Day is not 'one out of several' days of the week and does not belong to time, just as the Church is 'not of this world,' and cannot be a part of it. But at the same time the Lord's Day, the first and eighth day, does exist in time and is revealed in time, and this revelation is also the renewal of time, just as the existence of the Church in the world is its renewal and salvation."[57]

The purpose of the Lord's Day, as well as daily and yearly liturgical cycles, is not to sacralize (or sanctify) certain aspects of this world. That is an impossibility, for this world is dying, is passing away. The latter, however, is occurring in order that the world may be transformed into a new creation, become a new time, rise into a new life. The antinomy that marks the Church's authentic experience, or better, authentic construction of time, should generate a tensive energy in the Church. A sacred calendar does just the opposite. It delimits time by breaking it up with rest days and feast days that "introduce into time a kind of 'other world,' an alien reality" but "do not transform it into new time . . . do not renew it from within."[58]

The renewal of time and, thus, the world, but precisely a renewal *from within:* This, to my reading, is crucial to what Schmemann is claiming about the transformative power of Christian liturgy and sacramentality and, more foundationally, about Christ. As we have seen, Schmemann argues on the basis of scholarship that identifies a continuity between a "liturgy of time" in Judaism and that in the earliest Christian churches. Endorsing the work of Oscar Cullmann, Schmemann understands Jewish cult as having given "religious sanction" to the "natural" cycles of time by subordinating them to YHWH. Moreover, by constantly blessing the Kingdom of YHWH which is to come, the Jewish cult came to orient all temporal activity to the *eschaton,* "the light of the ultimate truth about the world, [humanity,] and history."[59] This Day of the Lord, eschatological in its revelation of the ultimate meaning of all things, constituted the "center" of time for Judaism and, subsequently, for early Christianity. The difference or

[57] Ibid.
[58] Ibid., 184.
[59] Ibid., 70.

discontinuity, however, lies in the latter's identification of the kingdom of God with Jesus the Christ. That identification entailed a shift
in how time is measured and perceived and, thus, lived. The pivotal
event of salvation in history has occurred; the Messiah has already
come; the kingdom of God is at hand. For Christians eschatology cannot be exclusively futuristic; rather, the normative Day of the Lord
has occurred in the events of Jesus the Christ.

THE INTERRUPTION AND INTENSIFICATION OF TIME

Metz's work has motivated my particular reading of Schmemann,
causing me to note, beginning with terminology, the latter's attention
to a messianism and apocalypticism endemic to earliest Christianity.
This has required a straightforward rehearsal of Schmemann's identification of those notions with the early Christian eucharistic liturgy,
celebrated on the "eighth day." The eucharistic action itself is an icon
of the new life that challenges and renews—transforms, judges, and
changes—the present (old) time in which we live. Through the life,
death, and resurrection of Jesus this old world is being renewed from
within or, to quote another of Schmemann's descriptions of this process, this is an "inner subordination of the old time to the Aeon of the
Kingdom."[60] Precisely that last point, however, requires an explicit
critique by and dialogue with Metz.

In the most global sense the two authors agree that eschatology is
essential to an adequate theological apprehension and practice of the
Christian faith. Both authors demonstrate that the noun "eschatology" refers to both (1) a doctrine and (2) a way of life, a life "in the
presence of God," as Metz is wont to say. Eschatological doctrine and
practice are essential to and mutually dependent within Christianity.
An absence of both aspects of eschatology in the churches and theological academies of both the West and the East has resulted, to use
Schmemann's analysis, in a division of religious life into the mutually
exclusive categories of sacred and profane, a division inimical to the
fundamental kerygma about the kingdom of God. Nor is either author unaware of the faults, perhaps each would passionately call them
failures, on the part of theological efforts to recover eschatology in the
course of the past hundred years or so. Those failures, as we saw in
Chapter 2, Metz summarizes as reductions of eschatology to "mean-

[60] Ibid., 183.

ingful teleologies" for human history or "existential" reflections on individual salvation.

The practical problem is that Christianity ends up simply confirming social processes currently under way and/or therapeutic methods widely practiced, often mimicking them, offering second-rate, more or less "spiritualized" versions of what is already happening. For that reason both Metz and Schmemann turn to a more specific notion of eschatology, namely, apocalyptic, but with differences in their approaches. Both recognize that an apocalyptic notion of eschatology does not necessarily entail a renouncing of the world. Engagement in some form of apocalypticism does not, indeed, should not imply a disinterest in the present circumstances of history. It does, however, mean that an apocalyptically-oriented faith does indeed reject crucial aspects of those present circumstances on the basis of the apocalyptic vision. For both authors the apocalyptic element of eschatology makes the practice of Christian religion an interruption of the normal course of time.[61] For both it places the world and history in question. The manner and content of that interruption, however, each author conceptualizes differently.

In view of the sense of timelessness that renders people apathetic in technological, market-driven societies, Metz argues that Christianity's interruption must be a shock to the socioeconomic system, an apocalyptic goad for a radically different praxis. As we saw in Chapter 2, the clarity Metz achieved by the late 1970s in evaluating the signs of the times was not matched by a comparable clarity in explaining or even describing how this apocalyptic goad is to take place. Metz was right, in theory, to recognize and insist upon the singular, essential role for narratives and memories of both the oppressed and forgotten and those courageous enough to act in solidarity with them. He thereby improved his practical response to his principle desire for a critical eschatology, shifting from an open-ended "eschatological proviso" to the definite memory of Jesus the Christ. The vagueness for Metz, however, persisted. He relied on the notion that the *idea* of the parousia can function critically for today's Christians. He introduced—clearly with the

---

[61] Here I employ the concept—a single word—wherein Metz effectively captures the force of his argument for political theology, and whereby he has captured the thought of such a wide range of theologians. "The shortest definition of religion: interruption." Metz, *Faith in History and Society*, 171.

expectation of some current benefit—the *memory* of how scriptural stories of catastrophe functioned as a "mystical analogy" for ancient Christians in their struggle with oppressive "political realities." Just how that all worked for those earliest Christians, that is, how they avoided despair, as well as how they integrated faith in the narrative-memory of Jesus' own life, death, and resurrection with their own trials, Metz did not address sufficiently.

As we further saw in Chapter 2, a development in Metz's thought emerged several years later, as he came to describe the life of faith as an eschatological dialectic between symbols of catastrophe and symbols of consolation. The appearance of the latter, in my estimation, resonates with Metz's growing appreciation for the potentially transformative role of symbols and sacraments amidst an instrumentally rational and consumerist society. But again, how do these latter moments in the dialectically Christian life impact upon those that wrestle with disaster? Metz tends to identify apocalypticism with catastrophe, while wanting symbols of consolation to nurture messianic virtues in late modern Christians. That there is little evidence of this happening in the first world societies for which Metz writes is demonstrated by the fact that he must cite his visitations to third world communities. Metz's narrative approach takes us to the threshold of insight; but is there a theory about sacramental liturgy that may provide insight into the mystery of the eschatological dialectic? Schmemann may provide such a theory, but from a radically different viewpoint. Schmemann perceives an apocalyptic eschatology within the symbols of consolation themselves, especially in the symbols that together comprise the practice of the eucharistic liturgy.

Schmemann recognizes that interruption is an essential characteristic of Christian apocalypticism. He finds the apocalyptic interruption not in narratives about immanent human, social catastrophe but in the weekly eucharistic liturgy of the Lord's Day. The messianic and apocalyptic interruption of time comes with each celebration of the eighth day, when the time of this old and fallen aeon is left behind, when a definite (redemptive) break in the regular (fallen) social and ecological ordering of things occurs:

"It is the day on which the Church assembles, locking the doors, and ascends to the point at which it becomes possible to say, 'Holy, holy, holy Lord God of Sabaoth, heaven and earth are full of thy glory.' Tell me, what right do we have to say that? Today I read the London

Times—a welcome change from the *New York Times*—but, whichever of them we read, does it make us say, 'Heaven and earth are full of thy glory'? The world which they show us is certainly not full of the glory of God. If we make such an affirmation in the Liturgy, it is not just an expression of Christian optimism ('Onward, Christian soldiers'), but simply and solely because we have ascended to the point at which such a statement is indeed true, so that the only thing that remains for us to do is to give thanks to God. And in that thanksgiving we are in him and with him in his Kingdom, because there is now nothing else left, because that is where our ascension has already led us."[62]

There is a critical edge to Schmemann's statement, an edge which Metz would undoubtedly appreciate. Schmemann's theological evaluation of the world as fallen is neither abstract nor focused exclusively on the sinfulness of individuals. It has, on the contrary, a potentially social (political) dimension, evidenced in his reference to a couple of the major newspapers of our day. Schmemann, moreover, has no patience for any sort of "Christian optimism," as if the glorious vision of heaven and earth that is revealed in the liturgy, the enacted symbols of consolation, simply reconciles (represses?) the real struggles in our time.

In his liturgical concept of ascension, however, Schmemann is asserting something that he believes is not only equally but even more real than worldly struggles. For this present study, his eschatology, so characterized by antinomy and paradox, must now unfold. The assembled Church both leaves the world behind, as symbolized by "locking the doors," and yet raises it up into its vision or experience of the kingdom of God. This experience of the kingdom is fundamentally one of joyous thankfulness. We must work through Schmemann's eschatology of the liturgy in order to see how liturgical participation in thankfulness can have a messianic and apocalyptic impact on the world.

In the long passage just quoted Schmemann exhibits the unabashedly, although not exclusively, realized quality of his eschatology. The assembled, worshiping church's "ascension" has *already* "led" its participants into the kingdom of God. Throughout his writings Schmemann never tires of, indeed, he clearly revels in, asserting that the eucharistic liturgy is the actual experience of the parousia:

[62] Schmemann, "Liturgy and Eschatology," 97–8.

"[The] messianic Kingdom or life in the aeon is 'actualized'—becomes real—in the assembly of the Church, in the [*ekklesia*], when believers come together to have communion in the Lord's body. The Eucharist is therefore the manifestation of the Church as the new aeon; it is participation in the Kingdom as the *parousia,* as the presence of the Resurrected and Resurrecting Lord. It is not the 'repetition' of His advent or coming into the world, but the lifting up of the Church into His *parousia,* the Church's participation in His heavenly glory."[63]

There is a boldness in Schmemann's identification of the eucharistic liturgy with the parousia that cannot but startle Western Christian readers, both Catholic and Protestant. If, however, one reflects carefully upon what Schmemann is asserting, one realizes that it amounts to a fundamental confession of faith in Christ and in the relationship of believers, as well as the world, to him. The statement is no more startling than a Protestant's confession that the Word of God speaks directly in the Bible or the Roman Catholic's conviction that Christ is really present to the adoring faithful at the Mass and before the tabernacle. Christian faith requires such intellectually outlandish affirmations (Metz too, as we have seen, has come to assert this). The value of turning to the Orthodox version lies not only in its jarring difference of expression (its otherness, if you will) but also, under Schmemann's tutelage, in its assertion of the irreducibly social (as opposed to individualistic) dimension of salvation. To assert Christ's messiahship requires that believers take history (time) and society seriously, but precisely on the basis of the vision of the kingdom of God.

For Schmemann, in his effort to recover what he considers authentic Orthodox theology, the most important question is one of priority. If the Church is to serve an obviously sinful and troubled world then it must, without excuse or compromise, assert that a vital, experiential knowledge of the kingdom of God is both the source and end for the world's redemption. The crucial issue lies in whether the Church allows the eschatological Gospel or various forces in society to establish the parameters of its world view and, thus, inspire the pragmatics of its mission. Schmemann argues that the Church began to let society set the agenda as early as the end of the second century, and more so in the third:

---

[63] Schmemann, *Introduction to Liturgical Theology,* 72.

"The emphasis shifted from the Church as an anticipation of the Kingdom of God to the Church as a sacramentally hierarchical institution, 'serving' the world and life in it in all its manifestations, providing it with a religious and moral law, and sanctioning the world with this law. There is no better evidence of this change than the gradual extinction in the Christian community of the eschatological doctrine of the Church, the replacement of the early Christian eschatology by a new, individualistic and futuristic eschatology. 'The Kingdom of God,' Salvation and Perdition came to be experienced as primarily individual reward or punishment depending on one's fulfilment of the law in this world. The 'Kingdom of God' or eternal life, having become 'ours' in Christ, paled in the experience of believers (not dogmatically, of course, but psychologically), and no longer appeared as the fulfilment of all hopes, as the joyous end of all desires and interest, but simply as a reward. It was deprived of the independent, self-sufficient, all-embracing and all-transcending content toward which all things were striving: 'thy Kingdom come!'"[64]

The fundamental problem, as rehearsed earlier in this chapter, is the attitude with which Christians, both clerics and laity, undertake the eucharistic action. The liturgy itself, as well as the Church, continues to have an eschatological *doctrine,* but its proper content is lost to the "worldly" attitudes of its practitioners. Rather than giving themselves over to an experience of worship whose *content* and pattern are markedly different, indeed, independent, from their daily ways of thinking and acting, Christians approach and perform the Eucharist on the basis of their own agendas. Schmemann is calling for Christians to stop trying to control the gospel by isolating the liturgical experience as a merely "sacred" one and reducing it to a dramatic ritual reenactment of past events. They must, instead, give themselves over to a pattern of gathering, proclamation, offering, and communion that instills joy and gratitude to God and compels with a mission for the world.

The issue of control, as I have noted, is a crucial one. For the Orthodox, in Schmemann's estimation, it is the problem of sacralization. Both clergy and laity place constrictive limits on the power of the liturgy by relegating the entire action to a sacred sphere. For middle-class American Catholics, as we saw in *The Awakening Church* project,

---

[64] Ibid., 137.

it is the conforming of the liturgical celebration to conventional ways of being "friendly" and "relevant." What Schmemann teaches through his theology of time, however, is that there must be a definite break from whatever people's patterns of action and interaction. This is not to say there is no continuity between liturgical symbols and gestures and the rest of our experience of the world. Neither Christian cosmology nor eschatology will allow that. The point, rather, is that Christians must break off their regular patterns of societal and inter-personal interaction, their ways of using words, bodily gestures, food, and drink (as subjects in society and the wider world), and, instead, consciously and actively enter into a different, ritualized and symbol-laden pattern. Christians need to know a way of living in relation to God, humanity, and all creation that can transform what they—due to arrogance, selfishness, indifference, resignation, or despair—already know and take for granted about the way the world is. The experi-ence of the "fulfillment of time" in the Eucharist "bears witness to [time's] finitude and limitedness, which constitutes the sanctification of time."[65] In other words, giving oneself over to the radical otherness, the transcendent, messianic, and eschatological content of the liturgy, changes the way one perceives and prioritizes all aspects of life— interpersonal, economic, familial, political.

In his last book Schmemann explicitly introduces the language of conversion: "[The eucharistic liturgy's] setting, its entire sequence, order and structure consist in manifesting to us the meaning and the content of the sacrament, in bringing us into it, in converting us into its participants and communicants."[66] Metz, as we saw in the previous chapter, came to recognize as well that conversion is an integral part of the Christian life. He describes conversion as Christians becoming *followers of Christ*, those who hear the narrative memories about Jesus and seek to imitate him. Schmemann, on the other hand, envisions conversion as participation in the Church, with the eucharistic liturgy as "the crowning and fulfilment of the entire faith, the entire life and the entire experience of the Church."[67] In assembling as the *ekklesia* in the liturgy, the Church, with all its various members and their various roles, undergoes over and again an experience of conversion by being

[65] Schmemann, *Introduction to Liturgical Theology*, 80.
[66] Schmemann, *The Eucharist*, 161.
[67] Ibid.

drawn through the elements of the rite into a participation in the life of the risen Christ.[68] The world of the kingdom of God, which is only a future concept in "this world," is "already revealed," "already 'anticipated,'" and "accomplished" in the culmination of the liturgy at the table of Christ—the proclamation of the anaphora and the sharing of communion.[69]

Schmemann turns the opening dialogue of the canon, "Lift up your hearts," into a prophetic interrogation of the ecclesial community: Is the "ultimate treasure of our heart in God, in heaven?"[70] He warns that if the answer is negative, then the Lord's sacramental epiphany comes as judgment. Such instruction could not but meet Metz's approval. Recall Metz's inquiry (really, indictment) of northern Christians: Do they really expect anything at all? Does an immanent expectation instill in believers a conviction for praxis? Schmemann is bringing to Metz a different possibility for this interrogation. It comes by means of joy and thanksgiving conveyed through eschatological symbols. Christians must enter into "the entire mystery" of Christ, his incarnation, redemptive mission and glorious ascension, and thereby receive the *"theoria,"* the knowledge and communion with God, which transforms their experience of the world.[71] This is only possible

---

[68] In a two-volume work, systematic theologian Donald Gelpi develops an extensive, five-part theory of Christian conversion—affective, intellectual, moral, sociopolitical, and religious—which he argues is essential for the furthering of sacramental theology and liturgical reform.

"The malaise haunting the revised liturgy of the Church dramatizes a serious pastoral problem that we must address if the liturgical reforms mandated by Vatican II hope to advance beyond mere formalism. Christian worship comes alive when it expresses integral conversion before God. It languishes in the absence of conversion."

Donald L. Gelpi, *Adult Conversion and Initiation,* vol. 1 of *Committed Worship: A Sacramental Theology for Converting Christians* (Collegeville: The Liturgical Press, 1993) 7. See also vol. 2: *The Sacraments of Ongoing Conversion* (Collegeville: The Liturgical Press, 1993).

[69] Schmemann, *The Eucharist,* 169.

[70] Ibid.

[71] Alexander Schmemann, "Symbols and Symbolism in the Byzantine Liturgy: Liturgical Symbols and Their Theological Interpretation," *Liturgy and Tradition: Theological Reflections of Alexander Schmemann,* ed. Thomas Fisch (Crestwood, N.Y.: St. Vladimir's Seminary Press, 1990) 123.

through a proper engagement with the liturgy, an adequate grasp of its (eschatologically) symbolic nature.

ESCHATOLOGICAL SYMBOLISM: REMEMBRANCE OF THE KINGDOM OF GOD

Throughout the wide range of his writings Schmemann always took great pains to explain the specific type or nature of symbolism proper to Christian liturgical action.[72] This he conceptualized as an "eschatological symbolism." Schmemann constructed his theory of liturgical symbolism constantly with a view to the unacceptable piety he observed in the Orthodox Church. From as early as the fourth century Eastern Christians developed what Schmemann calls an "illustrative" or allegorical or "mysteriological" understanding of the liturgy's symbolic actions and objects. With the *ordo* and elements of the Eastern liturgy in place by the middle of the patristic era, ecclesial authorities began to perform commentaries (homilies, letters) wherein they interpreted parts of the liturgy as illustrating specific historical events or, in another vein, theological or doctrinal notions. Examples of the former include identifying the Gospel procession with Christ's arrival at the Jordan to preach, and the Great Entrance (the introduction of the eucharistic rite) with Christ's burial.[73] Examples of the theological type of illustrative symbolism include identifying the seven vestments a bishop wears with the seven gifts of the Holy Spirit, and some sixteen different interpretations Schmemann found for the call issued at the beginning of the eucharistic rite, "The doors, the doors!" All sixteen provide a different illustrative meaning. That is precisely Schmemann's point. The wide varieties of illustrative symbolism, unfortunately considered "the very essence of the Byzan-

---

[72] See ibid., 114–28; see also Schmemann, "Liturgy and Eschatology," 95–7; Schmemann, *The Eucharist*, 25–48; Schmemann, *For the Life of the World*, 135–51.

[73] Schmemann cites the liturgical commentaries of Gregory of Nyssa, Pseudo-Dionysius, and Maximus as representing "different emphases, different varieties [of illustration or allegory], although with the same general, mystical, and mysteriological trend and orientation." Schmemann, "Symbols and Symbolism in the Byzantine Liturgy," 124–5. In his Catechetical Homilies, Theodore of Mopsuestia (d. 428) performed a veritable tour de force of such illustrative symbolism, commenting on each part of the eucharistic liturgy. For well-selected excerpts see Edward Yarnold, *The Awe-Inspiring Rites of Initiation: The Origins of the R.C.I.A.*, 2d ed. (Collegeville: The Liturgical Press, 1994) 165–250.

tine liturgical tradition," are in radical "discontinuity" from the ancient theology of the liturgy, "a comprehensive and consistent theological vision."[74] That original liturgical vision is the source from which Schmemann constructs his notion of eschatological symbolism. Before rehearsing the concept, however, brief attention to the flawed history and present notion of liturgical symbolism in the Roman Church is in order.

While the situation of Orthodoxy is Schmemann's admitted concern, at times he does accurately note the predominant problem for the eucharistic liturgy in Roman Catholicism.[75] The problem's origins lie in the eighth-century controversies over whether and how the eucharistic bread and wine are the body and blood of Christ. By the thirteenth century, theological inquiry was predominantly concerned with the causality by which the "elements" were transformed, and liturgical piety overwhelmingly focused on the object that resulted from this "transubstantiation."[76] In the words of Joseph Powers, "The Eucharistic life of the Church was a sad spectacle if it is compared with the meaning which is shown in its beginnings. 'Take and eat . . .' and 'Take and drink . . .' had become 'Gaze on the Host and find your salvation in the gazing.'"[77] The net result for the Catholic Church was the same as the one Schmemann perceives amongst the Orthodox: "the

[74] Schmemann, "Symbols and Symbolism in the Byzantine Liturgy," 124.

[75] Schmemann, "Liturgy and Eschatology," 96. Schmemann, as one would expect, gives the topic greater attention in his expansive project *The Eucharist*; see 214, 218–23.

[76] For a thorough scholarly study identifying three major models or approaches to the meaning of the Eucharist in the West from the eighth to the twelfth century see Gary Macy, *The Theologies of the Eucharist in the Early Scholastic Period* (Oxford: Oxford University Press, 1984). Another informative and insightful work is David N. Power, *The Sacrifice We Offer: The Tridentine Dogma and Its Reinterpretation* (New York: Crossroad, 1987) esp. 27–49. Power undertakes a historical examination of the practices and theologies surrounding the Eucharist in the three centuries leading up to the Council of Trent, as well as the questions that the Reformers had raised with regard to these. For further exploration of eucharistic theology and piety in the Middle Ages see Hans Bernhard Meyer, *Eucharistie: Geschichte, Theologie, Pastoral*, vol. 4 of *Gottesdienst der Kirche: Handbuch der Liturgiewissenschaft* (Regensburg, Germany: Verlag Friedrich Pustet, 1989) 226–36.

[77] Joseph M. Powers, *Eucharistic Theology* (New York: Seabury Press, 1967) 31.

excommunication, for all practical purposes, of the laity, for whom the partaking of communion, having ceased to have its source in their participation in the liturgy, became something exceptional . . . ."[78]

While it is true that the vast majority of North American Catholics now "receive communion" when at Mass, the problem of a radically flawed *practice* of eucharistic theology persists. Insofar as the *meaning* of the eucharistic liturgy is concerned, Catholics largely focus on two moments in the liturgy: first, the elevation of the host (and, secondarily, the cup), and second, the individual's reception of the host (and, at a significantly lower rate, the cup).[79] In Schmemann's astute terms, bad theology and piety obscure the goodness (redemptive capacity) of the rite. Whatever the given contemporary "style" of performing the Roman Mass, at the heart of the event most believers watch a ritual drama and individualistically receive a sacred wafer.[80] The liturgy of

[78] Schmemann, *The Eucharist,* 18.

[79] At the outset of his *magnum opus* on eucharistic theology, David Power assesses the problem as follows: "Though liturgical rites have been reformed and there is a much greater confluence at the communion table than had been the case for centuries, no coherent ritual edifice has taken the place of the old piety or of the doctrinal explanation that supported it." David N. Power, *The Eucharistic Mystery: Revitalizing the Tradition* (New York: Crossroad, 1992) vii.

[80] I make this statement fully aware that parochial leaders, such as those in the parishes of *The Awakening Church* project, would most likely protest that my analysis is harsh, simplistic, and inadequate to what one can observe at their liturgies. However, as a presbyter of the Roman Church who presides at numerous different parishes, as well as a Catholic who has long participated from the pews, I can readily offer much description in support of my analysis. At liturgies comprised of any range of age groups, musical styles (from a cappella Gregorian chant to guitar-led testimonial singing) and degrees of "friendly" interaction (exchanges of greetings at various points in the liturgy, holding hands, etc.), the "traditions" of adoring posture (bowing and kneeling) and/or gazing at the "moment" of consecration, as well as a variety of individual pious practices around the reception of the host, are universally evident. The problem resides both in the text and rubrics of the Mass of Paul VI and in the piety of the clergy and laity. The Eucharistic Prayers of the Roman Rite, upon arriving at the account of the Last Supper, all change in textual style and require the presider to drop his arms from the *orans* position. The address to the Father as blessing turns into a dramatic depiction (or "illustration," in Schmemann's terms) of an event. As for the posture of the assembly, paragraph 21 of the "General Instruction of the Roman Missal" (4th ed., 1975) calls for the people

the Lord's Day, on the contrary, should be a cultic action that culminates in sharing a ritual meal—specifically, the eschatological banquet.

The relationship between cult and eschatology is crucial for understanding what Schmemann means by the eschatological symbolism that is proper to Christian ritual. As we have seen, Schmemann roundly condemns all conceptualizations of Christianity as a religion of sacred practices. The category of the sacred isolates the content of the faith from the profane, "natural and secular life," protecting the latter "from the constant challenge and absolute demands of God," as well as depriving it of "the 'natural sacramentality' of the world."[81] The Christian doctrines of creation, incarnation, and redemption are incompatible with merely cultic religion. On the other hand, beginning with the early Church, Christianity has recognized its need for cultic activity

"because only a cult can express or manifest in 'this world'—this aeon—the holy, the wholly-other, the divine, the supra-worldly. But this cult was subjected to an eschatological transposition, since within the Church as the Body of Christ the wholly-other was realized as something given, fulfilled, communicated to people, something already belonging to them. Not a mediation between the sacred and the profane, but the fact of the accomplished consecration of the people by the

---

to stand "from the prayer over the gifts to the end of the Mass, except at . . . the consecration," when they should kneel. Bells may also be rung—a holdover from the Mass of Pius V. Again, the economy of the prayer is disrupted, effectively signaling that all the other words of the Eucharistic Prayer are supplementary. As some of *The Awakening Church* commentators noted, the prayer is, in fact, largely lost on the people. Despite the theological quality of the historical scholarship that informs the overall shape of the "renewed" eucharistic rite, its transformative intent for the *ekklesia*, the assembled church, is widely lost to practices whose origins lie elsewhere. In a word, Schmemann's theory is right.

For an insightful and pastorally sensitive discussion of the relation between liturgical posture and prayer see John F. Baldovin, "Introduction: An Embodied Eucharistic Prayer," *The Postures of the Assembly During the Eucharistic Prayer*, John K. Leonard and Nathan D. Mitchell (Chicago: Liturgy Training Publications, 1994) 1–13. For Schmemann's discussion of the Orthodox churches' failure to understand and enact the unity of the Eucharistic Prayer, which he condemns as "a deep decadence," see *The Eucharist*, 172–4.

[81] Schmemann, *For the Life of the World*, 130, 121.

Holy Spirit, their transformation into 'sons [and daughters] of God'—herein lies the newness of the content and significance of this cult."[82]

The fundamentally eschatological character of the Christian faith requires a cultic dimension to its practice; nevertheless, it prohibits Christianity from being a cultic religion. Here again, Schmemann's concerted attention to eschatology makes antinomy essential to his theology. As the height of Christian cultic ritual, the Eucharist is "the actualization of the identification of the Church with the Body of Christ and of the fact that she belong[s] to the Aeon of the Kingdom."[83] The Church realizes itself as the body of Christ through the symbolic words, objects, actions and, moreover, through the overall shape or structure of the eucharistic liturgy. This shape, however, is based on the eschatological principle that the liturgy is the one way that the Church, situated as it is in the old world, can experientially know, can envision, the new world to which God has ordered all things in Christ.

This eschatological dimension of the sacraments, long lost in the churches of both East and West, qualifies the way Christians should understand and, thus, perform their ritual symbols. What Christians are invited to know liturgically on the Lord's Day is that they are alive in Christ, that their lives are joined to (participate in) the entire economy of his life, death, resurrection, and sending of the Spirit. Attendance at the liturgy is not a matter of viewing representations of past or future events, nor of intellectually assenting to a metaphysical theory of causality that opposes symbol and reality, nor of adoring and receiving a sacred object.

"The essential character (I could say the particularity) of this eschatological symbolism, is not simply its realism in the sense of the presence in the sign of the reality which it signifies, for the same realism, as we have seen, is affirmed also by Saint Maximus and the other representatives of the symbolism we termed 'mysteriological.' The essential particularity of the eschatological symbolism is the fact that in it the very distinction between the sign and the signified is simply ignored. . . . The whole point of the eschatological symbolism is that in

---

[82] Schmemann, *Introduction to Liturgical Theology*, 102–3. See also Schmemann, *The Eucharist*, 219–20.

[83] Schmemann, *Introduction to Liturgical Theology*, 103.

it the sign and that which it signifies are one and the same thing. The liturgy, we may say, happens to *us*."[84]

The members of the worshiping community leave the regular order of life and the world and enter into the symbolic order of the liturgy, wherein they realize their life in Christ. They do not symbolize the presence of angels (Holy, holy, holy, Lord . . .), they join them in their unending divine worship. They do not merely represent the Last Supper (worse yet, Christ's death), they enter into the reality of the heavenly banquet of the kingdom of God. The heavenly banquet, however, is inseparable from the earthly events of Christ's life, all of which together comprise the reality of salvation. This is possible because "what eschatology does is to hold together things which otherwise are broken up and treated as separate events occurring at different points in a time sequence."[85] The liturgy functions eschatologically.

The Western reader, especially one influenced by Metz, might become wary in the turn my rehearsal of Schmemann's eschatology has taken at this point. Clearly Schmemann is making an ontological claim about what occurs in the Church's sacramental ritual. By claiming a transcendent reality he seems to contradict his earlier insistence that Christianity, when true to its messianic and apocalyptic origins, takes time with utmost seriousness. Schmemann, however, is not proposing an idealistic, "platonic," timeless realm for Christian faith. Such an "eternal" sphere would render believers utterly passive or indifferent toward creation and history. Schmemann is arguing that the liturgical action

"is an entry not into some abstract and motionless 'eternity' but into 'life everlasting,' in which all is *alive*, everything lives through the life-creating memory of God, and *everything is ours*—'the world or life or death or the present or the future'—all is ours, for we 'are Christ's; and Christ is God's' (1 Cor 3:22-23)."[86]

The realized eschatology *within the context* of the liturgy is fundamentally the experience of faith. Faith, once again, entails belief in a reality that, however essentially related to the contingencies of human existence,

---

[84] Schmemann, "Symbols and Symbolism in the Byzantine Liturgy," 126–7.
[85] Schmemann, "Liturgy and Eschatology," 96.
[86] Schmemann, *The Eucharist*, 129.

nonetheless exceeds their limits. Faith's origin is indeed in the past events of Jesus, but this Jesus is nonetheless by faith known now to be alive: "our faith and our life in essence consist in this memory and in this remembrance [of Jesus' life, death, and resurrection]."[87] Participation in the liturgy is a communion, an encounter (to use the language promoted by Schillebeeckx), with the living Christ, which empowers and encourages Christians in the midst of a world that is dying.

Our study thus arrives at a new theoretical meeting point for Metz and Schmemann: the equation of faith's essence with memory. In Chapter 2 we found that Metz regularly identifies the dangerous, transformative, anticipatory memory of Jesus with the phrase *memoria passionis, mortis et resurrectionis Jesu Christi*—a phrase whose liturgical origins he touches upon but does not explore. Schmemann teaches that "the whole liturgy is a *remembrance* of Christ," and that this liturgical *"commemoration"* gives to its participants, by means of words and symbols, the experience that enables them to accept and confess, *to know,* that God, through the same Spirit that formed and raised Jesus, is "transfiguring the old time into the new time."[88] Schmemann, fully aware that the liturgical term "anamnesis" has spawned numerous, divergent theological interpretations, wisely asserts that a profitable grasp of the notion requires its situation in the entire experience of the Church.[89] A thorough exploration of precisely that weighty but promising requirement will be the agenda of our next chapter. For the moment two of Schmemann's main points are important.

First, the eucharistic liturgy is the Church's *commemorative* practice that draws creation and history into a present experience that both remembers God's definitive salvific acts, especially Jesus' life, suffering, death, and resurrection, and anticipates the final deliverance of this fallen (still suffering) world at the parousia. The eschatological experience in the liturgy draws together disparate moments in history, even those that we, confined to the limits of this old world's time, yet await. That is Schmemann's point, a point at once ontological and soteriological: For God alone the disparate moments of the history of salvation are one: "What is accomplished in heaven is already accom-

---

[87] Ibid.

[88] Ibid., 199, 219.

[89] Once again Schmemann demonstrates his fundamental tenet concerning the authority of the Church's *lex orandi.*

plished, already *is*, already *has been accomplished*, already *given*."[90]
That, however, means that Christians, tossed about by the vicissitudes
of history in a fallen world, can and do indeed know that they belong
to the God of Jesus. This knowledge is, nonetheless, an act of faith.
God is far greater than what humans can know, as well as often silent
in the face of human suffering. More directly to Schmemann's point:
In the eucharistic liturgy Christians only have a partial, anticipatory
knowledge of the new heavens and the new earth, of life on high in
Christ Jesus. That anticipatory quality makes the knowledge no less
real in the Christian's life. Indeed, the anamnetic ascension to the eucharistic table is the most real of experiences amidst this world, a joyous gratitude that transforms believers for the life of the world. This
leads to a second, more expansive point.

THE TRANSFORMATIVE VISION OF JOY

A persistent theme throughout the corpus of Schmemann's work is
the identification of joy as the fundamental characteristic of Christian
liturgical experience.

"The *joy* of the Kingdom: it always worries me that, in the multi-volume
systems of dogmatic theology that we have inherited, almost every
term is explained and discussed except the one word with which the
Christian Gospel opens and closes. 'For behold, I bring you tidings of
great joy' (Lk 2:10)—so the gospel begins, with the message of the angels. 'And they worshipped him and returned to Jerusalem with great
joy' (Lk 24:52)—so the Gospel ends."[91]

Evangelical joy is not an "idea" subject to theological definition;
rather, it instills in believers a "different perspective" on the world
and its needs—the truth and righteousness of the kingdom of God.[92]

[90] Schmemann, *The Eucharist,* 221.

[91] Schmemann, "Liturgy and Eschatology," 99. While Schmemann is certainly free to do so, it must nevertheless be noted that, in developing his argument about joy, he chooses to identify the "Christian Gospel" here exclusively
with the Gospel of Luke. One might turn to what Scripture scholars widely
agree was the original ending of the Gospel of Mark—"and [the women] said
nothing to anyone, for they were afraid" (16:8)—to pursue a different trajec-
tory for theology.

[92] Don Saliers brings greater theoretical clarity to Schmemann's terminology of "experience" and "perspective" by (re)introducing the concept of "the

Only if "this experience of the joy of the Kingdom in all its fullness is again placed at the center of theology" can the Church perceive (1) the world's cosmic dimensions, (2) the "historic reality" of the eschatological "fight between the Kingdom of God and the kingdom of the prince of this world," and (3) the "plentitude" of the redemption, "the victory and the presence of God," given in Christ.[93] Once again, the experience of the liturgy is the *lex orandi,* the precondition for doing theology: "The remembrance, the *anamnesis* of the Kingdom is the source of everything else in the Church."[94] At this point, however, Schmemann zeroes in on the central feature of liturgical theology's vision, namely, joy, and argues that it is this joyous vision that theology brings to bear on the world.

The comparison and contrast with Metz's political theology could not be more compelling. The structures of their arguments for what theology, the Church, and contemporary society demand at this moment in history are remarkably alike. The experience of faith, which has a particular message and a practical content, must be recovered as the singular source for a theology that can serve a Church that has placed itself in service to the world. Christianity is not fundamentally about ideas but, rather, a way of life—messianic virtues (Metz) practiced in light of a vision that is known (Schmemann). Theology must support that mission. At the same time, the contrast between each writer's focal point or "center" (Schmemann) for theology is utterly stunning. Metz argues from the memory of suffering, Schmemann from the remembrance of joy. As we saw in Chapter 2, however, what Metz intends by his insistence on the centrality of the *memoria passionis* requires its situation in discipleship as followers of Christ. The messianic virtues include (among others) prayerfulness, gratitude,

---

religious affections." Circumventing "some of the problems connected with the term 'emotion,'" the concept of "the affections" enables Saliers "to denote a comprehensive phenomenon of life by which we understand the world in and through a 'sense' of the world. Affections thus always combine evaluative knowledge of the world and self awareness." Saliers argues further that there is "a pattern of particular affections which constitutes and governs the life of the Christian," and proceeds to explore that thesis in his work. Don E. Saliers, *The Soul in Paraphrase: Prayer and the Religious Affections,* 2d ed. (Cleveland: OSL Publications, 1991) 6.

[93] Schmemann, "Liturgy and Eschatology," 99.

[94] Ibid., 100.

and joy (all markedly counter to the culture of evolutionary reason). Schmemann is starting from the other pole of Metz's Christian dialectic. His is fundamentally a *theologia gloriae* (to employ terminology from an old theological debate). The question is whether he takes into adequate account the *theologia crucis*.

One of Schmemann's most thorough passages on joy (one especially helpful with Metz in mind) occurs within his discussion of the specifically Christian notion of the feast. As the reader may recall, early in this chapter I found Schmemann's critical evaluation of the feast within technological, market-driven society to be a point of gratifying comparison with Metz. Both authors perceive modern, middle-class Christians as having reduced the feasts of the liturgical year to mere cultural decorations. Bourgeois Christianity thereby deprives both itself and society of a communal form of experience that is not only humanly essential but drastically needed at this time. More so than Metz, however, Schmemann pursues what modern Christians and society are thereby missing:

"Feast means *joy*. Yet, if there is something that we—the serious, adult and frustrated Christians of the twentieth century—look at with suspicion, it is certainly joy. How can one be joyful when so many people suffer? When so many things need to be done? How can one indulge in festivals and celebrations when people expect from us 'serious' answers to their problems? Consciously or subconsciously Christians have accepted the whole ethos of our joyless and business-minded culture."[95]

Modernity's reduction of public life (and thus, people!) to what can be economically transacted and technically manipulated has caused the loss, in Schmemann's estimation, of an essential, "natural" cultural practice. More than a mere break from time's relentlessness and work's heaviness, the feast instills meaning in life's cycles and hard work. By its cosmic, incarnational faith, Christianity accepted this human need for the feast, but also transformed it.

Christianity transformed the socially essential practice of the feast, along with all that is "natural" to humanity, through its faith in Christ's death and resurrection:

---

[95] Schmemann, *For the Life of the World*, 53.

"Christianity was on the one hand the end of all natural joy. It revealed its impossibility, its futility, its sadness—because by revealing
the perfect man [*sic*] it revealed the abyss of man's [*sic*] alienation
from God and the inexhaustible sadness of this alienation. The cross
of Christ signified an end of all 'natural' rejoicing; it made it, indeed,
impossible. From this point of view the sad 'seriousness' of modern
man [*sic*] is certainly of Christian origin, even if this has been forgotten by that man himself [*sic*]. Since the Gospel was preached in this
world, all attempts to go back to a pure 'pagan joy,' all 'renaissances,'
all 'healthy optimisms' were bound to fail. . . . Because it relegated
the perfection of joy to the inaccessible future—as the goal and end of
all work—it made all human life an 'effort,' a 'work.'"[96]

Schmemann masterfully turns phrases here that at once add theological depth to political theology and point toward further reflection
within liturgical theology. As noted more than once in Chapter 2,
Metz has a tendency in his theology only to name or refer to Christian
dogmas, assuming rather than exploring their content. The *memoria
passionis, mortis et resurrectionis Jesu Christi* tends to be a symbol in
Metz's work. For all his advocacy of narrative for theology, Metz
rarely engages the narratives of Jesus' passion and death (let alone the
resurrection). Schmemann, far from shying away from the transcendent content of Christian belief, exploits it in this passage, providing a
succinct theological argument for why redemption can never be
equated with emancipation.[97] The argument strongly reflects the no-

[96] Ibid., 54–5.

[97] For the sake of brevity, I risk overstating my case here. Metz, like other
political and liberation theologians, has had to grapple with the distinction
and relation between emancipation and redemption. Indeed, he wrote an
essay under that title, which eventually became one of the chapters in the
scattered "Themes" section of *Faith in History and Society*. I remain critical,
however, of the degree to which Metz, even in that essay, falls short of exploring key doctrinal issues in greater depth. The reason for Metz's shying away
from such theological investigation seems to be his constant desire to provide
a corrective to the abstract quality of modern, transcendental theology. Interestingly, however, when Metz does—briefly—address the content of Christian
soteriology, he does so by quoting the work of Karl Rahner on guilt. Metz's
own contribution is to argue that Christianity "does not offer definitive meaning for the unexpiated sufferings of the past"; rather, it offers narratives of a
"distinct history of freedom." The two narratives Metz names (but does not

tion found extensively in patristic theology that humanity was created for participation in the life of God. Sin is alienation (a modern term) from that life, setting the agenda for both redemption and the ongoing tension in the life of the baptized.[98]

Furthermore, Schmemann's description of Christianity as work implies an essential link between the "effort" of Christian work in the world and the community's work in the liturgical assembly (leitourgia). Schmemann immediately proceeds to make that link explicit:

"Yet, on the other hand Christianity was the revelation and the gift of joy, and thus, the gift of genuine *feast*. Every Saturday night at the resurrection vigil we sing, 'for through the Cross, joy came into the whole world.' This joy is pure joy because it does not depend on anything in this world, and is not the reward of anything in us. It is totally and absolutely a *gift*, the *'charis,'* the grace. And being pure gift, this joy has a transforming power, *the only really transforming power in this world.*"[99]

Thus does Schmemann get at what makes the joy he is describing other-than-natural (supernatural, in Western theology), what makes it pure: the love of God in Jesus manifested on the cross. Schmemann is giving this instruction with his audience in mind, a Christian audience that is heavily influenced by the notions *and* practices of joy and

---

narrate and scarcely interprets) are "the cross of Jesus" and "the descent into hell." The latter, an apparent reference to the Apostles' Creed, is a strange and enticing idea that only fizzles into another Metzian call for an "apocalyptic sting" in Christian soteriology. The thought that Jesus descended into hell is indeed shocking, but so what? If this credal statement strengthens political theology (as I believe it does), then how does it do so? Metz, *Faith in History and Society*, 129. Metz has continued to address the relationship between emancipation and redemption in his later writings. See *A Passion for God*, 3, 36–7, 38–9.

[98] Schmemann engages the language of "tension" in his essay "Symbols and Symbolism in the Byzantine Liturgy," 126. Perhaps the strongest representative patristic text on the human condition as intended for but fallen from divine participation is Athanasius' *On the Incarnation of the Word*. See *Athanasius: Select Works and Letters*, vol. 4 of *The Nicene and Post-Nicene Fathers*, ed. Archibald Robertson (Edinburgh and Grand Rapids, Mich.: T. & T. Clark/Eerdmans, 1891, reprinted 1987) 31–68, esp. 37–45.

[99] Schmemann, *For the Life of the World*, 55.

love found in modern romanticism or increasingly, one might add, in jaded popular culture. Christian faith takes priority over such problematic views of love and joy, as it must, so as to transform people, their views, and their practices.

What Christians know paramountly in the eucharistic liturgy, Schmemann explains, is that love is sacrifice. Yet another concept with a troubled history enters the discussion. Schmemann warns that the fragmented, isolating practices of scholastic theologies have served this crucial Christian concept poorly, giving it a one-sided, juridical connotation that associates it almost exclusively with atonement for sin. Correction comes from the Eucharist, *"the sacrament of offering"*:

"In its essence sacrifice is linked not with sin and evil but with *love:* it is the self-revelation and self-realization of love. There is no love without sacrifice, for love, being the giving of oneself to another, the placing of one's life in another, the perfect obedience to another, is sacrifice. If in 'this world' sacrifice is actually and inevitably linked with suffering, it is not in accordance with its own essence but in accordance with the essence of 'this world,' which lies in evil, whose essence lies in the falling away from love."[100]

Love and sacrifice have their origin in the very life of God, the Trinity. Of that life God has imparted a share (a participation) to humanity. Human sin and evil have forced upon joyous sacrifice the necessity of suffering. Thus, the manifestation of God's love in Jesus, the Son, that is, his sacrificial offering of human life and love to God, entailed suffering from the start and, most acutely, at its climax on the cross. As the theology of the liturgy teaches, however, that climactic moment of crucified suffering cannot and must not be isolated from Jesus' entire life, from his ministry through his glorification. The liturgy teaches (manifests) this in the Eucharistic Prayer's formula of anamnesis. Often in that formula the Church explicitly names a number of the events in Christ's life, even those yet to come, and knows them all as gloriously joyful, for they are the source of life and salvation.

Schmemann insists that all his words about the joy of the kingdom experienced in the eucharistic liturgy, about the Church's actual ascension into heaven, must always be interpreted in this specific way: "These very words about joy and fulness would be truly *irresponsible*

---

[100] Schmemann, *The Eucharist,* 207–8.

words were they not referred—through the Church herself [*sic*], in the eucharist itself—to the *cross*, to the singular path of this ascent, to the means of participation in it."[101] Because the members of the Church are in this world, their ascension to life in God can only be known through the cross, through the inevitable suffering that this world exacts of sacrificial love. The earliest Christians experienced the gift of this freedom and knowledge of the world in *Eucharist*, in the entire liturgy of thanksgiving which gave them communion with God, "paradise," the consoling and "total joy of that little child of the gospels."[102] This is not the joy of knowing *about* the world: "As Kant has demonstrated once and for all, this 'objective,' *external* knowledge is hopelessly closed off from access to 'things in themselves,' . . . and thus to genuine possession of them."[103] The freeing, grateful knowledge of Christians, rather, is that they belong to Christ, which gives them true knowledge *of* the world and themselves: "'. . . the cross of our Lord Jesus Christ, by which the world has been crucified to me, and I to the world' (Gal 6:14). Need we point out that in these words the apostle Paul expresses the entire essence of the Christian life as a following after Christ?"[104] As followers of Christ, Christians cannot but expect suffering in the world. The Eucharist, being a remembrance of the kingdom inseparable from remembrance of the cross, transforms that suffering into joy.

Following after Christ: By means of a radically different theology Schmemann arrives at virtually the same phrase as Metz to summarize the life of faith. Schmemann has provided insight into the "mysticism" toward which Metz points in his practical christology of imitation. Schmemann's liturgical theology provides much understanding into

---

[101] Ibid., 209.

[102] Ibid., 175, 176. Whereas he refers to the faith and liturgical practice of the earliest believers, Schmemann does not quote any sources. The obvious one in reference to his argument about the joint experience of knowledge, freedom, and thanksgiving (see 175) is the tenth chapter of the *Didache:* "We give thanks to you, holy Father, for your holy Name which you have enshrined in our hearts, and for the knowledge and faith and immortality which you made known to us through your child Jesus; glory to you for evermore." Translated in R.C.D. Jasper and G. J. Cumming, *Prayers of the Eucharist: Early and Reformed*, 3d ed. (Collegeville: The Liturgical Press, 1987) 23.

[103] Ibid., 177.

[104] Ibid., 209.

how it is that the "message" of Christian faith (Metz's term) can be experienced, deeply known, and thus can be the source for following Christ through inevitable adversity.

On the question of describing that adversity, however, the two theologians diverge again. Schmemann interprets Paul's "I am crucified to the world" in an adamantly individualistic, self-referential manner: "but this sacrifice cannot but be my crucifixion, for 'this world' is not only outside of me but above all in my very self, in the old Adam in me."[105] Metz would not argue with this concern for the condition of the Christian subject; indeed, the assertion of a genuinely Christian subjectivity is integral to his political theology. Crucial to Metz as well, however, is criticism of middle-class Christians' lack of concern for other subjects in their suffering. Such concern is essential to following the kenotic Christ and, therefore, to genuine Christian subjectivity. Schmemann's impressive work on eucharistic joy and thanksgiving could easily lead to such a social (political) call, but he stubbornly resists it. In consequence, Schmemann's repeated rhetoric about the Church's (corporate, non-individualistic) salvific mission in the world is evacuated of any substantial content. An exploration of that significant problem in Schmemann's theology, along with a proposed corrective (with Metz's help), constitute the final section of this chapter.

CHRISTIAN MISSION IN THE WORLD: BUT WHAT MISSION?

Throughout his writings Schmemann's zeal for the Church's mission in the world takes the form of a passionate expectation of triumph known only in sacrificial service.

"'This world' will pass away, the Lord will reign in glory. The Church is expecting this fulfilment of time, is directed toward this ultimate victory. But this expectation is not a passive state, it is a responsible service—it is to 'be as He was in this world.' This is the time of the Church."[106]

Schmemann is well aware that this sense of an essentially kenotic mission of service has not been widely evident in the Church. Clergy

[105] Ibid., 210.
[106] Schmemann, *Introduction to Liturgical Theology*, 74.

and laity persist in understanding the joy which Christ brought by the cross as their "personal and private" possession, experienced within liturgical walls. Schmemann responds:

"Once again, were Christianity pure 'mysticism,' pure 'eschatology,' there would be no need for feasts and celebrations. A holy soul would keep its secret feast apart from the world, to the extent that it could free itself from its time. . . . The Church [however] is *in time* and its life in this world is *fasting,* that is, a life of effort, sacrifice, self-denial and dying. The Church's very mission is to become all things to all men [*sic*]."[107]

Schmemann uses the liturgical experience of feast and fast to open his contemporaries' minds and hearts to a broader theological vision. If Christians wish to be lavished by God in the feast of their liturgies they must follow Christ's life of service; they must fast in the world. The crucial point is that both desires are necessary. Moreover, the latter, difficult as it necessarily is, is only possible on the basis of the former, the liturgy's faith-engendering experience of joy and peace.

The question remains: What practical shape does this life of sacrifice and self-denial take today? Schmemann's answer: "'It all depends' on thousands of factors—and to be sure, all faculties of our human intelligence and wisdom, organization and planning, are to be constantly used."[108] At first blush Schmemann's reply seems reasonable enough. A text in theology is by nature a theoretical enterprise—so a conventional argument would run. A move to prescribing specific practical actions is beyond its scope. We cannot, however, allow Schmemann to hide behind such convention, not when he has made so explicit his call for theology to forswear its isolation of theory from practice. Schmemann might argue that his definition of practice is the *leitourgia* of the Church, that the specifics of the liturgy are the practice to which he attends. We cannot allow that either, for Schmemann has made the critique of modernity far too integral to his theological project. Over against his detailed criticisms of Orthodox piety and modern culture Schmemann offers a vague, abstract mission for Christians. They are to "witness," "manifest," "proclaim," and/or "preach" the faith in the

---

[107] Schmemann, *For the Life of the World,* 55, 59.
[108] Ibid., 113.

world, and thus "transform" it.[109] But what does that mean concretely and practically, especially at this time in history?

Let us return to Schmemann's scathing invective against politically-oriented theologies, quoted at the beginning of this chapter.[110] There, in the preface to his last book, Schmemann accuses the whole range of contemporary theologies of liberation of abandoning the "Christian vision of the world at the service of God," and casts aspersions on the characters of the "professional 'religious'" engaged in this work. Schmemann's early death from cancer made that preface one of his very last written contributions to theology. Unfortunately, Schmemann thereby did himself, liturgical theology, and the Church the tragic disservice of making that uncharitable statement a partial epitaph on the monument of his theological career. Schmemann meant those words. They betray a serious flaw in his theology. Nevertheless, the solid contributions Schmemann made to liturgical theology must not be allowed to languish in the misguided isolation to which his last words condemned them.

Years earlier Schmemann argued against giving priority to social justice in the Church's theological and pastoral work. He wrote, however, more respectfully of others and more carefully in relation to his own theological vision of the liturgy:

"Christianity begins to fall down as soon as the idea of our going up in Christ's ascension—the movement of sacrifice—begins to be replaced by His going down. And this is exactly where we are today; it is always a bringing Him down into ordinary life, and this we say will solve our social problems. The Church must go down to the ghettos, into the world in all its reality. But to save the world from social injustices, the need first of all is not so much to go down to its miseries, as to have a few witnesses in this world to the possible ascension."[111]

[109] Schmemann, *For the Life of the World*, 113, 149; Schmemann, *The Eucharist*, 90, 92, 93, 137; Schmemann, "Liturgy and Eschatology," 94, 98; Schmemann, "Symbols and Symbolism in the Byzantine Liturgy," 126; and Schmemann, "The Liturgical Revival and the Orthodox Church," *Liturgy and Tradition: Theological Reflections of Alexander Schmemann*, ed. Thomas Fisch (Crestwood, N.Y.: St. Vladimir's Seminary Press, 1990) 110, 111, 114. Schmemann's term of preference, statistically, is "witness."

[110] See above, pp. 76–77.

[111] Alexander Schmemann, "Sacrifice and Worship," *Liturgy and Tradition: Theological Reflections of Alexander Schmemann*, ed. Thomas Fisch (Crestwood, N.Y.: St. Vladimir's Seminary Press, 1990) 135.

If one gets past the polemical character of this statement, one can recognize, once again, that Schmemann is mounting an argument for the necessity of mysticism in the praxis of Christianity (to use Metz's terminology). A generous interpretation of Schmemann's statement finds allowance for an ecclesial mission of social justice. He is, however, insisting that the experience of faith known in the liturgy is the irreducible source for any such mission. The polemical quality of the statement, nonetheless, so opposes liturgical ascension to the descent (might we say, *kenosis?*) into political action and social advocacy that the subtlety of Schmemann's theology of the eucharistic liturgy is lost. Taken independently of the totality of his writings, the statement quoted could easily give the impression that Schmemann's notion of liturgical ascension, far from taking up the brokenness of the world, spurns the world in a manner akin to the Gnostic movements of old. A brief exploration of both the historical-contextual and the theological reasons for Schmemann's severe criticism (and ultimate condemnation) of the political dimension of Christian theology and practice can lead to the possibility of a more constructive appropriation of his theology.

That Schmemann, a pastor and scholar so deeply committed to the liturgy, found himself in a polemical environment on several fronts is beyond doubt. In the most immediate circle of his Orthodox Church, Schmemann was fighting a pervasive piety that claimed the title "traditional," as well as a form of seminary education that he found irreconcilable to the Church's *lex orandi*. As dean of St. Vladimir's Seminary for two decades, Schmemann made significant progress in that fight.[112] In the wider circle of the theological academy Schmemann observed movements afoot that directly assaulted liturgical life. In one essay Schmemann describes "a highly respectable seminary in the state of New York, which in the glorious 60s unanimously voted, faculty and students, to close the chapel and to repent for the useless time spent in prayer or contemplation when the world had to be helped."[113] Elsewhere Schmemann reports how a "well-known seminary" exerted much effort in developing "themes" for liturgy that focused on current "relevant" issues: the S.S.T., flooding in Pakistan, and the ecology.[114] Schmemann's criticism: This approach implies that

---

[112] See Meyendorff, "A Life Worth Living," 151.
[113] Schmemann, "Liturgy and Eschatology," 94.
[114] Schmemann, *For the Life of the World*, 125–6.

the Church's liturgical tradition has no revelation to offer these circumstances. Moreover, it reduces liturgical symbolism to new, arbitrarily illustrative roles, thereby squandering the genuine strength of the *lex orandi* for the Church and, thus, the world. Schmemann's points certainly deserve careful attention.[115]

Given the time and place (the context) of his writing, Schmemann's words on the liturgy's relation to liberation are most generously interpreted as correctives in what he experienced as extreme situations. In the ecumenical circles of liturgical theology perhaps the most extreme, threatening, and, to some degree, heart-breaking situation Schmemann observed was the "chaos" that the Second Vatican Council's mandate for liturgical reform immediately unleashed.

"On the problem of liturgical reform I can say this: it seems to me that the 'anarchy' mentioned by Dom [Bernard] Botte and which permeates, to a degree, the liturgical scene in the West, is due primarily and precisely to a deep discrepancy between the 'norms' as recovered by the Liturgical Movement and a new 'liturgical piety' which claims the authority of Vatican II, yet is in many ways directly opposed to its liturgical directives. Whereas the Liturgical Movement, in its best representatives at least, was oriented towards a recovery of traditional elements of Christian *leitourgia*, elements which were obscured and even abolished for centuries, the 'liturgical piety' which is behind modern 'experimentations' and 'anarchy' is inspired by an altogether different and indeed deeply *anti-traditional* set of aspirations. This obvious discrepancy between the 'letter' of Vatican II and what is everywhere proclaimed to be its 'spirit' and, thus, the justification for virtually every innovation, is a perplexing mystery for all watchers of the present Roman Catholic scene."[116]

[115] Aidan Kavanagh has pursued further those sorts of insights in Schmemann's work, as well as his methodological principles, in light of historic sources of the Roman tradition and sharp observation of the current North American context. See Aidan Kavanagh, "Reflections on the Study from the Viewpoint of Liturgical History," *The Awakening Church: 25 Years of Liturgical Renewal*, ed. Lawrence Madden (Collegeville: The Liturgical Press, 1992) 83–97; see also Aidan Kavanagh, *On Liturgical Theology* (New York: Pueblo, 1984).

[116] In a 1968 issue of the *St. Vladimir's Seminary Quarterly* Schmemann wrote these words in response to an essay by Bernard Botte, in which the Benedictine

Years of observation and theological reflection later enabled Schmemann to provide the following insight into the troublesome fate of the Roman liturgical reform: In the difficult effort to implement the council's mandate for an integration of the Church in the modern world, "the liturgy itself became a privileged place to carry out the struggle."[117] Given the notion of secularization regnant at that time, the result was inevitably chaotic and, predictably, gave rise to a conservative backlash equally uninformed by the scholarship of the Liturgical Movement. *The Awakening Church* project provides ample evidence for the extent to which the shape of parish liturgies has been informed not by the tradition but by modern criteria. The present writer can report at the end of the 1990s a widening of the conservative backlash Schmemann recognized more than a decade before. This backlash, which enjoys increasing official support, seriously deters the potential contribution that liturgical reform could make to the Church's mission in late modern society.

Recollection of *The Awakening Church* project prompts a further observation. The influences of modernity observed in the parish reports were only a selective representation of the secularist "principles" that Schmemann rehearsed in the late 1960s: "the famous 'relevance,' or 'urgent needs of modern society,' 'the celebration of life,' or 'social justice.'"[118] Some theological analysts of the project, notably Monika Hellwig and Peter Henriot, found an acute lack of connection between liturgy and social concerns on the part of not only the people observed and interviewed but also the fieldworkers and theologians themselves. Those crucial observations lend themselves not so much to Schmemann's (1960s) concern with secularism but, rather, to Metz's theory of the bourgeois, technocratic, "evolutionary" world view of late modernity. Schmemann's own social-political conservatism (in the 1970s he leveled criticism against the "whole idea of the welfare state")[119] seems to have impeded his critical awareness of the

---

liturgical theologian took issue with aspects of Schmemann's work. Alexander Schmemann, "A Brief Response," *Liturgy and Tradition: Theological Reflections of Alexander Schmemann,* ed. Thomas Fisch (Crestwood, N.Y.: St. Vladimir's Seminary Press, 1990) 28.

[117] Schmemann, "Liturgical Reform: Remarks on Method," 139.

[118] Schmemann, "Liturgical Theology," 46.

[119] Schmemann, "Sacrifice and Worship," 134.

causes that Metz identified for the inability of northern Christians to connect the work of the liturgy to their work in the world.

Schmemann did not completely avoid politics in his work as a liturgical theologian, however. In the light of the often painful history of the Orthodox churches in the twentieth century, Schmemann confronted theologically and pastorally a serious threat to the viability of Orthodoxy: ethnic nationalism. From his early years in France, Schmemann was troubled by the lack of cooperation and unity among the various ethnic Orthodox churches. He perceived how such divisions hindered Orthodoxy's viability and impact in Western societies. As dean and professor at St. Vladimir's, Schmemann saw to it that the seminarians were "taught the spirit of a universal and missionary Orthodox Church, transcending purely ethnic concerns."[120] That practical work in the classroom and chapel found its way into his theological writing.

In his text on eucharistic theology Schmemann raises the issue of nationalism in a chapter entitled "The Sacrament of Unity." His manner of doing this demonstrates not only (1) Schmemann's recognition of the potential for political conversion through liturgical practice, but also (2) crucial aspects of his theological method. Schmemann introduces reflection on the (inherently practical) theological implications of the kiss of peace by arguing that believers need "to hear [the rite's acclamation, 'Let us love one another!'] not only with our outer but also our inner ear."[121] Schmemann reports that throughout Orthodox churches the rite has been reduced to the acclamation, with only the clergy in the sanctuary, at best, exchanging the embrace. Schmemann believes that full implementation of the rite can have a transformative impact upon the people and thus, the life of the Church. Schmemann explains that the inner source of the acclamation is Christ's new commandment of love (John 13:34). His explanation exudes a sense of the Gospel's critical urgency that Metz would undoubtedly applaud.

Schmemann emphasizes the "staggering newness" of Christian love, at once a command and a gift, and thus a revelation.[122] As gospel, the command calls Christians to love their enemies, a disturbing, frightening sort of love that is anything but a mere crowning of what they already do. The latter is the love of one's family and

[120] Meyendorff, "A Life Worth Living," 151.
[121] Schmemann, *The Eucharist,* 133.
[122] Ibid., 136.

friends. In Orthodoxy that "natural love" has taken the now uncritically practiced form of a "religiously colored and justified nationalism [that] long ago became a genuine heresy, crippling church consciousness, hopelessly dividing the Orthodox East and making all our profuse talk about the ecumenical truth of Orthodoxy a hypocritical lie."[123] Schmemann observes that the Orthodox faithful, when at the liturgy, are actually fearful to reach out to those around them for the kiss of peace. They fail to understand that this action is paradigmatic of their work as members of the liturgical assembly. If they would but recover their authentic participation in the liturgy and thus open themselves to the Christ who is in the liturgical action, Christ might transform their minds and hearts, their attitudes and actions toward all people, especially the disconcertingly "other."

Schmemann demonstrates in his "Sacrament of Unity" chapter that his liturgical theology does include the possibility of making direct connections to the political aspect of the life of faith, that faith can be a praxis of mysticism and politics. Schmemann argues from the authority of the love and truth revealed to those who enter into full, conscious, and active participation in the liturgy. At least in that one instance of his writing Schmemann provides a more concrete example of how the ascension in the eucharistic liturgy manifests or reveals a new way of life, radically transformative of what is taken for granted by many in this fallen world. The problem that nonetheless remains is Schmemann's obstinate refusal to consider more carefully the oppressive conditions experienced by other peoples in the world—those, for example, in the southern hemisphere who endure relentless social, economic, and political oppression. Christian love for those peoples requires attention to the systemic conditions of their oppression, as theologians of liberation have shown. The liturgy, in its content and shape, is clearly not capable of being the sole authoritative source for Christians' ongoing conversion—in this case, Father Alexander's. Metz's argument for the authority of people's suffering enters the conversation, warning that modern theologies have a tendency to become abstract. Attention to the narratives of suffering expels abstraction and compels a shift (conversion) in northern Christians' perspectives.

To the Metzian critique, Schmemann might reply that he has had a consistent concern to banish abstraction. Consider a passage from the

[123] Ibid., 135.

chapter on baptism in his earliest book, wherein Schmemann describes the definite reality of evil in the modern world:

"In our world in which normal and civilized men 'used electricity' to exterminate six million human beings, in this world in which right now some ten million people are in concentration camps because they failed to understand the 'only way to universal happiness,' in this world the 'demonic' reality is not a myth . . . it is this reality that the Church has in mind, that it indeed faces when at the moment of baptism, through the hands of the priest, it lays hold upon a new human being who has just entered life, and who, according to statistics, has a great likelihood some day of entering a mental institution, a penitentiary, or at best, the maddening boredom of a universal suburbia."[124]

Here narrative does appear; history does break into Schmemann's theology; the authority of suffering has a word. Schmemann introduces his political observations as a commentary on specific elements of the baptismal rite. The liturgy reveals that the nascent Christian's response to such an evil, fallen world entails a renunciation of Satan, a pledge of unity (conversion) to Christ, and worship of the Trinity:

"And again it is difficult to convince a modern Christian that to be the life of the world, the Church must not 'keep smiling' at the world, putting the 'All Welcome' signs on the churches, and adjusting its language to that of the last best seller. The beginning of the Christian life—of the life in the Church—is humility, obedience, and discipline. The last preparation for baptism, therefore, is this order:

"'Bow down before Him.' And the Catechumen answers, 'I bow down before the Father, and the Son, and the Holy Spirit.'"[125]

Schmemann is clearly insisting that Christian conversion requires critical social and cultural awareness, but always through the truth revealed in the practice of the liturgy. Schmemann's critical reflection in the context of baptism is a notable reminder that the Church's *leitourgia* includes a broader range of sacramental rites, that the Eucharist does not bear *all* the weight of the liturgy. The Eucharist, nevertheless, does complete Christian initiation by admitting the individual to

[124] Schmemann, *For the Life of the World*, 70.
[125] Ibid., 71–2.

communion with fellow believers, the *ekklesia* at the Lord's table. Schmemann, of course, knows that. Our concern, however, is with how the communal experience in the eucharistic liturgy, the "realized anticipation" of the kingdom, can indeed convert its participants not just to (individual) self-responsibility but to forms of praxis in (social-political) solidarity with others.

In his commentary on baptism Schmemann offers a devastating depiction of modernity. The fates of individual subjects are inherently subject to societal conditions, to historical forces sweeping up entire masses of people without regard for their human subjectivity. Such critical social awareness would seem to imply an ecclesial mission in the world that confronts systemic, political, social realities. Schmemann, however, consistently presents the Church's mission in terms of individual effort and inclination. The closing lines of his text on the Eucharist are as follows: "We depart into life, in order to witness and to fulfil our calling. Each has his own, but it is also our common ministry, common liturgy—'in the communion of the Holy Spirit.' 'Lord, it is good to be here!'"[126] It seems that for Schmemann the communal or corporate identity of the Church is only manifested in the liturgy, wherein the actions of the assembly realize an experience of the Church as the kingdom of God. Once renewed and reinvigorated by the liturgy, the Church's members scatter into individual lives of ethical agency united only on the transcendent plane of "communion in the Holy Spirit." As Metz has argued, however, theology needs to take history more seriously through attention to the narratives of people's suffering and development of an ecclesiology for a truly *world church.*[127] Schmemann, on the other hand, for all his demands that the liturgy be purged of individual piety, lacks a sufficient ecclesiology. To what end are all his calls for communal participation in the liturgy if such experience does not manifest *and thereby inspire* forms of communal praxis of solidarity in the world?

Schmemann's commentary on baptism contains one more historical-contextual clue to his individualistic approach to the Christian life of "responsible service" in the world. His description of the millions

---

[126] Schmemann, *The Eucharist*, 245.

[127] See Johann Baptist Metz, *The Emergent Church: The Future of Christianity in a Post-Bourgeois World,* trans. Peter Mann (New York: Crossroad, 1987) esp. 48–81.

who languished in labor camps for failing to understand the "only way to universal happiness" is obviously in reference to the oppressive, totalitarian form that Marxism took in the Soviet Empire. The universalism touted by the communists belied the cruel reality of a social-political system that deadened the initiative and agency—the free spirit—of individuals, and banished to camps, asylums, and prisons those who actively resisted the obliteration of their human will. It seems that Schmemann's reaction to this historical reality (which visited no small measure of suffering on members of the Orthodox churches) contributed to his almost exclusive emphasis on individual responsibility and action and, moreover, to his dark suspicion of systemic approaches to the problems of human suffering, such as "the welfare state" and "any number of theologies of liberation."

Metz was neither unaware nor uncritical of the personal devastation inflicted by communism. At the outset of his construction of a fundamental theology, Metz analyzes the tenuous situation of the European subject in the late 1970s. An evolutionary, technically rational world view predominates in the West (rehearsed in Chapter 2), while a "historical and materialist dialectical system . . . is manifested . . . in the socialist societies of the East."[128] The latter has proven to hold an evolutionary logic of its own, a teleology of freedom based on material nature, that erases the human subject. Metz condemns this as "an evolutionary disintegration of the dialectics of liberation."[129]

Metz's careful theoretical work demonstrates invaluable knowledge and insight into the conditions of late modernity from which Schmemann needed to learn a great deal. Schmemann needed to do so precisely so as not to identify dialectical materialism with the dialectics of liberation. The latter is integral to a Christianity committed not merely to "preaching" or "witnessing" to the subjectivity of all persons but, rather, to a praxis that makes the free exercise of subjectivity possible for oppressed peoples. Such is the missionary vision and action of a world church. The next two chapters shall explore how the anamnetic aspect of the eucharistic liturgy, as well as other elements of the Christian tradition, are capable of forming the *ekklesia* in the memory of, concern for, and solidarity with others in their suffering.

We must, finally, address an integral aspect of Schmemann's theological method that, in part, hinders his theology of liturgy (and time)

---

[128] Metz, *Faith in History and Society*, 5.
[129] Ibid., 12, n. 7. See also Metz, *A Passion for God*, 34–9.

from realizing the prophetic impact on the Church which he so passionately desired for it. Recall that in his commentary on the kiss of peace Schmemann proceeds by inviting the reader to hear the invitation to the rite not only with one's "outer" but also one's "inner ear." This procedure points toward the key to how Schmemann conceptualizes the transformative power of Christian sacramental liturgy: it renews time and the world from within.[130] A certain metaphysics is operative in Schmemann's theology, as has been the case since the first efforts to enlist Greek philosophy for help in proclaiming the sacramental mystery of the incarnation. Schmemann argues:

"It would be wrong to ascribe such a theological interpretation in its full form to Judeo-Christianity and the early Church. But there can be no doubt that even at that time, and perhaps more strongly and clearly then than at any time after, all the elements of this future theological development were alive in the faith and experience of the Church."[131]

As we have seen, Schmemann argues that for the early Church the kingdom of God, experienced on the eighth day, is fulfilled. It is "eternal and actual" precisely because it is of God, that is, it exists "in God."[132] In the time of this world, however, the kingdom "is something in the future" that, nonetheless, is in time, is "within" the Church and, thus, is transforming the world from within. In the course of that argument Schmemann cites the scriptural teaching that believers' lives are "hid with Christ in God."

Elsewhere, Schmemann strikes a similar note:

"The kingdom of Christ is accepted by faith and is hidden 'within us.' The King himself came in the form of a servant and reigned only through the cross. There are no external signs of this kingdom on earth. It is the kingdom of 'the world to come,' and thus only in the glory of his second coming will all people recognize the true king of the world. But for those who have believed in it and accepted it, the

---

[130] See the conclusion to the fourth section of this chapter, "The Liturgy of Time: Time Made 'Eschatologically Transparent,'" p. 99.

[131] Schmemann, *Introduction to Liturgical Theology*, 72.

[132] Ibid., 73. Later in the text Schmemann engages explicitly metaphysical terminology: "The whole meaning of the Feast Day is to give us a vision of the eternal 'this day,' i.e. of the supra-temporal, ideal substance of the enacted 'mystery.'" Ibid., 178.

kingdom is already here and now, more obvious than any of the 'realities' surrounding us. 'The Lord has come, the Lord is coming, the Lord will come again.' This triune meaning of the Aramaic expression *maranatha* contains the whole of Christianity's victorious faith, against which all persecutions have proven impotent."[133]

The statement betrays a significant problem in Schmemann's theology, especially in his concept of eschatological symbolism. That the Christian faith and, therefore, its symbolic expression are paradoxical is certain. The way, however, in which Schmemann opposes the "kingdom of Christ" and its "external signs" in this world causes the paradox or antinomy to be debilitating for the *practice* of faith, both "in the world" and within the liturgy itself. Ironically, Schmemann often argues in his writings that symbol and reality should not be opposed, yet here he states both that there are "no external signs" of the kingdom on earth and, on the other hand, that the kingdom "here and now" is the most obvious of "'realities' surrounding us." Schmemann's error lies in identifying the signs of the kingdom *only* in the liturgy, where they are glorious. But is that the case? Are the signs of the kingdom only evident in the liturgy? No, signs of the kingdom, while only fragmentary now in the time or history of this world, are nonetheless powerfully real for people who see with the eyes of faith. The liturgy must enable Christians to perceive the poor and suffering as the special object of God's favor, as well as kenotic deeds of service as signs of the Christ who "came in the form of a servant and reigned only through the cross." If one overidentifies the signs of the kingdom in the liturgy with the signs of the glorious victory of the Second Coming, then it becomes difficult to expect the participants in the liturgy to be able to perceive the Spirit of the kenotic Christ acting in the world.

My argument with Schmemann here leads me to press him on the very notion of symbolism. It seems to me that Schmemann needs to consider more carefully how symbolism entails action, and what this implies about the relationship between symbol and reality. In the case of the liturgy, words and physical objects are engaged in the gestures and patterns of activity into which the participants are drawn. This activity or *leitourgia*, as Schmemann and all sound liturgical theologians teach, is the action of Christ's Spirit in the Church. The salvific import

---

[133] Schmemann, *The Eucharist*, 41.

of Christ's sacramentality, however, lies not simply in the mere appearance of God's Son in the incarnation, but rather in the deeds of redemption God brought about in the life and death of Jesus. Human decision and action, essential to the kenotic Christ and his kingdom, are what make Jesus the sacrament of all human encounter with God. Jesus is not simply an affirmation of the human inclination to use symbols for such encounter; rather, in the praxis of his kenotic service he is an eschatological transformation of sinful humanity amidst a fallen world. He is the sacrament of genuine humanity because people could see his actions, and through those actions they could perceive the eternal faithfulness of God, the God who "raises up the lowly." Schmemann is right to insist that the vision of the kingdom is most fully revealed in the liturgy; however, I am arguing that there is a more dynamic quality to this vision, as the temporal ambiguity in the ancient cry of *maranatha* implies. In other words, the practice of the liturgy has elements of "hiddenness" as well and, therefore, a certain dialectical quality, if the symbols of both consolation and crisis are given a role therein.

This criticism allows us to return appreciatively to Schmemann's laudable argument for the cosmological and eschatological dimensions of Christian sacramentality. Schmemann successfully argues for the way in which Christian liturgy (in the entire range of the rites) transforms human vision to perceive the sacramentality of the cosmos God has created and is redeeming. Despite his extensive, carefully argued work on the liturgy of time, however, Schmemann does not, in the end, take history—and thus, eschatology—seriously enough. As Metz has pointed out (with his mentor Karl Rahner in mind), modern theology has tended to mean by "history" the fact that (individual) human beings experience life in the conditions of time and space. The notion of history takes on an abstract quality that does not wrestle enough with the untidiness of historicity, of the narratives of actual events in all their (social-political) complexity. In Schmemann's case, one ends up with the ahistoric, abstract assurance that God is gradually transforming all of creation from within.[134] Does that do justice to all the work Schmemann has done on the eucharistic liturgy as the celebration of the Lord's Day, the eternal day that breaks into the regular weekly pattern precisely for the intensification of time?

[134] See Schmemann, *Introduction to Liturgical Theology*, 66, 77–9, 88; and Schmemann, *The Eucharist*, 126, 128.

Despite all the nuances in his theology of eucharistic joy, Schmemann's location of Christian sacramentality so extremely in the Church's majestic liturgy results in an "overworked Christian identity" wherein "all the safety signals are put out."[135] Despite his repeated arguments for the transformative purpose of Christian worship and the mission with which it compels its participants, Schmemann himself in his dismissive comments on theologies of liberation falls prey to making the Church's intercessory prayer a "eulogistic evasion" of the responsibility that a "mature attitude towards prayer presupposes."[136] I believe that a large part of the theological/theoretical problem resides in Schmemann's identification of the liturgy's eschatological impact with the gradual restoration of the individual human's memory and knowledge of God. On this point Schmemann's work is more akin to American approaches to sacramental theology that correlate the transformative activity of the rites with theories of developmental psychology.[137] The contribution those efforts have made to theology is unquestionable; however, their methodology cannot comprise an exclusive theory of Christian sacramental liturgy.

To his credit, as we saw earlier in this chapter, Schmemann both recognizes and condemns the reduction of transformative, sacramental faith to "inner feelings," as is so widely the case in the contempo-

---

[135] Metz, *Faith in History and Society*, 179.

[136] Johann Baptist Metz, "The Courage to Pray," *The Courage to Pray*, Karl Rahner and Johann Baptist Metz, trans. Sarah O'Brien Twohig (New York: Crossroad, 1980) 20.

[137] As Peter Fink has duly noted, the two theologians whose developmental-psychological approaches to the sacraments had the widest impact on a generation of American Catholic readers were Bernard Cooke (*Christian Sacraments and Christian Personality* [New York: Holt, Rinehart and Winston, 1965]) and Joseph Powers (*Spirit and Sacrament: The Humanizing Experience* [New York: Seabury Press, 1973]). See Peter Fink, "Sacramental Theology After Vatican II," *The New Dictionary of Sacramental Worship*, ed. Peter Fink (Collegeville: The Liturgical Press, 1990) 1110. Cooke continued his theory of the sacraments in terms of the symbolism inherent to genuine human personhood in subsequent systematic and historical works. See Bernard Cooke, *Ministry to Word and Sacraments: History and Theology* (Philadelphia: Fortress Press, 1976); Bernard Cooke, *Sacraments and Sacramentality* (Mystic, Conn.: Twenty-Third Publications, 1983); and Bernard Cooke, *The Distancing of God: The Ambiguity of Symbol in History and Theology* (Minneapolis: Fortress Press, 1990).

rary middle-class context. The problem, however, as Metz teaches, is that the metaphysics operative in classical (in this case, sacramental) theology is not only inadequate to the Enlightenment's recognition of history, but also unable to break the stranglehold that the middle-class values of technical reason, exchange value, and privatization have on the promise of the Gospel. Metz warns that if the pervasive influence of those three middle-class concepts is lost sight of, then "the consequence might be that the middle class may imperceptibly be given those theological, religious and ecclesiastical honours which were denied to it in the beginning because a better instinct prevailed and which will now help it at this late stage to justify itself."[138] Unfortunately, Schmemann's theology is a stellar confirmation of Metz's prediction. Schmemann's diatribes against theological and practical concern for social justice and the efforts of liberation theologies are borne out of (1) the ideological shortcomings in his critical analysis of contemporary religious piety and (2) the heavy theoretical reliance on classical metaphysics in his sacramental-liturgical theology.

As stated earlier, however, Schmemann's contributions to liturgical theology (and thus to the theory and practice of Christian faith) are far too valuable to allow them to perish because of his insufficiently critical awareness of the social (economic and political) consequences of the Enlightenment. As a monumental figure in the field of liturgical

---

[138] Metz, *Faith in History and Society,* 44. The English translation of Metz's original text is cumbersome here. Walter Lowe provides clarifying treatment of this crucial element of Metz's critique of the middle-class subject of religion, i.e., of why the middle class is so politically insensitive to the consequences of their "enlightenment" values for the overwhelming numbers of the poor in the world (and, one might add, for the earth itself):

"Savoring the benefits of an economic revolution and fearing that to couple the economic with an authentic political revolution might put those benefits at risk, the bourgeois individual was content to stop halfway [toward enlightenment]. But that meant that, for all their real and apparent power, the bourgeoisie themselves never thought and decided 'without the guidance of another.' They thought and decided, instead, within the predefined parameters of the system of exchange. Allowing this system to define (political) value, the middle class embraced an 'enlightenment' which came to them ready-made."

Lowe, *Theology and Difference,* 7–8.

theology, Schmemann is representative of problems to which the discipline as a whole has been prone. Fortunately, some of the best liturgical theologians have become attentive both to the inadequacy of classical and modern approaches to sacramental theology, as well as to various aspects of the overall dilemma that late modernity poses for Christianity. Precisely those two theoretical and practical areas of concern have caused many of them to give increased attention and authority to the concept of anamnesis.

The next chapter shall explore the concept of anamnesis along the lines of its biblical origins, situating it within the entire practice of the faith, before moving more specifically to its function in the theology and practice of the eucharistic liturgy. This process will unfold the integral relationship between the practices of worship and ethics in the Jewish and Christian traditions. The concluding chapter shall return to the topic of eschatology, so important to both Schmemann and Metz, as it is integrally related to liturgical anamnesis. The ancient Christian cry, *"maranatha,"* with its temporal ambiguity, will come forward for closer consideration in the context of the eucharistic commemoration. My wager is that the fundamentally anamnetic quality of the liturgy can point the way toward a liturgical theology that executes Metz's insightful call for a Christian theology that both in theory and practice is in a constant, genuinely dialectical movement between the "symbols of the [apocalyptic] crisis" and the "symbols of promise and consolation . . . of the kingdom."[139]

---

[139] Johann Baptist Metz, "Communicating a Dangerous Memory," *Communicating a Dangerous Memory,* ed. Fred Lawrence (Atlanta: Scholars Press, 1987) 53.

Chapter 4

Christian Memory: Anamnesis of Christ Jesus

INTRODUCTION

The dialogue constructed in Chapter 3 between the political theology of Johann Baptist Metz and the liturgical theology of Alexander Schmemann compared and contrasted (1) their appraisals of the crisis-situation of Christianity in late modernity, (2) their historical criticisms of ecclesial institutions (including academic theology) and practices (with Schmemann's special focus on liturgy), and (3) their constructive proposals for a renewal of Christianity that would empower the Church in service to the world. In the process of the study, two significant points of convergence in their undeniably different approaches to theology emerged: (1) the singular authority of the specific content of the faith in relation to all efforts at Christian theory (theology) and practice (praxis), and (2) the location of faith's essence in the memory of Christ's death and resurrection. Both authors identify the contemporary challenge for theology in the task of demonstrating how these two elements—faith and memory—are fundamental for realizing a praxis of Christianity that is redemptive (and, Metz would add, emancipatory) in late-modern society. Each author writes out of a passionate desire that his theological reflections serve the Church's practical mission. Chapter 3 demonstrated the similarities in Metz's and Schmemann's concerns for the specific, transformative content of faith.[1] Here we shall briefly consider each theologian's approach to the concept of memory, pressing the limits of each one's method so as to open the discussion to pertinent work that has been done by other theologians, especially those concerned with the history and theology of worship.

MEMORY AT THE CENTER OF THE PRACTICE OF FAITH

In Chapter 2 we found that Metz, in his most comprehensive effort to establish the concept of political theology, analyzed the threatening

---

[1] See the section of Chapter 3 entitled "The Contemporary Christian Crisis," pp. 77–87.

socioeconomic conditions of late modernity in order to argue that the Christian message can realize its salvific import today only if recognized as a "dangerous memory," the *memoria passionis*. Relying extensively on the critical theorists of the Frankfurt School, Metz describes the threat that the instrumental, "evolutionary" reason of technology and the market poses to humanity and ecology at this juncture in history. Remembrance of the victims of these social processes constitutes an interruption of the abstract arguments for progress. Metz then turns to the memory of Jesus, confessed as the Christ of God, the narrative of whose passion, death, and resurrection reveals God's identification with and promise of redemption for all victims of humanity's inhumanity. The pattern of Jesus' life and death, one of service to the oppressed, constitutes the pattern of life that can be salvific for Northern Christians now, a pattern that promises an authentic subjectivity and freedom. Metz thereby recovers the tradition of the *imitatio Christi*. This imitation is at once "dangerous" both in the conversion it requires of its practitioners, away from a privatized view of salvation, and in the threat it poses to the conventional (evolutionary) wisdom of society. This praxis of mysticism and politics is also the means by which believers can know, in an experiential or practical way, the deep joy and hopeful consolation (freedom) of a way of life in the presence of God, the God of Israel and Jesus, the God of the living and the dead.

While the phrase *memoria passionis, mortis et resurrectionis Jesu Christi* emerged as the central category of Metz's fundamental practical theology, his initial "historical and systematic" attempt to explain its essential role in the exercise of "practical critical reason" only minimally connected to the Christian content evoked by the phrase.[2] Gradually, however, Metz came to explicitly identify the phrase's origin in the eucharistic tradition of memorial or remembrance, formulaically summarized in the "anamnesis" section of the Eucharistic Prayer. Having first argued that this ritual enactment constitutes the one way the Church has avoided total neglect of the narrative memory essential to the practice of faith, Metz has advanced the even stronger position that the Jewish origins of this type of "remembrancing" contain further insights into the type of "anamnestic reason" in-

---

[2] Johann Baptist Metz, *Faith in History and Society: Toward a Practical Fundamental Theology*, trans. David Smith (New York: Seabury Press, 1980) 185.

herent to Christian tradition.[3] It is this type of reason, tenaciously committed to the narratives of history and the solidarity with the suffering and dead that these entail, that Christians can bring to the political context and social crises of the day. Metz does not, however, elaborate in detail the history and theology of the Jewish and Christian practices of liturgical remembrance, which could provide fuller elaboration on how this fundamental category of memory practically functions in Christian faith.

For his part, Schmemann approaches the concept of memory specifically in the context of the practice of the liturgy. Schmemann performs his most extensive theological reflection on the meaning and function of memory for Christian faith in his last book, *The Eucharist: Sacrament of the Kingdom*. This he does in a chapter on the first movement of the Orthodox eucharistic rite, the bringing forth of the offering of bread and wine to the sanctuary and table. Reflecting on the first words of the litany which accompanies the action of preparing the gifts ("Remember, O Lord . . ."), wherein the community recalls the many and various persons and concerns they gather up in the offering, Schmemann boldly asserts: "Without any exaggeration one can say that the commemoration, i.e., the referral of everything to the *memory* of God, the prayer that God would 'remember,' constitutes the heartbeat of all of the Church's worship, her entire life."[4] Schmemann quickly adds that by this statement he is not yet referring to the specific aspect of eucharistic memory (the Lord's command that the ritual sharing of bread and cup be done "in remembrance of me, *eis ten emen anamnesin*"); rather, Schmemann is situating the eucharistic action in the "constant remembrance" which is the very "essence" of the entire economy of the Church's liturgical celebrations and, thus, the Church's very existence.

---

[3] Johann Baptist Metz, *A Passion for God: The Mystical-Political Dimension of Christianity*, trans. J. Matthew Ashley (New York: Paulist Press, 1998) 64, 142. See also Johann Baptist Metz, "Facing the Jews: Christian Theology after Auschwitz," *Faith and the Future: Essays on Theology, Solidarity, and Modernity*, Johann Baptist Metz and Jürgen Moltmann (Maryknoll, N.Y.: Orbis Books, 1995) 45, 48; and J. Matthew Ashley, *Interruptions: Mysticism, Politics, and Theology in the Work of Johann Baptist Metz* (Notre Dame, Ind.: University of Notre Dame Press, 1998) 32, 123–4.

[4] Alexander Schmemann, *The Eucharist: Sacrament of the Kingdom*, trans. Paul Kachur (Crestwood, N.Y.: St. Vladimir's Seminary Press, 1988) 123.

The Church, however, both in its theology and piety, has long failed in what Schmemann would consider an adequate recognition of this essential role of memory in the profession and practice of faith. In both East and West the reigning scholastic theology, with its methodological criterion of scientific objectivity, has lacked both the interest and resources for exploring the undeniably ambiguous phenomenon of memory, both human and divine. Theology has thereby once again failed in serving the Church's life and mission, especially as these are manifested in the liturgy. Clergy and laity alike, in their pieties, have been left to an all too predictable, ever-burgeoning "subjectivism" and "'psychologization' of worship," whereby they reduce symbolic liturgical actions to illustrations of "the 'meaning' of [some past] event" and "commemoration in prayer" to "prayer *on behalf of* another human being."[5]

One must pause and ask why such attitudes are so objectionable to Schmemann. These sorts of ritual perceptions would seem to abet the larger religious attitude that egregiously divides life into sacred and profane spheres, thereby leaving activity in each isolated from the other. Moreover, practice in both the liturgical (i.e., sacred) and secular (i.e., profane) arenas of life are synchronically trapped by this mentality, cut off from both the past and the future. Rather than being formative realities, the events of the past and future are objects of nostalgia and speculation. Schmemann argues, in contrast, that *genuine* participation in the liturgy entails the people's entrance into the very memory and life of Christ, a recollection of "both the past and the future as *living* in us, as given to us, as transformed into our *life* and making it life in God."[6]

Schmemann's (liturgical) theology of memory is utterly christological in focus. Christ stands at the juncture of the divine and human capacities for memory. Having noted and dismissed the "thousands of books [which] have been written, from all possible points of view, on *memory*," Schmemann asserts that the topic, in the end, is basically "mysterious" and elusive of all efforts to "understand and explain its meaning and 'mechanism.'"[7] Schmemann's approach proves to be what I would consider a mythological one—accented, interestingly,

[5] Ibid., 123–4.
[6] Ibid., 130.
[7] Ibid., 124.

by tones of twentieth-century existentialism, patristic homiletics, and Chalcedonian dogmatics.

Schmemann proceeds by describing the sad condition in which humanity finds itself with regard to "the most human but therefore also the most ambiguous of all human gifts," namely, "'natural' memory."[8] The human exercise of memory is always an effort to "resurrect" the past, an exercise that entails painful awareness of absence and loss and, finally, death. With a quick bow to "biblical, Old Testamental teaching" (but not one citation of a specific text), Schmemann introduces divine memory to the scenario. God's memory, like all else "in" God, is reality itself; thus, God's activity of remembrance is the source of humanity's creation and sustenance. "Man's [sic] memory," in turn, "is his responding love for God, the encounter and communion with God, with the life of life itself."[9] Sin is nothing other than human forgetfulness or "obliviousness" of God, an ontological state of fallenness from God. Through the incarnation, Christ—"perfect God and perfect man"—saves humanity by bestowing divine remembrance of all the created order and offering, in turn to God, "perfect human remembrance of God," exercised as "love, self-sacrifice and communion with the Father."[10] The very essence of faith, therefore, consists in believers' memory of Christ, a knowledge of Christ that entails remembrance of all aspects of his life, death, resurrection, and glorification. Rather than being mere knowledge *about* Christ, such remembrance is a participation in life everlasting; it is the gift of new life in Christ.

Taken as a whole, Schmemann's reflections on memory amount to an alternate entree into his theological understanding of the practice of Christian liturgy. As we saw in Chapter 3, liturgy is the action of the people whereby they encounter God through symbols, gestures, and words. Each liturgical celebration is an experience of the redeemed order of creation through which God has always intended humanity to know God. In terms of memory, liturgy is the privileged, paradigmatic action wherein God's remembrance of creation and especially humanity, and, in turn, humanity's remembrance of God, takes place. The symbolic nature of this mutual remembrance, this encounter, makes it no less real; rather, it is a manifestation of

---

8 Ibid., 125.
9 Ibid.
10 Ibid., 128.

what the world and human existence are all about. As such, liturgy is eschatological. It is a moment in our present fragmentary experience that reveals the fullness of history that Christ will achieve in the *eschaton*. That final divine-human action, however, is consistent with all that Christ did and revealed in his earthly life. Eschatology is comprised of both memory and anticipation. God's faithful remembrance of humanity in Christ is presently known on the basis of what God has done and will yet accomplish. This remembrance is "narrated" in the liturgical assembly—the Word that is proclaimed, read, sung, and enacted.

Schmemann explicitly labels his understanding of memory as both "biblical" and "ontological."[11] The latter term basically indicates his conviction that memory is "lifecreating," that memory is the means by which God creates and sustains life in humanity. While this sort of reflection is not inconsistent with Metz's recognition of a metaphysical aspect in memory, still, Schmemann's approach cannot avoid the accusation of becoming too abstract. The problem of abstraction persists when one turns to the "biblical" aspect of Schmemann's theology of memory. In a manner quite similar to the way Metz merely names or cites elements of Christian dogma in his arguments, Schmemann merely draws in a global way upon the content of Scripture, rarely quoting a specific passage. The upshot of this twofold (biblical and ontological) abstraction is that Schmemann provides no convincing argument for how the liturgical experience or exercise of memory actually can and should transform the perceptions and actions of Christians in the world. In other words, Schmemann falls short of demonstrating how the action of liturgically commemorating the paschal mystery necessarily or intrinsically holds implications for Christians' ethical agency. Ironically, Schmemann has not made his case strongly enough to rescue the contemporary praxis of faith from the crippling religious dichotomy between the sacred and profane.

The dilemma in which I find Schmemann's theology is, however, an unnecessary one. The solution lies in a more careful and thorough consideration of how memory functions in the scriptural texts at the origin of Christianity. Toward the end of his theological construction of memory Schmemann himself invokes the practices of the earliest Christians as a justification for his argument:

[11] Ibid., 126.

"The essence of our faith and the new life granted in it consists in *Christ's memory*, realized in us through our *memory of Christ*. From the very first day of Christianity, to believe in Christ meant to *remember* him and keep him always in mind. It is not simply to 'know' about him and his doctrine, but to *know him*—living and abiding among those who love him. From the very beginning the faith of Christians was memory and remembrance, but memory restored to its life-creating essence."[12]

Neglecting once again to support this claim with even one passage from the New Testament, Schmemann is mistaken if he thinks that such a description of the earliest experience and practice of faith is simply obvious and self-evident to contemporary Christians. Schmemann's point is exactly the one that needs to be made, but it needs to be made in significant detail, that is, by means of direct attention to the biblical texts, both to their content and to their specific liturgical function as enacted in cultus and in life. During the twentieth century, especially its more recent decades, scholars of the Hebrew Bible, New Testament, systematic theology, and the history and theology of liturgy have been carefully researching and reflecting upon the concepts of commemoration and remembrance in the Jewish and Christian traditions. In my estimation, one particular essay by New Testament scholar Nils Dahl provides a survey of early Christian sources that singularly meets the challenge to which our explorations of Schmemann and Metz have brought us.

To summarize, then, the point to which Metz and Schmemann have brought us: We take as our own Metz's description of theology's mission in late modernity.

"If it is not to remain at the level of a pure assertion that is suspected of ideology, theology must be able to define and call upon a praxis in which Christians can break through the complex social, historical and psychological conditions governing history and society. What is needed, then, is a praxis of faith in mystical and political imitation."[13]

The Christian praxis of imitation is primarily (primordially) an imitation of Christ. For this reason memory is of irreducible importance to

---

[12] Ibid., 128–9.
[13] Metz, *Faith in History and Society*, 76–7.

the theory and practice of Christian faith. What Christians glean from the narrative remembrance of Jesus is the pattern of his life, a pattern of prayer and action, of (in Metz's specific terms) mysticism and politics. Metz's efforts at a theoretical explanation for Christian memory seem predominantly to serve the political aspect of his definition of Christian praxis. Narrative memory breaks into prevailing social consciousness and goads action. Schmemann's work, on the other hand, is clearly situated in the mystical end of the Christian dialectic of faith. As the previous chapters have demonstrated, both authors recognize and promote both the mystical and the political or prophetic elements of Christian praxis. Nonetheless, each understandably concentrates on one aspect, while pointing toward its relationship to the other. Both, however, fall short of establishing fully the narrative, noetic, and practical aspects of the biblical, Christian tradition of memory in its capacity as the dynamic, mediating force in the dialectic between mysticism and politics. What is needed is a framework for explaining the function of memory in the praxis of Christian faith, a framework which takes into account the elements of worship (mysticism) and ethics (politics). For that framework we turn to Dahl. A reading of his essay will draw out new features of our interrogation of Metz and Schmemann, as well as invite contributions from other scholars.

MEMORY AT THE ORIGINS OF CHRISTIANITY

Christian Memory in the New Testament

At the outset of "Anamnesis: Memory and Commemoration in Early Christianity," Dahl warns that one would search the New Testament in vain for any formal reflections on the nature and function of memory. Whereas Aristotle had provided Greek culture with a precise psychological explanation for the verb *mnemoneuein*, "to remember," the authors of the New Testament employed the word (and other analogous terms) in manners typical of ordinary Greek usage. Aristotle limited the concept of memory strictly to referents from the past, a matter of recollecting them. The New Testament authors differed from Aristotle in their usage of the Greek terminology for memory on two fundamental counts. First, in the New Testament the exercise of memory can concern not only something in the past, but also something at present or in the future. Second, the exercise of memory does not entail the mere recalling or recollection of its object but, rather, entails a far greater degree of subjective involvement: "*Mnemoneuein* and other analogous terms signify not only to recollect but also to think of something or someone."[14]

The distinction Dahl is making between merely recalling some person(s) or situation and "thinking of" them lies in the recognition that the latter entails a commitment or action on the part of the subject. Examples include the act of mentioning persons or situations, especially in prayer, such that the remembrance leads to intercession. Dahl cites several thanksgivings at the beginnings of Pauline letters which demonstrate how commemoration integrates both memory and intercession (1 Thess 1:2ff.; Phil 1:3ff.; 2 Tim 1:3ff.). Dahl's introduction of the term "commemoration" indicates the qualitative difference in the act of remembering that he is trying to distinguish from mere recollection. This manner of remembering entails bringing the object of one's memory into linguistic expression. Such expressive activity has an impact upon those who perform it or participate in it. To remember those presently in need can also carry the implication that the persons doing the remembrance are committed to coming to the aid of the needy. This is demonstrated in Gal 2:10, where Paul refers to the collection as "remembering the poor of Jerusalem."

Dahl concludes his survey of the general usage of *mnemoneuein* in the New Testament by considering passages wherein the object of remembrance is in the past. Here again he finds a pattern in which the act of remembering is integrally related to one's present thought and decisions for action. In John 16:21 the woman who has given birth no longer remembers the anguish of her labor because of the joy she now feels for having brought her child into the world. The latter feeling does not obliterate the possible recollection of the difficult experience of labor. The woman, however, is pro-active in the exercise of her memory; she makes the decision on how she stands in relation to the past. Likewise, in Phil 3:13-14, Paul describes how his "straining forward" toward the fullness of life on high in Christ has led him to forget "what lies behind." Although he is certainly capable of recalling it, Paul no longer allows his past to shape his life. For Paul the formative

---

[14] Nils Alstrup Dahl, *Jesus in the Memory of the Early Church* (Minneapolis: Augsburg, 1976) 12. Although first written as the inaugural lecture for his appointment at the University of Oslo in 1946, the essay appears (unaltered) as the "programmatic paper" for this later collection of essays. Ibid., 9.

remembrance is that "Christ Jesus has made me his own" (v. 12). Dahl concludes: "'To remember,' in the New Testament, signifies almost always to recall something or to think about it in such a way that it is expressed in speech or is formative for attitude and action."[15]

Dahl's initial observations about the function of memory and commemoration in the New Testament lend immediate support to Metz's arguments that the Christian exercise of memory is for the purpose of transforming believers' perspectives and praxis. In other words, Dahl demonstrates the practical character of human memory, as appealed to in the New Testament literature. Remembering is an activity performed by people which has a significant impact upon their further decisions and actions. At the conclusion of this first step of his essay, Dahl reiterates that this New Testament usage of the verb "to remember" is unremarkable in relation to the ordinary Greek of that period; he further notes that it is analogous to the common usage in modern languages. In the context of this present study, the significance of that observation lies in its recognition of the pervasive function of memory in people's daily decisions for action, let alone in their more careful reflection in the context of making more formidable decisions.

When considering the modern context, Metz brings to the discussion his analysis of the pervasive forgetfulness in society. The instrumental reason of technology and the market, increasingly concerned with short-term or immediate goals, discourages careful (one can even say, theoretical) reflection upon the longer implications of present decisions. The means for producing short-term results (i.e., "science" or profit) become ends in themselves. This sort of practical thinking has a pervasive effect upon the subjects in modern society. Historical remembrance of the victims of such instrumentalist thinking in the past (which may include not only people but also the ecology), as well as remembering that future generations will wrestle with the results of present practices, disrupts the sort of thinking that raises immediate means to the status of ends in themselves.[16] Metz signals a warning call: People's capacities for remembering (in all the senses) are deteriorating, and the results are proving humanly catastrophic.

---

[15] Ibid., 13.

[16] Max Horkheimer who, as we saw in Chapter 2, has influenced Metz's thought, theorizes about this issue in an essay entitled "Means and Ends." See Max Horkheimer, *Eclipse of Reason* (New York: Continuum, 1947, 1992) 3–57.

That the Christian religion has not been spared this crisis is not surprising, given the fundamental role that tradition, with its backward and forward looking memory, plays therein.

The subjects of Christian memory, however, are not only people but also God. This crucial point returns our attention to Dahl, whose next move in his essay is to introduce the relationship between human and divine remembrance as found in the earliest sources of the tradition. Dahl reports that the primary influence in this regard at the origins of Christianity is Judaism. In so doing, Dahl introduces to the theology of Christian memory a source that, as we saw above, Metz has come to argue is essential for understanding memory as a crucial category for political theology. Dahl's brief treatment of the Jewish view of remembrance also invites some expansion on the topic which, as we shall see, can strengthen Schmemann's work on liturgical commemoration.

Commemoration in Jewish Tradition

Dahl acknowledges that the New Testament's usage of the verb "to remember" in terms of a recalling that is formative for attitude and action is analogous to common contemporary Greek usage. Still, he argues that the pervasiveness of this usage in the New Testament is primarily due to Jewish influence. The Hebrew verb *zakar*, "to remember," signifies the calling forth "in the soul" of a thing or event such that what is remembered effects the subject's disposition, decision, and action.[17] Old Testament passages in which God is the subject markedly exemplify this concept of remembering. Citing passages in Exodus, Leviticus, and the Psalms,[18] Dahl explains that when God remembers the covenant or when God either remembers or no longer remembers the people's sins, God acts accordingly, intervening on their behalf, punishing them, or pardoning them (respectively). The God of Israel is one who acts in history; thus, Israel's memory of God, of God's deeds and commandments, is of fundamental importance to their religious practice. At the time of Christianity's beginnings, Jews actively remembered God's deeds and commands through the rabbinic school tradition and by means of their cultus. Dahl reports the latter as having exercised significant influence on Christian tradition.

---

[17] Dahl, *Jesus in the Memory of the Early Church*, 13.
[18] Exod 2:24; 6:5; Lev 26:24; Ps 105:8.

Dahl explains that the cultus of the Israelite religion included practices by which not only the people remembered God but God also was prompted to remember the people. Israel remembered YHWH by means of numerous mnemonic signs, but especially by the ritual symbols and actions and the accompanying words, psalms, and hymns which comprised their great festivals. Moreover, the prayers, sacrifices, showbread, trumpeting, and other cultic objects included in their religious ceremonies had the purpose of making YHWH recall his former mighty deeds and causing him thus to remember his people again.[19] The overall import of these practices Dahl summarizes as follows: "By this cultic 'commemoration,' past salvation became once again an actual and present reality."[20] Dahl provides an illustration of this principle from the Mishnah, which instructs the members of every generation to consider themselves as having come forth from Egypt.

Unfortunately, Dahl does not elaborate on the question of what is meant by saying that the reality of Israel's historical deliverance is again made real or actual in each ritual celebration of Passover. Interpreting a similar teaching in the Passover Haggadah (which Dahl also cites in a footnote), C.J.A. Hickling understands the phenomenon in corporate terms:

"The Haggadah does not imply that the Exodus is in some way brought out of the past into the present, but that each successive generation of Israelites is so fully identifiable with its predecessors back to the Exodus generation itself that all subsequent ones may be thought of as included in the latter."[21]

Hickling appends the following endnote: "to such an extent that the Wicked Son is reproved by a formula excluding him from this partici-

[19] For detailed treatment of these Jewish ritual forms of memorial see Max Thurian, *The Eucharistic Memorial: Part I—The Old Testament,* trans. J. G. Davies, ed. J. G. Davies and A. Raymond George, *Ecumenical Studies in Worship* 7 (Richmond, Va.: John Knox Press, 1960) 40–93.

[20] Dahl, *Jesus in the Memory of the Early Church,* 14. See also Clemens Thoma, "Memorial of Salvation: The Celebration of Faith in Judaism," *The Meaning of the Liturgy,* ed. Angelus A. Häussling, trans. Linda M. Maloney (Collegeville: The Liturgical Press, 1994) 48.

[21] C.J.A. Hickling, "Eucharistic Theology and Eucharistic Origins," *Liturgical Review* 4 (November 1974) 20. See also Thoma, "Memorial of Salvation," 49.

pation."[22] This augments Dahl's treatment of remembrance in the Jewish cultus by explicitly introducing an ethical dimension. One whose conduct is evil cannot be identified with the saving reality shared by one's forebears. The ritual performance of remembrance has implications for the attitudes and actions by which one conducts one's life. Given the importance of this latter point for this present project, the question of what is meant by saying that remembrance or commemoration makes a past event in salvation history "actual" or "real" warrants closer consideration.

In his *Memory and Tradition in Israel* Brevard Childs produced a landmark study on the meaning and function of memory among the various sources, traditions, and books in the Hebrew Scriptures. Relying largely on the method of form-critical analysis, Childs examines the use of verbs and nouns signifying remembrance in relation to both God and Israel as subjects, and in the context of such issues as cultic activity and the dynamic processes of history. In so doing, Childs does not shy away from the problematic concept of "actualization" *(Vergegenwärtigung)*, about which he reports "a wide divergence of scholarly opinion."[23] The difficulty of reconciling the function of cultic activity in relationship to belief in a God who brings about salvation for humans through historical events forms the nexus of the problem that Childs conceptualizes in the term "actualization."

At an important transitional point in his study, Childs asserts:

"Although the same verb *zkr* is used to express both God's and Israel's remembering, the comparison makes evident that a totally different process is involved. Only in terms of Israel's memory can we correctly speak of an actualization of a past event. Only in relation to Israel's memory is the problem to contemporize past tradition."[24]

God's act of remembering, as conveyed in the psalms and various texts of the prophets, is not an actualization of the past, for God is not confined by the strictures of time and space. Rather, God's exercise of memory is inseparable from God's constant justice and faithfulness to the covenant (cf. Psalms 105, 106, 98, 136). On the basis of that faithfulness

---

[22] Hickling, "Eucharistic Theology and Eucharistic Origins," 26, n. 12.

[23] Brevard S. Childs, *Memory and Tradition in Israel* (Chatham, England: W. & J. MacKay, 1962) 81.

[24] Ibid., 75.

God, when petitioned by psalmist or prophet, remembers the people and gives the promise of future blessing. "Only from Israel's point of view is each remembrance past. God's memory is not a re-creating of the past, but a continuation of the selfsame purpose."[25] Here the issues of God's "time" and God's being eternally active in relation to human temporality is not a speculative problem.

When Israel is the subject of the act of remembering, Childs reports that in many texts the verb denotes the general psychological function of recalling a past event so as to evoke some action. However, when Israel during the Deuteronomic period of its history, found it necessary to reinterpret the meaning of its tradition, "a new and highly theological usage of *zkr* emerged."[26] In Deut 8:1-6, God instructs the people to keep the commandments. These, however, are not presented as abstract rules but as "events," in conjunction with the memory of how God salvifically led Israel out of Egypt and gave them the Promised Land. The present people of Israel are in a situation *analogous* to that of their ancestors. The great events of deliverance happened once and for all in history. Successive generations have no direct access to them, but neither are they cut off from their salvific significance. Keeping remembrance provides the link between past and present. This is not a matter of reliving the past; rather, observing the Sabbath and the festivals is for the purpose of the continuation of the history of redemption now and in the future. This history can occur only insofar as the present generation receives the divine command and makes the decision to be obedient, just as their ancestors had done. This active sense of decision and commitment, precisely in the context of narrative and ritual memory, is what Childs means by saying that the people actualize the event of salvation. They "participate again in the 'event,'" and by obediently doing so, they thoroughly "internalize" the tradition.[27]

In the texts of Deuteronomy, Deutero-Isaiah, Ezekiel, and the complaint psalms, Childs identifies the emergence of a theology of memory in the Hebrew tradition. While cultic practices, including many

---

[25] Ibid., 42. Childs notes that even in the Priestly tradition, with its undeniably cultic notion of the memorial sign *(zikkaron)*, a historical sense of memory functions in relation to God and the covenant: "This history is merely a working out of the one eternal act of divine grace" (43).

[26] Ibid., 50.

[27] Ibid., 53, 79. See also, Thoma, "Memorial of Salvation," 52.

types of *zikkaron* or mnemonic objects, continued to be essential to Israelite practice, the sense of what takes place in such ritual acts of remembrance underwent a transformation. The authors of those texts recognized the historical discontinuity between the experiences of earlier generations and their contemporaries due to both the passage of time and the crises brought about by the people's unfaithfulness. Through narrative and ritual—texts, gestures, and cultic objects (*zikkaron*)—each generation "encountered anew these same determinative events," they became "noetically aware" of the desperate circumstances of their ancestors and the love with which YHWH elected and delivered them.[28] The impact of such remembrance was more than reflection on the significance of those events or mere recognition of their importance; rather, the redemptive purpose of those events continued "to reverberate in the life of the people."[29] In the case of Deuteronomy, the criterion for obedience to the law of God encountered through such events was responsibility to the weak and disinherited. This amounted, in Childs' judgment, to a *secularization* of the cultic tradition.[30] In Deutero-Isaiah and Ezekiel, YHWH's constant faithfulness is revealed, despite Israel's disasters. YHWH is bringing about new things, but this future is nonetheless consistent with God's singular purpose of justice in history.

Childs' work substantiates not only Dahl's brief description of the Jewish concept of memory but also Schmemann's reference to "biblical, Old Testamental teaching" as the basis for his own theology of divine and human memory. Schmemann's assertion that the "heartbeat" of the Church's worship and very life rests in "the referral of everything to the memory of God" finds ample support in Childs'

---

[28] Childs, *Memory and Tradition in Israel*, 83, 52. Concerning the topic of the noetic aspect (the "noetic moments") of ritual activity see Theodore W. Jennings, "On Ritual Knowledge," *Journal of Religion* 62 (April 1982) 111–27. Angelus Häussling identifies a "linguistic form" whereby Israel remembered the saving deeds of God in their acts of worship, which he describes as follows: "self-definition by imitative assumption of the roles of the leading historical figures of the normative era of salvation through situative identity." Angelus A. Häussling, "Liturgy: Memorial of the Past and Liberation in the Present," *The Meaning of the Liturgy*, ed. Angelus A. Häussling, trans. Linda M. Maloney (Collegeville: The Liturgical Press, 1994) 111.

[29] Childs, *Memory and Tradition in Israel*, 84.

[30] See ibid., 78.

explanation of the ontological and objectively active aspects of God's remembering. Moreover, Schmemann's description of the human experience of memory in relation to the events of salvation (specifically, Christ) in terms of "encounter" and "participation" resonates with Childs' language for describing each Jewish generation's experience in the act of remembrance. Childs' use of such terms as "reverberation" and "internalization" to describe the unusual, conceptually evasive character of the commemorative event's impact on its human participants coincides both with Schmemann's words on the mysteriousness and elusiveness of the experience of memory and with the humanly transformative quality inherent to acts of liturgical remembrance.

Childs, however, succeeds in one crucial respect where we found Schmemann to be wanting. By both performing a close analysis of biblical texts and approaching the topic of remembrance in the social context of salvation history, Childs is able to demonstrate that the biblical category of memory essentially includes an element of ethical, moral, and/or social decision for action on the part of its human participants. In this way, faithfulness to God in worship, especially in commemorative rituals (Sabbath, festivals), cannot be isolated or reduced to merely cultic or "sacred" activity. This social ethical connection could not emerge in Schmemann's theology of memory due to his framing of the argument in terms of the abstract figure "man." Schmemann seemed to proceed in that manner in order to construct his christological argument. In light of Childs' work, however, we see the need for a more ecclesial perspective on christology, one that promotes the body of Christ as the Church, whose members are ethical subjects in society. If we consider the entire corpus of Schmemann's work, of course, we find that the ecclesial sense of the Church's liturgy is anything but lacking. Indeed, Schmemann posits liturgical action on the Lord's Day as constitutive of the Church. Among the key reasons why that is so resides in liturgy's manifestation of the newness of life that has been fully revealed or given in Christ. The definite content of faith is not merely an idea but a reality in which believers participate, a knowledge that transforms their view of the world and their roles within it. The key element from the Jewish Scriptures that establishes the historical, societal, and ethical dimensions of the reality of salvation is the concept of the covenant between God and the people. As we shall see further on in this chapter, this covenantal aspect will exercise a crucial role in understanding the Eucharist as a commemoration of Christ which necessitates decisions for the practice of faith in community.

Practices of Remembering in the Apostolic Communities

We have found in the Jewish roots of Christianity a cultic pattern of remembrance at the heart of religious life that also comes to carry prophetic and secular implications. Remembrance is essential to human living, to social living, and, for the Jewish and Christian faiths, to religious living. Dahl emphasizes the ordinariness of the New Testament writers' usages of verbs designating the act of remembering in order to demonstrate the fundamental, practical role that memory plays in the attitudes, decisions, and actions of believers. In a confirmation of Metz's thought, one of Dahl's crucial concerns here is to show that the earliest believers did not dwell upon abstract theories ("classical ideals") of memory and knowledge; rather, caught up in the "freshness and spontaneity" of the experience of faith in Christ, the New Testament writers sought to convey the lively impact that the memory of Jesus was bringing about in the Church.[31] While the content of the message of faith was astonishingly new, however, the pattern of its revelation was consistent with the Hebrew tradition of the covenant: God has acted through key historical events for the salvation of the people of Israel. Through cultic acts of worship, prayer, and the proclamation of God's word the people's remembrance or commemoration of those events enables them to participate in the reality of salvation.

This brings us to the main body of Dahl's essay, where he begins with the thesis, "The church's memory grew spontaneously out of its missionary experience."[32] Dahl develops his thesis by turning to 1 Thessalonians, the letter most scholars consider the oldest writing in the New Testament. While noting that Paul begins the letter by assuring the community of his constant remembrance of them, Dahl identifies as Paul's essential concern that the Thessalonians remember what Paul had said to them. Paul peppers his exhortation to the community with the formulas, "just as you know" (1:5; 2:1, 4, 11; 3:3, 4; 4:2; 5:1) and "just as you are doing," with the implication that they must strive to do those things more perfectly (4:1ff.; 4:9ff.; 5:11). Dahl recognizes these phrases as serving more than just polite or ingratiating purposes;

---

[31] Dahl, *Jesus in the Memory of the Early Church*, 12.
[32] Ibid., 15.

rather, Paul's use of them indicates a significant, practical theological agenda:

"The initial acceptance of the gospel puts the whole of life under obligation. A community of baptized Christians which has come to share in the gospel and which has received basic catechetical instructions already knows what must be done. They have received the Holy Spirit and are on the right road. They need to preserve what they have received and to remind themselves of it in order to live out the reality into which they have been introduced. The first obligation of the apostle vis-a-vis the community is to make the faithful remember what they have received and already know—or should know."[33]

Dahl identifies this same pattern of exhorting the faithful on the basis of the memory of what they have already received and possess throughout not only the Pauline epistles but numerous others in the New Testament, as well as the letters of Ignatius of Antioch and 1 Clement.[34]

Dahl readily points out that he is by no means claiming that all of the New Testament is a matter of recollection. First Corinthians has its practical ordinances, Hebrews its scriptural interpretations, the Apocalypse its visions. Still, all these writings "refer to the foundations that have been laid once and for all."[35] The epistle of Jude summarizes these foundations in a word: faith, "the faith which was once for all delivered to the saints" (v. 3). The author of the letter goes on in the fifth verse to say that although the faithful "were once for all fully informed," still the apostolic writer needs to remind them of certain things. Here begin to resound echoes of both Metz's and Schmemann's critical theological agendas. Both insist upon the definite content of Christian faith and recognize, as well, that it is precisely this message, with its practical implications, that contemporary believers (and even academic theologians) widely ignore. In terms of Dahl's study, one would do better to say that modern Christians *forget*, they fail to *remember* the content of the tradition they have received. Attention to texts from the earliest Christian communities demonstrates that the ex-

---

[33] Ibid.

[34] See ibid., 15–16, nn. 26–30, for Dahl's citations of passages from 2 Thessalonians, Galatians, 1 Corinthians, Romans, Colossians, Ephesians, Jude, 2 Peter, James, 1 John, Ignatius' letters, and 1 Clement.

[35] Ibid., 17.

ercise of memory is essential to the knowledge and practice of Christian faith. Closer attention reveals the liturgical and catechetical means by which the faith was so definitively bestowed upon believers.

Dahl argues that the predominant way by which the authors of the epistles in the New Testament kindled the fires of faith in the members of the Christian communities was to refer them to the memory of their initiation into Christianity. By initiation Dahl is referring to the entire process through which people came to belief in Christ and committed their lives to him as members of the Church.[36] Dahl expends few words on describing that process. His concern, rather, is with its foundational result for those who have undergone it: "Those who have been led to faith and who have received baptism know already what is necessary for salvation."[37] The apostolic writers appealed to their audiences' memories of having been cleansed, or reborn, or raised up into the life of faith (various New Testament metaphors for baptism), and then instructed them to let that specific memory shape their present attitudes, perceptions, decisions, and actions. At this point Dahl introduces the word "anamnesis," explaining that by this Greek term he does *not* intend the Platonic concept, that is, the reminiscence of Ideas a soul has already contemplated in its preexistence. Rather, by this term Dahl intends to say "that for the early Christians, knowledge was an anamnesis, a recollection of the *gnosis* given to all those who have believed in the gospel, received baptism, and been incorporated into the church. In effect, in Christ 'are hid all the treasures of wisdom and knowledge' (Col. 2:3)."[38] Without doubt, members of the Church can always acquire more knowledge, but Dahl explains that the early Christian leaders perceived this in terms of growth, in terms of ongoing assimilation and greater application of the wisdom

---

[36] Biblical and liturgical scholars have come to stress Christian baptism or initiation as a continuum of practices, of which the water bath is but one (albeit, culminating) part. On the basis of a comprehensive study of baptism in the New Testament, James Dunn explains that the word "baptism" is a "concertina" word, one which can refer simply to the actual water rite or can be "expanded to take in more and more of the rites and constituent parts of conversion-initiation until it embraces the whole." James G. D. Dunn, *Baptism in the Holy Spirit* (London: SCM Press, 1970) 5. See also Aidan Kavanagh, *The Shape of Baptism: The Rite of Christian Initiation* (New York: Pueblo, 1978) 18–23, 172.

[37] Dahl, *Jesus in the Memory of the Early Church*, 16.

[38] Ibid.

they have received once for all. Dahl notes that the pattern of letting remembrance of baptism shape conduct corresponds to what scholars have come to identify as the indicative-imperative tension in Paul's view of the Christian life.[39]

Although he himself makes little more of the point, Dahl's use of the term "gnosis" is a notably apt means for conveying the quality or character of the knowledge that believers received in baptism. As was true for the pursuit of any philosophy-of-life during that time (Stoicism,

---

[39] Pauline scholars have expended much effort upon what Gunther Bornkamm identifies as the "peculiar and apparently contradictory joining of indicative and imperative words" in Romans 6. Gunther Bornkamm, *Early Christian Experience* (London: SCM Press, 1969) 71.

Robert Tannehill provides a clear and convincing framework for interpreting Romans 6: "While dying and rising with Christ was connected in the [earliest Christian] tradition with baptism, it has a broader significance in Paul's thought." Tannehill classifies dying and rising with Christ a "motif," a set pattern in Paul's thought which is present "when Paul relates two elements, death and life, in a construction that contrasts them—and sees in this precisely what the believer participates in." The motif is present in numerous Pauline passages, including much of Romans 6–8; thus, Tannehill concludes that the Christian's participation in Christ's dying and rising is neither totally passive nor limited to the experience of initiation. Robert C. Tannehill, *Dying and Rising with Christ: A Study in Pauline Theology* (Berlin: Verlag Alfred Topelmann) 3, 6.

Bornkamm argues for the importance of the nature of "decision" in this entire context. The decision that has happened to humanity is the death and resurrection of Christ (Rom 6:10). Christ alone, however, has experienced the completeness of physical death and the totality of the resurrection. Believers live in the dominion of grace but nevertheless in their mortal bodies. Until they enter into the final completion of their death (i.e., when their bodies expire), believers are still vulnerable to being at the disposal of the master of sin and death. The gracious decision received by faith in baptism is the basis for the daily decision against sin and for righteousness that the believer is able to and must make. Bornkamm further explains that the sense of Rom 6:4 is not mystical initiation, since Paul fails to reflect on the symbolic character of the baptismal rite; rather, Paul is stressing the future character of the believer's resurrection as already present by conducting one's life as a person freed from sin. Paul has established a tension between the degrees to which one can identify with Christ's death and resurrection, and out of this tension arises Christian ethics and conduct, which Paul develops in the subsequent three chapters of Romans. See Bornkamm, *Early Christian Experience*, 73–4. See also James D. G. Dunn, *Romans 1–8*, Word Biblical Commentary Series (Dallas: Word Books, 1988) 330–1.

for example) the earliest believers were immersed in a kind of knowledge that was not merely intellectual or rational but, rather, comprehensively touched upon all aspects of human living. The indicative aspect of that life took its shape precisely in the knowledge that, to use Metz's terminology, was mystically known. By the water-ritual of baptism the believer knew that he or she had entered into a new mode of existence in Christ (whether the image is new birth, or dying and rising, or cleansing). This knowledge was a mystery, a participation, to use Schmemann's terminology, in the very life of Christ and, thus, of God. This belonging to Christ is final, bearing within it the continuity of God's singular faithfulness and the believer's ongoing growth and assimilation to God through the practices of mysticism and ethics. Still, the knowledge is known now, in the body, only as mystery. The indicative carries an imperative precisely because the believer still lives amidst this world, with its daunting challenges that at times so overwhelm as to impede the believer's memory as to whom she or he truly belongs. Thus, the practice of mysticism does not result in an inordinate assurance of the resurrection victory that Christ *already* has won for "us"; rather, the believer is placed in a tensive life that requires the interruption, over and again, of faith's message and memory.[40] The gospel must break into each person's life as well as the corporate life of an entire Christian community—a continuous series of interruptions. This occurs through narrative, but narrative in the broadest sense of the term, narrative in a variety of linguistic and performative genres. The earliest Christians kept the narrative memory of Christ through a number of different forms. Dahl particularly addresses the forms of (1) preaching and (2) prayers and thanksgiving.

The Church's preaching is fundamentally about a singular past event, namely, what God has done in the life, death, and resurrection of Jesus the Christ. A point on which Dahl lays great emphasis,

---

[40] On this point I explicitly have in mind Metz's criticism of an inordinately realized eschatology, "the overworked . . . Christian identity that, at every opportunity, insists on the salvation that has already been given in Christ." Metz, *Faith in History and Society*, 179. Not only does such a false spirituality or mysticism impede the intrinsically social and political aspect of the imitation of Christ, Metz observes that it has produced "a special kind of weariness" for many of the contemporary believers who practice Christian religion in this way.

however, is that the purpose (and therefore the style) of preaching that selfsame gospel changes in the course of people's being evangelized, converted, initiated, and encouraged in the ongoing life in the Church. The initial preaching is a public heralding of a message, the *kerygma* about Jesus. The instruction given to those undergoing the process of initiation is a catechetical indoctrination into the stories, traditions, and ethical practices that comprise the Christian way of life. While both these types of "preaching" are evident in the various epistles, they do not constitute the bulk of the preaching given in these letters because they are not the type of instruction needed by their audiences, namely, communities of fully initiated believers.

"The faithful already knew the message; they had been made participants, they had been made part of the divine work of which the kerygma was a proclamation. That is why, precisely when it is a question of the very core of the gospel, the preaching to the communities was more recollection than proclamation. Thus what we understand generally by 'to preach'—namely, to deliver a sermon in the church—no longer corresponds to the *keryssein* of the New Testament, but rather closely to *hypomimneskein,* to restore to memory."[41]

The difference in the three types of preaching Dahl describes resides in the pastoral, practical purpose of each. The third type, the task of apostolic leaders in relation to the communities, Dahl identifies as exercises in the restoration of memory. The notion of restoration implies that believers had forgotten or misunderstood what they had received. The way in which the apostle goes about the preaching, therefore, carries both the continuity of repeating the singular message of the gospel while also needing to do so in a way that meets the needs of the communities in their current circumstances.

What Dahl is pointing out is that the memory which the apostolic writers sought to restore was two-fold in nature. The Christian communities, both corporately and as individuals, needed to be reminded both of the memory of Jesus (the content of the gospel) and of their own memories of having been baptized into Christ. This

---

[41] Dahl, *Jesus in the Memory of the Early Church,* 19. Texts Dahl cites here in a footnote include 2 Tim 2:14; Titus 3:10; Jude 5; 2 Pet 1:12; 1 Clem 62:2; and 1 Cor 4:17.

point needs to be considered from the side of the believers as well: Why are they in need of remembering Christ? Dahl seems to be indicating two different, but related, reasons. When Dahl describes the apostolic preaching to the communities as an effort to restore believers' memories, the "memory" being restored is "the very core of the gospel." I take this as referring to the possibility that believers can forget essentials of that message, or may have misunderstood the content or its implications, or may have undergone some experience that places the meaning of the gospel in question. The causes for this failure to remember are what Dahl does not describe. One way to summarize the situation, however, is to say, with Metz, that faith is always threatened in the world. However, there is a second aspect to the need for remembering Christ. This is not due to a forgetfulness of specific content but, rather, to the processual character of the very reality into which believers were initiated. In Christ God has given to the world the fullness of wisdom, but this definitive gift is a mystery whose content continuously realizes measures of disclosure, amidst suffering, until Christ returns in glory. Christian memory, then, functions not only for the purpose of correcting believers in their lapses in remembering the content of the faith, but also as the means whereby communities and individuals receive further riches of the mystery of redemption. Although he does not explicitly use the term in his exposition, Dahl is pointing here, as well, to the eschatological orientation of the faith. Taken all together, the praxis of living the faith in these last days requires, to return to Dahl's essay, exhortation.

The New Testament contains numerous christological formulas which, Dahl explains, in several cases function not so much as credal confessions but as the motivating force for apostolic exhortation. Dahl considers 2 Tim 2:8 to be exemplary in this regard: "Remember Jesus Christ, raised from the dead, a descendant of David—that is my gospel." The passage is exemplary in two ways. First, the attachment of relative clauses, participles, or declarative or causal clauses to the name of Jesus Christ is characteristic of the christological formularies in the New Testament. These clauses or declarations designate the important events that constitute the messiahship of Jesus and, thus, his significance for the faithful. Second, in light of the concrete instructions to the community that follow it (2 Tim 2:14-26), this christological passage also demonstrates the purpose for remembrance: "To 'remember Jesus Christ' does not mean to preserve in memory an

image of him but to let this memory form our thoughts and actions."[42]
Dahl's conclusion amounts to a paraphrase of Metz's argument for
the intrinsically practical nature of christology: One only knows
Christ by imitating him.[43] Thus, Dahl's work with New Testament
texts provides further content to the "mysticism" or "contemplation"
which Metz recognizes as essential to the praxis of Christian faith.
The contemplation of the mystery of Christ in the narratives about his
person, life, actions, and death necessarily compels believers to their
own praxis in society, a praxis that finds both its model and strength
in Christ.

My reading and interpretation of Metz's christology as a kenotic
christology of imitation finds further textual support in Dahl's work.
Among the christological formularies that are specifically hortatory in
nature Dahl notes Phil 2:6-11. The passage, most likely an early Christian hymn, is a call to believers to remember the manner in which
Christ lived and died in faithfulness to God so as to let that attitude
shape their own approach to life. Dahl identifies this type of remembrance, again, as "an 'anamnesis of Christ,' a commemoration of
Christ."[44] In this case, however, Dahl does not employ the broad
Greek concept of *gnosis* to provide a sense of what Christian "anamnesis" entails. Rather, taking his clue from the strong likelihood that
the passage in Philippians 2 is liturgical in origin, Dahl turns to Judaism for an explanation:

"One finds similar formulas [to Phil 2:6-11] in the prayers of the early
church and in its thanksgiving, hymns, and praises. There Christ and
the salvation of God are remembered in the same way that Israel remembered the mighty deeds of its God in former times. To pray and
to give thanks in the name of Jesus does not mean simply that one
made use of the formula 'in the name of Jesus,' but that in prayer and
thanksgiving one mentioned the name of Jesus and generally also
what made him Savior and Lord of the church (cf. e.g., Act 4:24-30)."[45]

[42] Ibid., 20.

[43] See the section of Chapter 2 entitled "The Christology of Imitation," pp.
34–40.

[44] Dahl, *Jesus in the Memory of the Early Church*, 20.

[45] Ibid., 20–1. Dahl cites the following passages as further examples of hymns,
thanksgivings, or prayers: Col 1:9-15; 1 Tim 3:16; 1 Pet 1:18-21; 2:21-25; 3:18-22.

With this comparison between Jewish and early Christian patterns of prayer, hymnody, praise, and thanksgiving, Dahl substantiates his earlier assertion that the Jewish cultic forms of remembrance were strongly influential at the origins of Christianity. Moreover, Childs' detailed study of the meaning and function of memory in the Jewish Bible, succinctly rehearsed above, begins to show its implications for the Christian traditions of worship, prayer, proclamation, and a covenant-based way of life. The key difference, of course, is the belief in Jesus as Messiah and, thus, a change in the content of the memory of God's salvific deeds amidst the people. The crucial element of continuity, however, is the pattern of worship and prayer wherein the community's remembrance of God, now the remembrance of Christ, occurs through forms of narrative and ritual performance that intrinsically carry implications for the way the people are to live.

EUCHARISTIC ANAMNESIS

Priority Among the Church's Commemorative Practices

In light of the work of Metz and Schmemann, we have been reviewing Dahl's study of the New Testament in order to establish the following three points. First, memory has an essential role in Christianity, not only on the part of the faithful but also on the part of God. Second, there is a noetic aspect intrinsic to each of the various practices of remembrance Dahl has thus far described. Performative acts of remembrance impart to their participants a knowledge of God, Christ, the world, and each other that would otherwise be inaccessible. Third, narrative and ritual acts of remembrance precipitate moments of decision in their participants, decisions for attitude and action that arise from the mystical knowledge of Christ experienced in commemorative performances.

For his part, Dahl simply provides a brief reprise at this point in his essay: "'Remembrance' and 'commemoration' have thus held a central place in early Christian worship, in the preaching to the churches, and in thanksgiving and prayer."[46] Dahl has demonstrated both a number of different forms which the prayer, worship, and preaching of the early churches took and a consistent pattern to the remembrance performed in each. The memory of Jesus, the memory of his faithful service to God and humanity and, in turn, of God's raising

---

[46] Ibid., 21.

him up, bears knowledge of God's redemption of the created order. This knowledge prompts praise, thanksgiving, intercession, and the motivational source for living a life shaped by the gospel. Taken as a whole, Dahl's exploration of earliest Christian memory amounts to a narrative description of the life of Christian faith in community. In order to grasp the content and praxis of faith, one must describe—by means of a sort of narrative rehearsal—the ways in which the earliest believers shared the faith through specific practices. Having summarily listed the practices discussed thus far, Dahl next turns to the Eucharist, the "celebration" in the early Church whereby "the 'commemoration' of Jesus was most firmly established."[47]

Dahl bases his claim for the superlative role of the eucharistic celebration among the various anamnetic practices of the earliest believers on two types of scriptural sources. First, he cites passages which report the communities' regular and faithful observance of the Lord's Day (Acts 20:7; 1 Cor 6:2; Rev 1:10). This day took pride of place in the prayer-life and worship of the churches. Central to the day itself was the celebration of the Lord's Supper. Second, Dahl substantiates his claim for the singular importance of the Eucharist among the Church's commemorative practices in the dominical command, "Do this in remembrance of me" (1 Cor 11:24-25 and Luke 22:19b). Surprisingly, Dahl provides no detailed commentary on that text. Spurred by the controversial interpretations and theses of Joachim Jeremias and Odo Casel concerning the meaning and implications of the Lord's instruction that the bread and cup be shared *eis tein emen anamnesin*, liturgical scholars have throughout the better part of the twentieth century conducted extensive research and offered many constructive proposals about eucharistic anamnesis. Since the time of Dahl's own writing, close work with not only the Pauline and Lukan texts but also with all of the Lord's Supper pericopes has yielded numerous insights into the words and events at the origins of the Church's eucharistic faith and practice. In the following pages we shall pursue elements pertinent and helpful to the present project.

Dahl proceeds by providing the following general report:

"Historians of liturgy belonging to diverse confessions agree in seeing in *anamnesis*, commemoration, a fundamental theme or, one can justi-

[47] Ibid.

fiably say, *the* fundamental theme of the celebration of the Lord's Supper in the early church. The commemoration was not something that took place essentially within individual believers, in their subjective memory. The celebration itself, i.e. thanksgiving, sacrifice, and sacrament *(mysterion)* was a commemoration, an *anamnesis* of the death and resurrection of Jesus where the history of salvation was re-presented by the sacramental commemoration."[48]

Dahl's basic equation of *anamnesis* with commemoration and his definition of commemoration as a ritual re-presentation of the key event(s) of salvation in history is readily comprehended in light of Childs' work on the Jewish concepts of *zkr* and *zikkaron*. His introduction, however, of such further synonyms as thanksgiving, sacrifice, and sacrament indicates the need to explore more closely what is unique to this specific type of commemoration, namely, the eucharistic liturgy, especially in terms of the continuities and discontinuities that scholars have come to recognize between the Christian Eucharist and Jewish festive meals. On that point Dahl's work is minimal.

The crucial contribution of Dahl's essay is his establishment of the pervasiveness of memory, remembrance, and commemoration in the entire Christian life of faith, as conveyed in the New Testament. Dahl thereby situates the Eucharist in continuity with the other aspects and forms of early Christian worship and prayer, as well as preaching. Dahl accentuates that continuity in his choice of quoting just one other passage of the New Testament that deals with the Eucharist, Paul's commentary that follows immediately upon his account of Jesus' words and actions at the Supper: "For as often as you eat this bread and drink the cup, you proclaim the Lord's death until he comes" (1 Cor 11:26). Focusing on the verb *kataggellein*, Dahl argues that Paul is referring to the proclamation or words that are said in thanksgiving over the bread and wine and that the shape which those words of commemoration took must have been similar to the hymn-like passages of Philippians 2 and Colossians 1. Thus, the key elements of those forms of remembrance, which we summarized at the

---

[48] Ibid. For equally emphatic conclusion about the biblical priority of "memorial celebration" among interpretations of the Eucharist see Philipp Schäfer, "Eucharist: Memorial of the Death and Resurrection of Jesus," *The Meaning of the Liturgy,* ed. Angelus A. Häussling, trans. Linda M. Maloney (Collegeville: The Liturgical Press, 1994) 63.

beginning of this section, provide insight into the manner and purpose of the Christian community's remembrance of Jesus in the Eucharist—most notably, the noetic and performative aspects of commemorating Christ and the decision to imitate him, in Dahl's words, "as a way of life" which these entail. This interrelatedness between the performance of the Eucharist and other forms of Christian remembrance is important, for it demonstrates that the celebration of the Lord's Supper does not function in isolation from the rest of the Church's practices of proclamation, commemoration, and decisions for action in the world. Still, we need to consider what is unique to the eucharistic form of commemoration, the commemoration of Jesus' death and resurrection, in order to understand why this ritual is so central and how it informs all other aspects of the praxis of faith— both mystical and political/ethical.

Analysis of the Anamnesis Rubric in the New Testament

Given the complexity of this topic and the extensive research and publication it has engendered in this century, the decision on how to proceed here has not been easy. Given the extent, however, to which we have reflected upon Dahl's study of New Testament texts, the most profitable approach would seem to lie in paying closer attention to the scriptural sources for eucharistic anamnesis which Dahl has cited. Precisely this procedure comprises the body of an essay by David Gregg, based on research he did while in a degree program at the University of London. Gregg's work functions as a sort of enchiridion of the research, theses, and debates on the topic at the time of his writing (the mid-1970s); it still serves that function well.[49] We shall, therefore, explore Gregg's work in some detail, while also introducing other scholarly contributions to crucial issues that he raises.

At the outset of his monograph *Anamnesis in the Eucharist*, Gregg distinguishes three ways in which the word "anamnesis" can be used in reference to the Eucharist. First, anamnesis functions as a general term designating the remembrance quality of the eucharistic liturgy, which corresponds to the "'remembering' aspect" in the original

---

[49] See also David N. Power, "The Anamnesis: Remembering, We Offer," *New Eucharistic Prayers: An Ecumenical Study of Their Development and Structure,* ed. Frank C. Senn (New York: Paulist Press, 1987) 146–68.

event of the Last Supper.[50] This definition obviously coincides with the general use which Dahl makes of the term anamnesis throughout his essay and in his basic reflections on the Eucharist. Second, Gregg identifies the "Anamnesis rubric," at 1 Cor 11:24-25 (cf. Luke 22:19), wherein Jesus instructs his followers, "*touto poieite eis ten emen anamnesin* (do this in remembrance of me)," along with the further qualification in relation to the cup (v. 25), "*hosakis ean pinete* (as often as you [pl.] drink it)." From that rubrical instruction in the Last Supper account Gregg distinguishes a third definition of anamnesis, the verbal "formula" which appears in the Eucharistic Prayer of Christian liturgy, "by which is articulated the mode and content of the worshippers' response to the dominical command, and which may sometimes include a further element known as the 'Oblation,' an articulation of the act of offering."[51] It is Gregg's analysis of what he calls the Anamnesis rubric, i.e., the dominical command in First Corinthians, that comprises the better part of his study.

Before moving into that analysis Gregg articulates contextual assumptions governing his approach, some of which are worth noting. His crucial philosophical presupposition, one which accords with the work of Dahl and the vast majority of contemporary scholars of the Eucharist, is that the profitable means for comprehending the scriptural accounts of the Lord's Supper lie in "the unitive Sacramentalism of the Semitic thought-world, rather than the dual categories of physics and metaphysics of the Aristotelian dichotomy."[52] The primary

[50] David Gregg, *Anamnesis in the Eucharist*, Grove Liturgical Study 5 (Bramcote Notts., England: Grove Books, 1976) 3.

[51] Ibid.

[52] Ibid., 9. Louis-Marie Chauvet argues extensively for the inadequacy of metaphysics as philosophical theory for the practice of Christian sacraments, proposing instead a theology drawing upon a non-instrumental, symbolic theory of discourse. See his *Symbol and Sacrament: A Sacramental Reinterpretation of Christian Existence*, trans. Patrick Madigan and Madeleine Beaumont (Collegeville: The Liturgical Press, 1995) 21–98. Edward Kilmartin judges that "the average modern Catholic theology of the Eucharist," developed as a loose synthesis of scholastic concepts during the second millennium, "is without a future." He argues that the promise for a comprehensive theology of the Eucharist in the third millennium starts from the theology inherent in the classical Eucharist Prayers, an understanding of which requires attention to their origins in Jewish meal ritual. Edward J. Kilmartin, "The Catholic Tradition of Eucharistic Theology: Towards the Third Millennium," *Theological Studies* 55:3 (September 1994) 443, and see 445–9.

antecedents for the rubric in 1 Cor 11:25 reside in the texts of the Old Testament and Apocrypha, rather than in the philosophical thought forms of the Classical World. Moreover, citing the work of W. D. Davies, Gregg describes New Testament faith and thought as reflective of the first-century Jewish milieu: a faith dominated by memory of salvific events in the past and yearning for a future whose character is determined by that past. As for semantic considerations, Gregg adopts J.F.A. Sawyer's principle for biblical research that New Testament texts be studied in relation to writings contemporary to them. In addition to a sizable list of Semitic literature (including Jewish texts written in Greek) Gregg includes the Jewish Passover Haggadah, noting the caution which reference to the latter requires.[53]

While Gregg sides with those scholars who see the weight of evidence supporting the view that the Last Supper was a Passover meal, he nonetheless argues that little is at stake hermeneutically so long as all agree in recognizing the basic framework to be the Jewish pattern of the great festive meal. First Corinthians 5:7b-8a establishes the framework: "For our paschal lamb, Christ, has been sacrificed. Therefore, let us celebrate the festival." Particularly influential to the Christian Eucharist is the Passover's role in the *establishment* of the covenant community, the Feast of Unleavened Bread in the New Year's celebration of *renewal* and, moreover, the relationship between the two. Gregg's final note concerning the Passover meal as the key antecedent for the Christian Eucharist is the recognition that the latter came to replace all Jewish sacrifices and feasts and thus "it is the *whole* of the Jewish cultus (e.g. Covenant, Circumcision, Sabbath, Priesthood, Sanctuary etc. etc.) that forms the milieu of the NT writings."[54] Gregg acknowledges (and we concur) that by specifically focusing on anamnesis the intention is neither to deny nor to obscure the richness and complexity of the eucharistic symbol as a whole.

Among the three occurrences of the Anamnesis rubric in the New Testament (1 Cor 11:24, 25; Luke 22:19) Gregg chooses to study 1 Cor 11:25 for the following reasons: In comparison with Luke, the Pauline letter is "the earlier and more liturgically-oriented (let alone undis-

---

[53] "In evaluating the evidence of the Seder Service and the Haggadah however, the crucial changes post–70 AD must be borne in mind, as must the evidence of the considerable variation in Passover practice prior to that date." Gregg, *Anamnesis in the Eucharist*, 11.

[54] Ibid.

puted) account.["55] Second, within the Corinthians text, verse 25 contains the additional qualifier, "as often as you drink it," which provides further insight into the rubric's meaning that is lacking in verse 24. Our rehearsal of Gregg's exegesis must necessarily be selective, highlighting key points that contribute to our agenda. The acutely critical reader, of course, is encouraged to examine the exegetical details and references of Gregg's argument more closely. We shall augment certain points in his argument, referring especially to the work of New Testament scholar Xavier Léon-Dufour.

The rubric begins with the words *touto poieite."* While the common translation for this phrase in English-language Bibles and liturgical texts is "do this," Gregg is more careful in his translation: "Perform this action."[56] Gregg's concern is to counter two types of misconceptions. First, there is the mistake of taking the object of Jesus' command, i.e., the "this," as referring to the exact way in which Jesus spoke over and gestured with the bread and cup. Were that the case, Gregg argues, then the object of *poieite* would not be *touto* but *houtos,* which means "thus," implying that the manner demonstrated is to be exactly followed.[57] Although he does not explicitly say so, Gregg most likely has in mind certain Protestant churches which take the scriptural account as the literal, mimetic model for performing the Eucharist, to the exclusion of a Eucharistic Prayer or anaphora, which would include (anamnetic) blessing and (epicletic) intercession. To put the problem in Dahl's terms, many Protestant churches, by merely

[55] Ibid., 9–10. The dispute to which Gregg refers concerns the earliest authoritative sources of the Lukan passage. The Study Edition of the revised New Catholic translation of the Bible provides the following note:

"22, 19c-20: *Which will be given . . . do this in memory of me:* these words are omitted in some important Western text manuscripts and a few Syriac manuscripts. Other ancient text types, including the oldest papyrus manuscript of Lk dating from the late second or early third century, contain the longer reading presented here."

The New American Bible, with Revised New Testament (Nashville: Thomas Nelson Publishers, 1987) 1181.

[56] Gregg, *Anamnesis in the Eucharist,* 15.

[57] "*Houtos* would require exact imitative repetition, and would make the Last Supper the Model, rather than the Source, of the Christian eucharist." Ibid., 12.

reciting the scriptural "warrant" at the Lord's Table, reduced the eucharistic euchology to "praying in the name of Jesus," rather than proclaiming a narrative rehearsal of Jesus' life, death, and resurrection whereby the memory of Jesus might form and transform the thoughts and actions of the participants.

A second mistake, according to Gregg, is to consider the object of the command to be the bread or cup in itself. Were this indeed the case, then the object would require the appropriate accusative pronoun, *touton*. Gregg's concern here seems to be the correction of an inappropriate sacrificial or oblationary view of the Eucharist, especially in the Roman Church, whereby the bread and wine are isolated as sacrificial objects being offered. A nearly exclusive focus (gazing) upon the raising of the host and chalice, coupled with the priest's silent recitation of the Eucharistic Prayer, left the people with a ritual of adoration but not a liturgy for participation in the transforming, narrative remembrance of Jesus. In both cases, the misconceptions (albeit in different ways) lead to a lack of awareness of the entire ritual action of the supper as the source for the Christian Eucharist.[58] Failing in that awareness, Western churches of all kinds have lost the richness of the narrative recital and gestures which comprise the commemoration that occurs in the Jewish festive meal. Gregg points toward that richness when he explains how the verb *poieite* is best understood as "describ[ing] not only the performing of a cultic act but also the performing of a prophetic symbolic act."[59] This linking of the cultic with the prophetic is of great importance for the transformative capacity of the eucharistic celebration in the lives of believers—an issue, of course, of great concern both to Metz and Schmemann. We shall address this prophetic aspect more explicitly below.

Gregg draws further important implications from *poieite*, the present-continuous plural imperative form of the root *poiein*. First, the tense

"introduces the keynote of *continuation* and *renewal* to the sacrament. It gives the opportunity to draw attention to the eucharist as the *ongo-*

---

[58] Here Metz's characterizations and criticisms of both the Protestant and the Catholic attitudes and approaches to the sacraments (the former distrustful of symbolic engagement with the gifts of creation, the latter ritualistically rigid and negligent of narrative) begin to receive a corrective response. See the section of Chapter 2 entitled "Mysticism III: Symbols and Sacramental Ritual," pp. 57–62.

[59] Gregg, *Anamnesis in the Eucharist*, 15.

ing sacrament of the New Covenant, for which baptism is the initiatory sacrament. It therefore invites analogy with the Sabbath observance of the Old Covenant which stood in similar relationship to circumcision."[60]

This recovery of *covenant* as the fundamental reality constituting the life of faith and demanding ongoing decisions and commitments to praxis is essential to the Church's eucharistic renewal. The covenant, moreover, is a corporate reality whereby God establishes and maintains a people for service to God, to one another, and to the world. Hence the plural tense, *poieite*. This corporate, communal sense of the command corresponds to Paul's teaching in the previous chapter—"we who are many are one body, for we all partake of the same loaf" (10:17)—and to his introduction of the problem that occasions his recounting of the Lord's Supper here in the eleventh: "when you assemble as a church, I hear that there are divisions among you" (11:18).

Both the corporate and temporal aspects of the sacrament are further conveyed in the qualifying phrase *"hosakis ean pinete."* Gregg considers the clause to be the answer to the questions that naturally arise from the continuous imperative just given: When, on what occasion, and how often shall we perform this action? Gregg reports that amidst the debates about the apparently fluctuating practices of Jewish festive meals prior to 70 C.E., scholarly consensus has been reached in recognizing a common practice of observing "a weekly communal festive meal, at the start of the Sabbath, at which the Cup of the Berakha (Blessing), the symbol of the Covenant fellowship, was drunk."[61] Judging that the Passover Seder fit the pattern of these festive meals, the deduction follows that Jesus attached the Anamnesis rubric to the Cup of Blessing and, by means of the further qualifier under consideration, "ensured that the Sacrament he was instituting would be repeated at each communal festive weekly meal of the fellowship of his disciples."[62] With controversies and disparities among

---

[60] Ibid. See also Thoma, "Memorial of Salvation," 51–2.

[61] Gregg, *Anamnesis in the Eucharist,* 16. Gregg, following in the line of such scholars as G. Dix, G. J. Bahr, and G. Dalman (and I would add L. Bouyer), refers to the cup ritual for Passover as disclosed in the Talmud and Mishnah.

[62] Ibid. In his thorough "synchronic reading" of the four New Testament accounts of the Supper, Xavier Léon-Dufour establishes the temporal and ecclesial dimensions of the Lord's command to perform the meal ritual from a

the eucharistic practices of various churches in mind, Gregg argues that Jesus' attachment of the rubric to the Cup of Blessing provides the "essential hermeneutical clue" to the time-factor (weekly celebration) and the communal, covenantal (not private devotional) nature of the Eucharist.

These findings agree with Schmemann's work on the Lord's Day as the eighth day that celebrates the renewal of creation and covenant. The celebration enables the Church to realize its nature as a communal and social reality in service to the mission of the kingdom of God. The unique value and importance of the eucharistic ritual among the Church's ways of commemorating Christ lies in its singular ability to continue and renew the covenant which God shares with the body of Christ, the community Jesus establishes in the power of the Spirit.

The meaning and purpose of commemoration, Gregg explains, finds its focus in the subsequent phrase "*eis . . . anamnesin.*" The Hebrew root that corresponds to the Greek term *anamnesin* without doubt is *zkr*, "remember." Since the Greek term is a nominal form, Gregg turns to the Septuagint and finds in various places a total of four Hebrew nouns translated as *anamnesis*. Gregg examines all four and finds the most general, *zikkaron*, to be "the most obvious original for *anamnesis* in our rubric."[63] The term designates "something" which directs attention to a prior reality, of which the *zikkaron* itself is a derivative. The "something" may be a cultic object, a cultic act (a festive

---

different perspective—that of the disciples at the meal. Léon-Dufour notes the silence of the disciples in the accounts, a silence that contrasts with the manner in which they usually react to Jesus' miracles or respond to instructions which he gives them. The absence of that pattern of explicit response on the part of the disciples, Léon-Dufour argues, distinguishes the Supper narratives from other gospel accounts of Jesus' instruction to his followers. The silence of the disciples implies their carrying out of the Lord's instruction and leaves open the role of all subsequent disciples, who faithfully respond in kind. The Supper account is not limited to the setting of Jesus' meal with those particular disciples on the eve of his death but, rather, its setting is every celebration of the Supper that follows. Jesus' commands are valid now and always. The narrative describes both an episode in Jesus' life but also the festive meal of the community that continues until he comes in glory (cf. 1 Cor 11:26). See Xavier Léon-Dufour, *Sharing the Eucharistic Bread: The Witness of the New Testament,* trans. Matthew J. O'Connell (New York: Paulist Press, 1987) 65–6.

[63] Gregg, *Anamnesis in the Eucharist,* 20.

meal, blowing horns), or a written record (preserving lists of names, facts, words spoken). Comparison with the Septuagint, two specific passages in the book of Sirach, and Hebrew writings most contemporaneous with the New Testament all point toward *zikkaron* as a cultic act. Gregg takes special note of a passage in the Passover Haggadah to which M. Thurian and many other liturgical scholars have given much weight. At the point when the Cup of the Berakha is being blessed, God is asked to hear and accept the "remembrance" of the patriarchs, the Messiah, Jerusalem, the people, and thus to be gracious and merciful to all of these. In the Hebrew text the word *zikkaron* occurs at each remembrance, providing

"strong evidence that, in Mishnaic Hebrew, and in the context of the Passover Meal, and at a most suggestive point, the word *zikkaron* indicated a commemorative cultic *act*—because the passage seems to be summarizing all that has gone before it throughout the Seder service, which whole service is itself the distinctive commemorative act for the due observance of the Festival day."[64]

Finally, Gregg reasons that the intention of repetition implied in both Jesus' command and in the annual celebration of the Passover cannot be realized by a cultic object or written record. Only a cultic action is repeatable. He thus concludes that the Hebrew original for *anamnesin* in the rubric of the Lord's Supper is *zikkaron*, in the sense of a cultic act.

Thus far, Gregg's investigation of the Anamnesis rubric has yielded a sense of continuity and repeatability with regard to the practice of celebrating the ritual meal of the Lord's Supper. This is evidenced in the continuous-present tense of the command (*poieite*) and, as we have just seen, in the "cultic action" meaning of the Hebrew *zikkaron*. When Gregg, however, momentarily changes his method by reversing the study's pattern of moving *from* the Greek terms *to* the Jewish roots, the result is an awareness of how the eucharistic celebration causes an interruption in the regular course of people's time. I approach Gregg's

---

[64] Ibid., 22. Study of numerous early Christian Eucharistic Prayers, especially Eastern ones, reveals in many of them a similar pattern, in which the anamnesis formula serves as both a reprise or summary of all that has been recalled in "blessing" to the Father (reaching a climax in the narrative of the supper on the eve of Jesus' death), and a transition into the supplicatory part of the prayer.

argument having in mind the dialogue and debate I discovered between Metz and Schmemann over the question of how an element of interruption is essential to practice of Christian faith.

Having posited *zikkaron* as the type of ritual action (more specifically in the form of the festive meal) that comprises the Jewish context of Jesus' words and actions at the Last Supper, Gregg asks why the New Testament renders *lezikkaron* as *eis . . . anamnesin*, rather than *eis . . . mnemosunon*. The latter is the far more common translation for *zikkaron* in the Septuagint. Disagreeing with Thurian and others, Gregg argues that these two Greek referents for memory are not interchangeable. He first notes that in Sirach and the New Testament the uses of *mnemosunon* correspond more closely to the three other nominal forms of *zkr* (whose treatment I have foregone). The key is that the referents of those other Jewish nouns, as well as the Greek term *mnemosunon*, designate "a certain intrinsic continuing, abiding permanency about them, unless and until they are deliberately destroyed or consumed or blotted out."[65] *Anamnesis*, on the other hand, tends to designate something that is momentary or discontinuous. Philo makes this exact distinction in his discussion of the two terms. Moreover, occurrences of the root *anamneskein* in the New Testament entail the recollection of things forgotten, whereas the uses of *mimneskomai* depict the continual keeping of something in mind. Gregg correlates this quality of "*ad hoc* recollection" in the term *anamnesis* with W. D. Davies' observation of the differences in first-century Judaism between (1) the *perpetual* presence of YHWH in the Temple and (2) the festivals (especially Passover), whereby the people became "connected" with God's *interventions* at certain moments in Israel's history. Gregg concludes: "There is a distinctive sense of *renewal*, of remembering *again*, about *eis . . . anamnesin*, which made it far more appropriate to use to render *lezikkaron*."[66]

The discontinuous and intervening character which Gregg recognizes in the ritual concept of *anamnesis* invites a comparison with the function of temporal interruption in the theologies of Metz and Schmemann. Despite significant differences in their theologies, both insist that the content of Christian faith demands that its practice include an interruption in the regular flow of time. Metz explicitly in-

[65] Ibid., 23.
[66] Ibid.

troduces the concept of interruption in relation to apocalypticism. The images or stories of future catastrophe disrupt complacency or rationalizations about the present state of things, and thereby goad action. Interruption, however, also readily characterizes the function of dangerous memories in the face of the evolutionary world view, with the *memoria passionis Jesu* grounding both trust in God's faithfulness and the hope that the victims shall yet be raised up by God.

Christian faith, then, is experienced in interruptive practices that draw on memory and expectation. Such, however, is what Gregg is arguing about the function of *anamnesis* in the ritual meal of the Eucharist. In their weekly gathering Christians keep the remembrance of God's greatest intervention in the history of salvation, Christ's death and resurrection. They break for a moment in which to realize and share the remembrance of Jesus and the promise of life even for the dead. Schmemann introduces the concept of the eighth day, a concept from Jewish apocalypticism, now the Day of the Resurrection, when the faithful break from the perceived reality of this fallen world and experience the vision of what God will yet bring about in the redeemed creation. The liturgy is, nonetheless, grounded in the memory, the commemoration of Christ. For Schmemann, the liturgy is anamnetic in the very sense which Gregg describes—a moment of renewal, a remembering once again which enables and compels the life of faith in the volatile flow of the world's time.

The discussion of the eucharistic celebration in terms of an intervening moment, an interruption in time, might come as a challenge to Roman Catholics, for whom theological and pious reflection on the sacrament has long been dominated by a narrowly focused notion of real presence. If that is the case, then one of my purposes in writing will have been met. Just as Metz has developed his political theology for the purpose of critiquing society and Church and arguing for a new perspective on the praxis of faith, so the promotion and renewal of the liturgy cannot be realized without a degree of humble openness to the change in perspective that genuine reform requires. On the other hand, reform is for the purpose of continuing a valued tradition. The belief in and experience of God's presence in the Eucharist is not an inheritance to be squandered. Herein, however, lies the great value of the work of such theologians as Schmemann and Schillebeeckx in their efforts to recover for their respective churches the sense in which the eucharistic celebration is an *encounter* with the saving presence of God, manifested in Christ through the power of the Holy Spirit. It is the unique divine-human encounter in the liturgy that discloses the reality of God's creative and redemptive activity in the world. This, in turn, reveals humanity's vocation as the worship of God through just and loving praxis in the world.

As we have seen, Childs' study of the Jewish concept of commemoration (zikkaron) has provided Christian theologians with invaluable insight into the character and dynamics of the divine-human encounter that occurs in the performance of the festive meal. It is primarily to Childs' work (along with some reference to the earlier contribution of J. Pedersen)[67] that Gregg turns to explain the significance of the root zkr, the Jewish source for eucharistic concept of anamnesis.

Gregg begins with an observation that corroborates Dahl's assessment of the philosophical problem that the theological study of memory currently faces:

"When modern western man [sic] talks about 'memory' or 'remembrance' he does so in a framework of thought vastly different from that of the ancient Semite or Homeric Greek. Because he is heir to a philosophical framework in the dichotomous tradition of Plato, Aristotle and Posidonious, sharply differentiating between 'matter' on the one hand and 'spirit' on the other, he is inclined to equate the words solely with *mental recollection*."[68]

The Semitic world view, on the other hand, conceives reality as a single, unified whole. The exercise of zkr revitalizes this totality. In the case of the human being (here Gregg follows Pedersen), the totality of the person is conceptualized as the soul (one wonders whether one could substitute the term subject). When a person remembers she or he is not merely recalling an objective event; rather, the person is calling forth an image which assists him or her in determining a direction for action. Moreover, God is the all-pervading "soul" in this total reality and, thus, any act of zkr involves both God and people. For both, remembrance is never done in a vacuum; rather, every commemorative act entails "dynamic consequences, as both God and man [sic] grasp the whole and act accordingly. . . . There is always a volitional

[67] See Johannes Pedersen, *Israel, Its Life and Culture* (Oxford: Oxford University Press, 1926, 1940).

[68] Gregg, *Anamnesis in the Eucharist*, 24.

implication, a 'remember-and-do-something-as-a-result.'"[69] As has already been done earlier in this chapter, Gregg summarizes Childs' explanation of how the *zikkaron* stirs the memories of both God and the people, eliciting action on the part of both. In the commemorations of Israel's deliverance and the establishment of the covenant the people enter into a lively awareness or knowledge of their reality in the presence of God, of their participation in God's plan for history and its implications for their own lives.[70] Gregg notes that the significant function of commemoration for the vitality of the Jewish Covenant demonstrates the compatibility of the ritual practice of *zikkaron* with the perpetuation of the New Covenant in Christ's blood.

The gap between past events in history and the present, Gregg duly continues, constitutes the thorniest problem in our effort to understand and appropriate the Jewish tradition of commemoration. Childs' explanation, as we have seen, is in terms of how the cultic act (*zikkaron*) "actualizes" the past event for those who enter into the decision that the narrative performance demands. Gregg summarizes this principle of actualization as a narrative and ritual performance whereby the participants are *as if there*, that is, present to the salvific event. This means that the past event is neither brought forward to the present, as in the sacred drama of a myth, nor is the historical event so static by nature as to be only capable of eliciting mere recollection. Rather, a "real event" occurs in the commemorative celebration, in its present contextual import, whereby a redemptive event of the past enables a "genuine encounter" in the present.

[69] Ibid.

[70] Edward Kilmartin, strongly influenced by the work of Cesare Giraudo and Hans Bernard Meyer, provides a supportive summary on this point:

"The commemorative feasts of the Jewish tradition are not understood to contain the historical saving events which are commemorated, but rather, are considered to be the media by which the participants of the feasts are, as it were, presented to the foundation event that is commemorated. The return consists in the sharing of the blessings analogous to those imparted in the historical event. Thus the strict theological application of the biblical notion of *anamnesis* supports only the idea that the Christian liturgical assembly is, in some sense, represented to the foundation event of the death and resurrection and, as a consequence, enabled by faith to participate in its salutary effects."

Edward J. Kilmartin, *The Eucharist in the West: History and Theology*, ed. Robert J. Daly (Collegeville: The Liturgical Press, 1998) 367.

Gregg concludes that Childs' explanation of actualization in the Jewish tradition of memory provides Christianity with a suitable and profitable way of understanding *anamnesis* in the Eucharist. Gregg thereby arrives at the following summary for the meaning of Jesus' rubric in the Supper narrative: *"Take, give thanks, break the bread and say the interpretative words, at each weekly festive communal meal, as the commemorative act in which you initiate a genuine encounter in the present by means of a moment of redemptive time from the past."*[71] The one notable problem with Gregg's summary is that the concept of "genuine encounter" takes no object. Participants do not encounter the past event itself, for that is an impossibility. The genuine encounter is "in the present." I raise the issue because Gregg seems hesitant to say that the participants encounter God, that the act of remembrance on the parts of both God and the people brings about a real meeting and exchange between them. In other words, on the basis of the covenant, God has promised to be present to the people when they perform their ritual act of remembrance; otherwise, what could "genuine encounter" mean? Likewise, Jesus' words over the bread and cup, along with his command for his followers to perform this ritual, constitute a promise of presence to them, in the mutual act of divine and human remembrance. These reflections, in any event, point toward the last phrase of the rubric. Gregg's treatment will invite a more extensive commentary by Léon-Dufour.[72]

The prepositional phrase *ten emen* (of me), Gregg observes, is what distinguishes the commemorative act commanded at the Last Supper as the *zikkaron* of the New Covenant. That the phrase grounds the eucharistic commemoration of Jesus in the specific historical event of his death, Gregg argues, is manifestly evident. The context is clearly a

---

[71] Gregg, *Anamnesis in the Eucharist*, 25.

[72] Concerning the reflections I have offered in this present paragraph, especially the relationship between Jewish remembrance of the covenant and encounter with the presence of God, see Léon-Dufour, *Sharing the Eucharistic Bread*, 104–7. Hans Bernard Meyer asserts the biblical notion of the mutual presence of God and the people through the liturgical act of remembrance: "Gedächtnis ist eine Grundkategorie biblischen Gottesdienstverständnisses . . . . . Indem Gott und sein Volk einander gedenken, vergegenwärtigen sie sich einander, geben sich Anteil aneinander." *Eucharistie: Geschichte, Theologie, Pastoral*, Gottesdienst der Kirche: Handbuch der Liturgiewissenschaft 4 (Regensburg: Friedrich Pustet, 1989) 448.

covenantal one, in which Jesus has, in his interpretive words over the bread and cup, linked the cultic meal to his impending death, "just as the Passover commemorates the slain lambs and their redeeming blood."[73] In addition, Paul provides in the subsequent verse of his letter the commentary that as often as believers eat the bread and drink the cup they proclaim the *death* of the Lord until he comes. Early writers such as Justin and Melito of Sardis testify to this interpretation of the Lord's Supper as a commemoration of the Lord's death, as do a wide range of contemporary scholars.

In light of that evidence, Gregg is sharply critical of the way in which "modern liturgiology" takes what he judges to be the unwarranted and misleading liberty of understanding the referent of the eucharistic meal to be not only Jesus' death but also his resurrection and, in various cases, his ascension and other events. Gregg has in mind the anamnesis formulas of the new Eucharistic Prayers of various churches, as well as the writings of liturgical theologians, all of whom he faults due to "the fact that one is unable to elicit any serious attempt at a biblically-based theological rationale for any diffusing of [the anamnesis'] focus at all."[74] Gregg does not state sufficiently for this reader the reason why such a diffusion is a problem, that is, what theological and pastoral issues are at stake. In light of our study of Metz one wonders if the problem, in part, might not have to do with a suspicion that modern, bourgeois religiosity exhibits the faulty tendency of wanting to ignore the memory of suffering and death, as well as Christian ritual's anchoring in historical events. The tendency of some Christians to downplay, ignore, or even deny the death of Jesus has existed from the Church's origins, as is evident in the way Paul perceived and confronted the problems in Corinth and, in subsequent generations, various "Gnostic" groups produced stories of how the dead body on the cross was not really that of Jesus (he having somehow escaped).

As for the Eucharistic Prayers that began to appear at that time and in the next few centuries, Gregg oddly chooses to ignore them. Beginning with the text of Hippolytus we see an anamnesis formula remembering Jesus' death and resurrection, with later texts expanding the list of events. Even if we stay with the New Testament text, Gregg

---

[73] Gregg, *Anamnesis in the Eucharist*, 26.
[74] Ibid.

has clearly thrown down the gauntlet (as it were). Scripture scholar Léon-Dufour has taken up the challenge in a way that not only answers Gregg's complaint but also sheds important light on the implications of the Anamnesis rubric for the theology and practice of the Eucharist, especially as it nurtures the Christian way of life.

Time of the Church: Christ's Presence in Remembrance

Like Gregg, Léon-Dufour recognizes the content of the dominical command "Do this in remembrance of me" as primarily and fundamentally linked with the death of Jesus. Unlike Gregg, however, Léon-Dufour is not worried about the *diffusion* of that focus into a list of other events that surrounded the death; rather, he is far more concerned that the *depth* of the meaning of Jesus' death, as communicated in the celebration of the Eucharist, be recognized and comprehended, shared and appropriated by the faithful.

The context is the Supper, the festive meal in which Jesus and his disciples commemorate God's faithfulness to the covenant of salvation and thereby renew their faithfulness to this saving God. The daring innovation which Jesus introduces is the identification of "the effective salvation of humankind with the fulfillment of his own destiny. God's fidelity is henceforth mediated by the fidelity of Jesus and specifically by his death."[75] Léon-Dufour, however, is quick to point out that Jesus' instruction to his followers is not to perform the ritual meal "in memory of my death" but, rather, "in memory of me." The "me" summarizes Jesus' words over the bread and cup ("my body . . . my blood"); thus, it indicates that in the commemorative celebration of the Supper his followers' attention "is to be on the presence of a person."[76] Jesus establishes for his followers a new form of his presence that will not only sustain but be formative of them in the period of his absence after his death. Léon-Dufour's interpretation introduces the complex issues of (1) the "personal" character of the eucharistic encounter and (2) the tensive relationship between the presence and absence of Jesus experienced now, in the time of the Church. These points warrant closer consideration.

In his own interpretation of Jesus' command of anamnesis Léon-Dufour, like Gregg, recognizes significant parallels between the ritual

---

[75] Léon-Dufour, *Sharing the Eucharistic Bread*, 67.
[76] Ibid.

action of the Last Supper and that of the Jewish Passover. Whereas Gregg, however, surveys numerous biblical and other contemporary literary sources to establish the Semitic roots of the rubric, Léon-Dufour finds one passage in the Bible sufficiently compelling:

"The parallelism between [the anamnesis command] and the commandment of Passover remembrance shows clearly where it came from:

"This day shall serve you for a remembrance (lezik karôn). You shall celebrate it (Ex 12:14).

"Do this for a remembrance (eis anamnesin) of me (Luke/Paul).

"Eis anamnesin clearly corresponds, at least in its form, to the lezikkarôn of the ancient Passover."[77]

Léon-Dufour goes on to demonstrate, to a greater extent than Gregg, how the resemblance between the Lord's Supper and the Passover extends beyond these two sentences to the entire organization of the two accounts. Both accounts tell of how a salvific event of utmost importance is prefigured, on the night before its occurrence, in a sign ("leôt," in Exod 12:13). The sign is comprised of elements of food and nourishment in the context of a ritualized meal. The sign refers not only to the immediate future (the Exodus/Jesus' death) but also, by virtue of the command of repetition, to a distant future. In reflecting more carefully on this last point Léon-Dufour introduces the crucial issue of eschatology, which up to this point has been largely at the margins of this chapter.

The symbolic action has both a cultic and a prophetic character. On the eve of the actual historical event, it is prophetic of what will soon follow. For all subsequent generations who commemorate it, however, the ritual meal is also prophetic (forward looking) and not only cultic (a link with the past):

"It is noteworthy that the account repeated in cult is not of the saving event which is to be commemorated, but of its prefiguration. Is this because the sign, being originally prophetic, continues to be pregnant with the future? As a matter of fact, the deliverance of the ancestors, which is commemorated over and over again by the Passover meal,

---

[77] Ibid., 110.

ensures the eschatological deliverance of the children of Israel. In the case of Christians, Jesus' gift of himself, which is signified by the eucharistic sharing, ensures their own future 'passover' and the final banquet."[78]

When celebrated, therefore, the commemorative event is the means by which believers encounter and appropriate the meaning of God's decisive, salvific intervention in the past but also receive the "pledge of a definitive future fulfillment."[79] We shall return to this point in greater detail in the concluding chapter.

The crucial difference between the two parallel accounts and their ritual traditions is, of course, Jesus' establishment of the meal as a commemoration of himself. In his exegesis of the "me" in Jesus' command of remembrance, Léon-Dufour explicates why he puts such value on the sign as a commemoration of the "person" of Jesus. In so doing, he further shows how the command establishes the Christian framework of time.

What is remarkably new about the Last Supper in comparison to the Passover, Léon-Dufour explains, is that the event being remembered is now identified with a person. The meal is still a celebration of God's action, but the divine action is specifically "in the person of Jesus."[80] In his symbolic identification of the bread and wine with his body and his blood, Jesus is referring not only to the mystery of his death but also to his "person" in the "full sense" of the word: "the act includes by implication all that led Jesus to acceptance of the cross, namely, the mission which he continues to the end in fidelity to God

---

[78] Ibid., 111. For a briefer treatment of the New Testament pericopes of the Last Supper that agrees on numerous points with Léon-Dufour see Shäfer, "Eucharist: Memorial of the Death and Resurrection of Jesus," 60–3.

[79] Léon-Dufour, *Sharing the Eucharistic Bread,* 111. Léon-Dufour discusses elsewhere the explicitly eschatological element in each of the synoptic pericopes of the Last Supper: In Matt 26:29 and Mark 14:25, after the words over the cup, Jesus says he will not drink of it again with his disciples until he does so anew with them in the kingdom of his Father/God. Luke places the eschatological tone at the front of the institution narrative, where Jesus says that he will not eat "this Passover" with his disciples until it is fulfilled in the kingdom of God, nor will he drink "of the fruit of the vine until the reign of God comes" (14:16, 17). See ibid., 80, 200–1, and 71–2 (which I shall discuss below).

[80] Ibid., 112.

and human beings."[81] Moreover, in using the signs of the cultic meal whereby the Jewish people celebrated the covenant, Jesus signified that in his person and death all of YHWH's salvific interventions in history are fulfilled. "This 'me' is astonishingly comprehensive,"[82] furthermore, not only as the crown of all of God's great deeds that had occurred before, but also in Jesus' invitation to his disciples to eat and drink. Jesus gives them and all who follow the invitation to share in his very self, his life, his mission, and his destiny and, thus, to be assimilated and transformed by him. Here we find something of the mystery (mysticism) that makes the Eucharist the source and summit of the entire Christian life as a following or imitation of Christ. The invitation to imitation comes in the invitation to share at the Lord's table, to an intimate communion in the very person (body) of the crucified but risen Jesus encountered with joyous thanksgiving in the meal of the covenant (in his blood).

Jesus' gift to his disciples of a sharing (*koinonia*, communion, participation) in his life, mission, and destiny, in conjunction with his command to perform this cultic and prophetic action in remembrance

---

[81] Ibid. Léon-Dufour is able to make this identification of the bread and cup of wine with the "person" of Jesus on the basis of his presentation, earlier in the text, on the significance of these two ritual foods:

"In the biblical world bread is a food which no one can do without; it also stands metaphorically for food in general. Since it is that which sustains daily life it comes to human beings from the mighty Creator, who gives it to those who ask him for it. Especially in the context of the Passover, bread suggests the good will of Yahweh toward his special people and therefore his constant presence. Bread is meant to be shared, especially with the hungry; this sharing is the fundamental characteristic of the righteous. . . . In the account of the supper wine is called 'fruit of the vine'; like bread it is a gift from the Creator and one sign of the promised land's prosperity. Observe, however, that the word used in the eucharistic verses is not 'wine' but 'cup.' The choice of word doubtless depends on Jewish usage which distinguished various 'cups' in the course of a festive meal, but in the present context the word can also have harmonics of its own. Especially in the psalms 'cup' is associated with sacrifices of thanksgiving; as 'cup of salvation' that 'brims over,' it celebrates communion with the God of the covenant, with him who is himself said to be the 'cup' that is Israel's lot."

Ibid., 58–9.

[82] Ibid., 112.

of him, establishes the framework by which Christians are to understand time and their situation in history. In the supper account Léon-Dufour is able to distinguish three "successive periods" for the course of time:

"before the conclusion of the covenant in Jesus; between this and the reunion of Jesus and his disciples; and, last, the heavenly 'time' of God's reign. In this perspective, the heart of the account is the anamnesis or remembrance that dominates the intermediate period, the period of the sacramental meal."[83]

Believers live now in the time of the Church, the intermediate time of anamnesis and sacrament established for them "in the space that is opened up yet left empty by the Master's departure."[84] Anticipating his absence from them, Jesus provided his followers with a new form of presence for the indefinite period that would follow. This presence, Léon-Dufour argues, is one which cannot be forced upon them but, rather, comes to those who choose to remember him in their own action, at the table of communion and in their obedient decision to participate in the mystery of his life for the sake of the world. Christ's followers live the ongoing passage between the "night" of Jesus' suffering and death and the *new* "day" when he shall share with them the banquet in heaven. For the duration of this intermediate period the celebration of the Eucharist constitutes a "dynamic" remembrance of Jesus which "gives a forward thrust to the Church" by renewing "its contact with its Lord" and thereby empowering believers to live in their everyday lives "what Jesus himself experienced and lived on earth: the love of God that grounds love among human beings."[85]

Léon-Dufour concludes his discussion of the temporal dimension of the Last Supper accounts with a paragraph that contains deep resonances with key elements of both Metz's and Schmemann's writings:

"What Jesus does here, then, he does in anticipation: not only his 'dying' (which he anticipates in order to bring out its meaning and to express his free consent to it), but also the giving of his presence in symbols. Through the commemoration which the disciples will make

---

[83] Ibid., 72.
[84] Ibid., 61.
[85] Ibid., 116.

of him, this 'real' presence of Jesus will light up, from within, the night of the passion that lasts through the centuries in countless sufferings of human beings and their real 'dying.' The liturgical action will enable believers to express ever anew their confidence that love has conquered death."[86]

The obvious, most immediate affinity between Léon-Dufour's conclusion and Metz's political theology is the reference to the great numbers of suffering humanity. The affinity, however, runs much more deeply than the level of a general reference. As should be evident from my foregoing rehearsal of his text, Léon-Dufour does not make suffering—either the suffering of Jesus or of others—an abstraction. That he has the actual, historical suffering of victims in mind seems all the more evident in this concluding passage, in which he seems to play with quotation marks around the word "real." Intriguing is his decision to place those marks around the term when it modifies the presence of Christ in the Eucharist but not when it modifies the "dying" (i.e., the suffering and, so often, the actual deaths) of so many in history. I interpret this difference in accent as indicating that Christians' genuine perception (and thus, appropriation) of the reality of Christ's presence in the Eucharist depends upon their (practical) awareness of the reality of the suffering in their historical midst. The mutual dependence of believers' awareness of these two realities prevents the sacramental presence of Christ in the Eucharist from becoming an abstract, symbolic totality or, to put the tendency in Metz's own words, "the overworked . . . Christian identity that, at every opportunity, insists on the salvation that has already been given in Christ."[87]

With a painful, realistic awareness of suffering and death, however, also comes the genuine (and often urgent) need for hope and for confidence in the power of a divine love that is yet working out its purpose for the world. Léon-Dufour argues that the Church's eucharistic remembrance and anticipation of Jesus, whereby the covenantal relationship with God is actualized (becomes real) for its participants, illuminates *from within* the darkness of historical existence. This language of an illumination or a transformation occurring "from within" accords with the rhetoric of Schmemann's liturgical theology.

---

[86] Ibid., 72.
[87] Metz, *Faith in History and Society*, 179.

But what does this phrase "from within" mean in this context? The phrase is an honest acknowledgment that the world (creation and humanity) is not yet fully transformed by the redemption God has wrought in Christ. Christians perceive themselves now as continuously in the "passage" from death to life, for Jesus was in that passage on the night he gave them a share in his very life, his mission of kenotic service to humanity in faithful communion with God. The liturgy is the manifestation and proclamation of God's faithfulness and love to the kenotic servant Jesus, whom God has now raised up in glory. The kenotic life of the faithful is a praxis requiring struggle. Resources for the struggle are required. The fundamental resource is a gift, the experiential knowledge of God which comes in the practice of Christian mysticism, of which the eucharistic celebration is central. The performance of narrative and gesture, in the power of the Spirit of the crucified and risen Lord, creates the life-giving memory of God in the community of the faithful, who carry out the grace of that covenant in the world.

CONCLUSION: PROCLAMATION AND IMITATION

A vision for praxis in the world comes from the joy and confidence experienced in the liturgical remembrance of Jesus, who proclaimed and enacted a kingdom of God, which in this world and its history is ever a seed awaiting the full yield of its eschatological harvest. This is not to imply that joy and confidence are always and univocally the experience of each and every participant in the eucharistic action. The liturgy is, however, primarily the possession not of individuals but of the Church; it is fundamentally a communal entity. In commanding his followers to enact the gestures with bread and cup as a remembrance of him, Jesus gave what he commanded. Only if people perceive the command and the gift as given to the Church as his body now in the world (and not as the possession of individuals) is its power to transform able to be realized.

These last reflections return us to Paul's correspondence to the Corinthians. As Gregg pointed out, the imperative verb with which Jesus commands the performance of his commemoration is in the plural *(poieite)*. The corporate, communal nature of the command accords with Paul's theology of the Church as the body of Christ, whose many members are so mutually related that the condition of any one effects the condition of all. The failure of some in the Corinthian community to recognize the ecclesial reality of Christ's body and the mission of mutual service it entails occasions Paul's charging them with a fundamental misconception of what they do when they gather for the supper on the Lord's Day (11:20). Selfish feasting to the neglect of the poorer members of the community betrays a character inimical to that of Christ, whom they claim to commemorate in their performance of the Lord's Supper.

Scripture scholar Jerome Murphy-O'Connor argues that Paul's concern to correct the failure of those Christians in Corinth necessitated his adding his commentary to the account of the Last Supper: "For as often as you eat this bread and drink this cup, you proclaim the death of the Lord until he comes" (11:26). Concerning the word "proclaim," *kataggélete*, Murphy-O'Connor argues that analysis of the verb in various New Testament passages (1 Thess 1:8; Phil 2:14-16; 1 Cor 4:16-17; 11:1) disqualifies "any attempt to limit 'proclamation' to the purely verbal level."[88] The proclamation is of a definitive, completed event in history, but the act of proclaiming participates in the content and character of the message itself. Murphy-O'Connor describes this participatory quality of proclamation in existential terms:

"Paul was fully conscious of the importance of the existential affirmation that is manifested by quality of life, and this dimension would seem to fit the context here perfectly. The eating of the bread and the drinking of the cup are a statement, and what is 'said' is the death of Christ."[89]

Murphy-O'Connor proceeds to explain how the death of Jesus, in Paul's thought, is the consummate act of what was most characteristic of his life, a self-giving for others. The message or lesson of Jesus' life unto death is to be so fully assimilated by believers that the "dying" (*nekrosis*) of Jesus characterizes their own lives (see 2 Cor 4:8-11). Only with the "realism of Paul's approach" to the message and life of the gospel in mind can one understand what he means when he says that partaking of the eucharistic food is a proclamation of the Lord's death. "The attitude of those who eat and drink is essential to the proclamation, because if their imitation of Christ (11:1) is defective, then, as Paul expressly insists, 'it is not the Lord's Supper that you eat' (11:20)."[90]

---

[88] Jerome Murphy-O'Connor, "Eucharist and Community in First Corinthians," *Worship* 51 (January 1977) 61.

[89] Ibid.

[90] Ibid., 62.

Murphy-O'Connor thus returns us, at the close of this chapter on Christian memory, to the theme of *imitatio Christi*. It is Paul's exhortation to the Corinthians to imitate him as he imitates Christ that opens the chapter of the letter in which he recounts Jesus' words and gestures, as well as the command of anamnesis, at the Last Supper. The life of the apostle and, by implication, of all Christians must exude the character of Christ's love if the gospel is to be proclaimed effectively in the world. Paul is not hesitant to insist that the authenticity of the Church's eucharistic celebration depends on the existential attitude by which its members conduct their lives. The variety of practices—preaching, worship, prayer, and ethical action—whereby the Church keeps the memory of Jesus together comprise the praxis of faith whereby Christians know themselves as subjects in the presence of God. In the sacramental celebration of the Eucharist this memory and identity converge in the Church's most compelling moment of knowledge. The Church's ritual action reveals the love unto death that made Jesus' words at the Last Supper true so that this truth might be realized in the ethical actions of believers until Christ comes again in glory.

Chapter 5

Conclusion

PRACTICAL KNOWLEDGE BORNE BY
AN ANTICIPATORY MEMORY

The past several decades have witnessed a passionate concern for the reform and renewal of Christianity as a life of faith in which practices of prayer and worship are inextricably related to ethical and political practices in society. Our study has located this concern among: ecclesial leaders (the bishops of the Second Vatican Council); systematic, liturgical, and pastoral theologians (of *The Awakening Church* project); Johann Baptist Metz (the political theologian); Alexander Schmemann (the liturgical theologian); and Scripture scholars. Epistemological issues have pervaded the three central chapters. Analysts of Metz have generally approached his political theology as an exercise in epistemology, an exploration of the implications for Christian theology that Kantian philosophy set in motion. The rub of the question has focused on what Metz means by a practical fundamental theology.

My own interpretation of Metz is as follows: The *telos* of theology, its motivation and ultimate goal, cannot be a *system* of thought. The knowledge endemic to Christian faith is not that of a pure or abstract reason but, rather, of a practical following of Christ. As imitation of Christ, faith is itself a praxis, a purposeful way of life shaped by the definite content of narrative memories about Jesus and by narrative images of the final break in history when God shall bring about the full realization of the kingdom. Just as the narrative memory of Jesus is of his kenotic service in solidarity with the suffering even unto death, so the *imitatio Christi* is about a life lived with interest in the suffering of others, for which the apocalypse will be the definitive revelation of the God of Jesus as the God of the living and the dead. In the end will come the moment of judgment, an event at once consoling and catastrophic: catastrophic for all those whose interests lie in the continuation of the world as it is (an alleged limitless "progress" at the cost of others), and consoling for those who have faithfully pursued compassion for the suffering and justice for the oppressed.

While the latter's reward shall come in the final judgment, Christians' lives now are not, for all the pain that the absence of justice entails, simply lives of grim endurance and empty expectation. Rather, the life of imitation is a praxis in the presence of God. The practice of faith is a life lived in genuine hope of encountering something of God's boundless love and mercy *in* the very desire and effort to bring about that love and mercy where it is absent. For this reason Metz introduces the ethical concept of *virtues*. He specifically calls them *messianic* virtues, dispositions for action that are redemptive because they recover such genuinely human and, thus, religious capacities as sorrow, joy, friendship, mourning, expectation, playfulness, pain, and gratitude. The practice of these virtues, messianic in their imitation and expectation of Christ, is the experience of freedom. This constitutes the practical knowledge at the heart of Christian faith.

The life of messianic virtues, following in the memory of Christ and anticipating his return, has a fundamental need for narrative and symbol, word and sacrament, vision and prayer. Together, these practices of Christian tradition constitute the praxis of mysticism in Metz's theology. It is within these practices that Christians receive and develop a moral imagination that enables them to make a vital and original contribution in the social and political arena—the praxis of politics. For Metz, however, mysticism's role is not merely an instrumental one in relation to ethics and politics. Such instrumentalism is the "trap" of the evolutionary world view. Metz, on the contrary, also recognizes the value of mystical practices in themselves. Profound human freedom (so greatly inhibited in late-modern culture and society) is experienced when believers give themselves over to the narrative and symbolic world of the sacramental liturgy, as well as to a whole range of prayer, reading, contemplation, and divine adoration, in which language soars freely, the body opens up its senses, people join in communal bonds of fellowship, or individuals center on the depths of holiness in humanity, the cosmos and history. Metz perceives in the praxis of mysticism a retention or recovery of integral human capacities for knowledge that the instrumental rationality of technology and market have both denigrated to the "private" realm and depleted in the very subjects who might yet seek to realize them.

Mystical activity, however, is certainly not unrelated to the commerce of life in society, where so often believers experience the absence of compassion and justice as a "suffering unto God." Precisely for that reason their mystical practices of prayer, biblical proclamation, and bodily gestures include no small measure of lament, supplication, mourning, protest, yearning, and contrition. Thus is Metz able to summarize Christian life as a *praxis of mysticism and politics,* a genuine dialect between these two types of practices. The dialectic affirms the integrity and irreducible importance of each of these general types of human action, as well as their mutual impact upon each other.

The entire praxis of Christian life is also apocalyptically eschatological. In the realm of politics, belief in the parousia subverts the timelessness of the evolutionary world view and, thus, the rationalizations for injustice which it regularly fosters. In the realm of mysticism, apocalyptic belief and narratives provide both assurance to the beleaguered that Christ will come quickly and definitively, as well as the goading yet consoling awareness of the final judgment he will execute then. The story of judgment in Matthew 25 contains images of both consolation and catastrophe, of welcome and banishment resulting from people's ethical praxis in this world. Metz came to recognize an eschatological dialectic between symbols of crisis and consolation within the *present* praxis of mysticism as well. The whole range of mystical practices must include utterances, symbols, and ritual gestures of both joy and pain, praise and lament, in a mutually intensifying eschatological dialectic.

It was Metz's recognition and call for mysticism, including sacramental worship and liturgy, that initiated our turn to the work of one of this century's foremost liturgical theologians, Alexander Schmemann. I chose Schmemann because in his own work he explicitly argued for the practice of liturgy as a privileged form of knowing, indeed, the fundamental way in which believers know and appropriate the content of faith *(lex orandi statuat lex credendi).* In addition, like Metz, Schmemann recognized the essentially eschatological character of Christian faith and, thus, made the recovery of what he considered an apocalyptic eschatology integral to his theological project. Schmemann's *liturgical* approach to eschatology has both affinities and contrasts to the apocalypticism of Metz.

Focused on the recovery of the Jewish and early Christian apocalyptic notion of the "eighth day," Schmemann's eschatology entails an interruption of time, an interruption which manifests God's redemption of this fallen world through the mystery of Jesus' *pasch,* his passage through death into a life-conferring resurrection. Liturgical celebration of the Lord's Day is not a sacral religious practice that simply complements the rest of the week's profane activity or, in Metz's terms, merely satisfies contemporary people's needs for celebration and ritual. The apocalyptic eighth day, while breaking out of conventional time and behavior, nonetheless is integrally and paradoxically related to these. The divine and human realities revealed (and thus known) in the liturgy stand as judgment and inspiration in relation to Christians' understandings of and actions in the world. This eschatological knowledge is symbolically conveyed; the redemptive reality experienced in the liturgy is an indirect form of knowing in that the redeemed order it reveals is only known at present through the symbolic use of words, objects, and gestures. The assembly of believers themselves is a symbolic manifestation of the Church. All of this language of the symbolic, however, Schmemann argues, makes the content of faith conveyed in the liturgy no less real; rather, the liturgy, as the inspired action of the Spirit, raises its participants into an experiential knowledge of the love of a God whose glory is revealed in the salvation of humanity. Christians are to witness to this redemptive knowing in the world. This is the experience of faith. The contrast between the world manifested in the liturgy and this world which is passing away establishes, according to Schmemann, a fundamental antinomy or paradox in the Christian world view.

Schmemann provides an extensive, critical theological investigation of one tradition of the mysticism for which Metz calls, namely, the eucharistic liturgy celebrated on the Lord's Day. Perhaps the most dissonant aspect of Schmemann's work, nevertheless, when compared with that of Metz is the extent to which he asserts a realized eschatology within the eucharistic celebration—the liturgy as the very *parousia* into which the ecclesial assembly ascends. Schmemann's nuanced explanation for symbol as the conveyance of reality tends to get lost in numerous passages in which he revels in the actual ascension into the glorious heaven and earth that the liturgical action brings about. The liturgical experience of ascension engenders a paradox of such magnitude that it seems to hinder the translation and appropriation of its vision of the kingdom into, in his words, "a responsible service in this world," which is "pass[ing] away."[1]

Schmemann's notion of ascension, which he says would be "irresponsible" if not understood by way of the cross, must basically be respected as a viable (Russian Orthodox) interpretation of the concept

---

[1] Alexander Schmemann, *Introduction to Liturgical Theology,* trans. Asheleigh E. Moorhouse (Crestwood, N.Y.: St. Vladimir's Seminary Press, 1966, 1986) 74.

of liturgical anamnesis. As we saw in Chapter 4, biblical and liturgical scholars explain anamnesis in terms of an encounter with the reality of salvation which, although accomplished by God at a definite point in past history, is experienced anew through a commemorative action. The ritual performance of anamnesis is the celebration of a covenantal relationship between God and people. The commemoration strengthens the people's commitment to living the ethics of that covenant by remembering God's faithful actions in the past and renewing hope in the promises of the covenant's fulfillment in the *eschaton*. For Christians, the new covenant has been established in the body and blood of Jesus, his person and mission, given in freedom to the point of death. In the Eucharist Christians perform with praise and thanksgiving the remembrance of the crucified and risen Christ whom they encounter in liturgical word and gesture and, moreover, anticipate joining in the heavenly banquet. The anticipatory memory of Christ in the Eucharist nurtures their own lives now as his followers, who imitate him in kenotic service in the Church and to the world.

In his normative understanding of the Eucharist as a commemoration Schmemann places greatest emphasis on the aspect of real, genuine encounter with the risen Christ. In the end this emphasis, although certainly consistent with the eucharistic tradition, seems to result in an excessively realized eschatology within the liturgy. The liturgy is the "experience of *heaven on earth*,"[2] an icon of the new life "which is to challenge and renew the 'old life' in us and around us."[3] Schmemann's eschatology tends to lack the palpable quality of yearning and anticipation for the promised return of Christ, for the day when he will drink anew the fruit of the vine and share the Passover meal with his followers, not in sacramental signs but reclining with them at table in the kingdom of God (see Luke 22:15-18). By focusing so much on the reality in the symbols of the liturgy Schmemann gives insufficient attention to the function of narrative, to the ways in which the scriptural readings and preaching in the Liturgy of the Word and the recital of God's deeds and the Church's intercessions in the

[2] Alexander Schmemann, *The Eucharist: Sacrament of the Kingdom of God,* trans. Paul Kachur (Crestwood, N.Y.: St. Vladimir's Seminary Press, 1987) 220.

[3] Alexander Schmemann, "Liturgy and Theology," *Liturgy and Tradition: Theological Reflections of Alexander Schmemann,* ed. Thomas Fisch (Crestwood, N.Y.: St. Vladimir's Seminary Press, 1990) 52.

anaphora serve the definite purpose of remembering past events, as well as promised future ones. Only by virtue of narrative form can memory and anticipation acquire definite content and thereby have a (trans)formative impact upon life in the present. For just this purpose Metz called for a recovery of an integral role for narrative in the celebration of sacrament. In this concluding chapter we turn to one more liturgical scholar, Geoffrey Wainwright, whose study of early Christian worship recovers resources in ancient liturgical tradition that correct an overly-realized eschatology in the eucharistic liturgy precisely by means of narrative's role in the ritual.

ANAMNESIS AND ESCHATOLOGY

Anamnesis as Promise

In *Eucharist and Eschatology* Wainwright discusses the relationship between the presence of Christ in the Eucharist and his final coming precisely through an investigation of the notion of anamnesis. Wainwright cites in full the Pauline source, 1 Cor 11:23-26, noting how recent scholarship has focused predominantly on the meaning of the Eucharist as a *memorial* of Christ's death, especially as a solution to the ecumenical impasse over sacrifice. Wainwright's primary concern, however, is the relationship between the memorial or commemoration and Christ's "final advent," recognizable in the "mutual proximity" in the Pauline text of the two phrases, "in remembrance of me" and "until he comes."[4] Wainwright turns to Eucharistic Prayers of the first several centuries, noting that in some instances the text becomes a first-person statement by Jesus (you proclaim my death until I come). More common to most of the Eucharistic Prayers is a section which liturgiologists call the anamnesis (Gregg's "Anamnesis formula"), which picks up the institution narrative's theme of remembrance.

In the earliest known example of a formal anamnesis, found in Hippolytus' *Apostolic Tradition*, remembrance is of Christ's death and resurrection.[5] In later anaphoras the anamnesis sections include oth-

---

[4] Geoffrey Wainwright, *Eucharist and Eschatology* (New York: Oxford University Press, 1971, 1981) 61.

[5] For a recent survey (with references) of the problems scholars face concerning the dating, authorship, and content of this ancient text, see Maxwell E. Johnson, *The Rites of Christian Initiation: Their Evolution and Interpretation* (Collegeville: The Liturgical Press, 1999) 78–80.

ers or an entire series of events in Jesus' earthly life, death, and glorification. Some end with the mention of his Second Coming. Among
those that include the latter, Wainwright notes two features: First, several (e.g., the *Apostolic Tradition*, the anaphoras of Sts. James, Basil, John
Chrysostom) place the Second Coming "on the same continuous line
with the *past* events of Jesus' earthly life."[6] Later churches apparently
found the notion of *remembering* a *future* event untenable and inserted
a phrase such as "looking for" before the Second Coming. Second, in
several anaphoras, including some of the earliest, the mention of the
Second Coming is accompanied by a description of the final judgment
that will occur. Wainwright quotes in full a particularly stunning
anamnesis in a West Syrian anaphora, in which an extensive description of and reflection upon the judgment at the parousia invites comparison with Metz's theological agenda. Such comparison with Metz
also lies in Wainwright's effort to demonstrate at the origins of the eucharistic tradition a genuine sense of anticipation or expectation of the
second advent. Wainwright's main points about the anticipatory quality of the Eucharist, therefore, warrant closer attention.

Wainwright provides a rapid and insightful survey of the literature,
debates (sparked by the theories of Casel and Jeremias), and basic
principles which have shaped contemporary scholarship on liturgical
anamnesis or remembrance. Given our extensive treatment of the topic
in Chapter 4, that discussion need not detain us here. Wainwright
finds the key to understanding the future-oriented aspect of liturgical
commemoration in the recognition that in the Jewish tradition of
memorial both God and the people perform acts of remembrance.
Having recalled God's creative and redemptive deeds in the past, the
people call upon God to be gracious still. Their prayer of intercession,
especially at Passover, came to include an eschatological dimension,
the request that God remember the promise of the Messiah, of the fulfillment of God's kingdom. Indeed, they developed the expectation
that the Messiah would come in the Passover season.

With regard to the Christian Eucharist, Wainwright argues, while it
is fundamentally a memorial of Christ's sacrificial death, it nonetheless is a commemoration of the entire person and life-story of Jesus.[7]

---

[6] Wainwright, *Eucharist and Eschatology*, 62.

[7] Wainwright's point here invites recollection of Xavier Léon-Dufour's
treatment of the integral relationship between the meaning of Jesus' death

This is the reason why the anamnesis passages of so many of the classical anaphoras remember all of Christ's "saving dispensation" (to use a characteristic Eastern phrase), including his second advent. In the eucharistic sacrifice the assembly experiences anew the grace which Christ's definitive sacrifice on the cross wrought. Citing Theodore of Mopsuestia, Wainwright presses further: The salvation in Christ celebrated at present sacramentally is, nonetheless, the action of the self-same God who will accomplish its fulfillment in Christ's return. The eucharistic action is a promise, a pledge, an earnest of Christ's final coming, bearing resurrection for all the faithful.[8] In phrases resonant with our study of Xavier Léon-Dufour, Wainwright concludes:

"The eucharist is celebrated in the time of *hope* before the second coming of Christ, of which the first coming of Christ was a *promise*. The church recalls before the Father in thanksgiving the first coming of Christ and prays for the second coming of Christ in final fulfillment of that promise. And because the Blessed Trinity is Lord of time, the one Christ who came and who is to come can come even now at the eucharist in answer to the church's prayer, in partial fulfillment of the promise and therefore as its strengthening, even though the moment of the final coming remains a divine secret. At every eucharist the church is in fact praying that the parousia may take place at that very moment, and if the Father 'merely' sends His Son in the sacramental mode we have at least a taste of that future which God reserves for Himself to give one day."[9]

In order to substantiate his claim that the eucharistic commemoration of Christ's first coming entails the two-fold expectation of both Christ's sacramental advent in the celebration and his final advent, Wainwright argues that the "until he comes" at the end of 1 Cor 11:26 echoes the primitive Christian cry, *maranatha*.

---

and the meaning of his entire life. I turned to Léon-Dufour in order to move beyond Gregg's admittedly strict focus upon the "Anamnesis rubric" in 1 Corinthians 11 as a remembrance of Jesus' death. As we saw, the death is central, but grasp of its salvific import necessitates a broader anamnetic awareness of Jesus' life and mission.

[8] See Wainwright, *Eucharist and Eschatology*, 67, 89.
[9] Ibid., 67.

Maranatha!

The Aramaic phrase *"marána thá"* occurs in the closing sentences of First Corinthians at 16:22. Numerous Scripture scholars, Wainwright reports, suggest that this concluding passage itself "forms part of the properly eucharistic liturgy which Paul knew would follow the reading of his letter in the service of the word in the Corinthian congregation."[10] Appreciation of the liturgical interpretation of the Aramaic phrase, however, has received its strongest impetus from the nineteenth-century discovery and translation of the *Didache*. The expression *maranatha* occurs in *Didache* 10:6, a passage which H. Lietzmann convincingly argued is a liturgical dialogue between the president and people:

"*President:* Let grace come and this world pass away.

People: Hosanna to the Son of David.

President: If anyone is holy let him [*sic*] come.

If any is not, let him repent.

Maranatha.

People: Amen."[11]

Although scholars disagree over the placement the dialogue most likely took in the primitive Christian Eucharist (a discussion we must forego here), Wainwright concludes that the association of *maranatha* with earliest eucharistic practice has been sufficiently established.

As for the eschatological significance of *maranatha* in the Eucharist, Wainwright explains that the best clues are philological. In the Aramaic original (transliterated, of course, into Greek in the Christian documents) the letters comprising the phrase may be divided in two ways: *marana tha* or *maran atha*. In both cases the first word in the Greek transliteration of the Aramaic means "our Lord." If the second word is *tha*, then the meaning is clearly, "Our Lord, come!" If, however, it is *atha*, then the Greek may represent either another Aramaic imperative or the perfect. The patristic authors, who had lost the eucharistic context of the phrase, assumed the latter tense and interpreted

---

[10] Ibid., 69. Wainwright relies especially here on the work of G. Bornkamm, but he also cites works by J.A.T. Robinson, C.F.D. Moule, and K. G. Kuhn.

[11] Ibid., 68.

the phrase as a statement of belief in the incarnation. However, it is possible, Wainwright explains, to recognize here the Aramaic *"present perfect*, with the meaning 'Our Lord has come and is now here, is present,' and this could then be understood of the cultic presence of Christ."[12] Given the exclamation *erkou Kyrie Iesou* (Come, Lord Jesus) in Rev 22:20, *maranatha* was most likely originally an imperative. In the eucharistic assembly at Corinth, however, it could very well have been a prayer with a double implication, beseeching both the final parousia and the Lord's present coming in the mystery (word and symbolic gestures) of the Eucharist. The eucharistic liturgy is thus an encounter with Christ's presence which anticipates his Second Coming. Although the Aramaic phrase vanished from the liturgy, its trace persists, Wainwright argues, in the *Benedictus qui venit*, which follows the *Sanctus* in both the Western and Eastern liturgies. Wainwright concludes that the phrase "found its place in eucharistic liturgies for the good reason that it can suggest, in a usefully ambiguous way, the present coming of the one who has come and who is still to come."[13]

Urgent Expectation

Wainwright does not, however, suggest or discuss how the temporal ambiguity of the maranatha tradition in the Eucharist is indeed useful.[14] This point invites a dialogue with Metz. As we saw in Chap-

---

[12] Ibid., 70.

[13] Ibid., 71.

[14] Although Wainwright does not discuss at this point in his text the contemporary significance of the eschatology he has recovered from earlier sources, he does provide the following comment in the preface to the 1981 "American" edition of his book:

"The vigorous social and political concerns of the churches and of Christians pose, implicitly or explicitly, questions of eschatology, for it is the nature and realization of 'the kingdom' which is ultimately at stake in them; and, without indulging in cheap apocalypticism yet bearing in mind that the universalization of horizons is a characteristic of biblical apocalyptic, it is permitted to wonder whether, in our global epoch, things may be 'coming to a head' for the entire human race as has never happened before, except proleptically in the life, death and resurrection of Jesus Christ. Eucharist and eschatology are vital to Church and world, and much may depend on their proper linkage." Ibid., v.

ter 2, Metz identifies the expectant plea "Come, Lord Jesus!" (Rev 22:20) as the honest and inevitable desire which erupts from the hearts of Christians committed to following the kenotic Christ:

"Following Christ when understood radically, that is when grasped at the roots, is not livable—'if the time be not shortened' or, to put it another way, 'if the Lord does not come soon.' Without the expectation of the speedy coming of the Lord, following Christ cannot be lived; and without the hope of a shortening of the time it cannot be endured. Following Christ and looking forward to the second coming belong together like the two sides of a coin. His call to follow him and our plea, 'Come, Lord Jesus,' are inseparable. The testament of the early Church, which committed itself to the demands of the radical following of Christ, has a purpose in ending with the plea, 'Maranatha, come, Lord Jesus.'"[15]

For Metz, the purpose of imminent expectation of the parousia, belief in a definite end of time, prevents Christian faith (the praxis of imitating Christ) from succumbing to resignation and apathy. Metz asserts that the *maranatha* plea testifies to a life "based on absolute hope."[16] But how is this basis established? Where is the base located, as it were? Here again, Metz does not provide a specific answer. Certainly the reading of Scripture is crucial, for it is the means by which the apocalyptic element of Christian tradition is conveyed. What our study of the liturgical tradition of anamnesis has uncovered, however, is the way in which the definite content of both the Old and New Testaments is communally shared in the eucharistic action, in the combined and irreducible roles played by both narrative and symbolic gesture as the Church encounters Christ in his commemoration. Just as we found the anamnetic aspect of the Eucharist to be the crucial mystical praxis linking memory of Christ with the dangerous but redemptive demand of imitating him in service to the lowliest, so we find the same anamnetic

---

[15] Johann Baptist Metz, *Followers of Christ: The Religious Life and the Church,* trans. Thomas Linton (London/New York: Burns & Oates/Paulist Press, 1978) 75. In his later writing, Metz has come to interpretively paraphrase this cry as, "What is God waiting for?" See Johann Baptist Metz, *A Passion for God: The Mystical-Political Dimension of Christianity,* trans. J. Matthew Ashley (New York: Paulist Press, 1998) 58.

[16] Metz, *Followers of Christ,* 76.

tradition to be the bearer of a definite eschatological expectation. The Eucharist is the tradition within Christianity that affords a practical knowledge of the "anticipatory memory" Metz theoretically posits at the center of theology and, thus, the praxis of faith.

The Eucharist, nonetheless, only *affords* this possibility, this invaluable contribution, to the life of faith in the Church and for the world. The history of actual eucharistic theology (its practice and theory) demonstrates, of course, the extent to which both the genuine remembering and anticipatory aspects of anamnesis have been obscured in East as well as West. Schmemann, as we have seen, was adamant about the disastrous consequences of the loss of genuine commemoration and eschatology in the liturgies of all the churches: pieties and theologies that have strayed from the transformative content of the gospel. While Wainwright, like Schmemann, recognizes the traces of eschatology continuously borne by the liturgical texts in the East, he also notes the abandonment of eschatology in the Roman eucharistic liturgy from the medieval era onward. Not only did the anamnesis formula in the Eucharistic Prayer lack mention of the Second Coming and the ensuing judgment, but the Roman understanding of how the Eucharist remits sins differed from the East as well.[17] In the classical Eastern tradition, forgiveness is one of the fruits of communion—a sacramental participation and partial realization of the fullness of redemption Christ will bring at the *eschaton*. The Roman view, on the other hand, shifted attention away from communion to offertory, the offering of a sacrifice of propitiation. Strictly linked to the memory of Calvary, the Roman view came to focus narrowly on the Mass as a representation of the sacrifice of the cross for the forgiveness of sins in the present moment.[18]

[17] See Wainwright, *Eucharist and Eschatology*, 84, 87–8.

[18] Wainwright focuses upon the Eastern notion of the eucharistic remittance of sins and does not elaborate upon the Roman position. I wish, however, to provide a word of clarification: When I characterize the Roman view of propitiation as oriented to the present moment, I have in mind the extent to which—by the Middle Ages—the offering of Mass was linked to the remittance of the sins of people who were already dead. By the thirteenth century belief in the doctrine of purgatory was not only popularly held but systematically elaborated by theologians in the universities. The Council of Trent taught that the souls in purgatory are aided by the prayers of the Church, especially by the sacrifice of the Mass. Hence the Roman Church's association of the forgiveness borne of the Eucharist with the present situation of an

Given the almost total lack of eschatological awareness that has been characteristic in the Roman practice and theology of the Eucharist, one can appreciate Metz's limited recourse to the Eucharist as a traditional resource for the recovery of an apocalyptic consciousness in the praxis of faith. As we saw in Chapter 2, Metz turned to the sacraments for their festive, symbolic, and narrative qualities, so that these might provide a redemptive alternative to the unimaginativeness, banality, lack of spontaneity, and alienation from creation and the body that pervade the bourgeois lifestyle and result from the evolutionary world view. Metz, however, seems to have difficulty bringing the joyously liberating potential of sacramental ritual together with his descriptions of prayer as both a passionate search for the loving God of Jesus and an urgent lament to God in the face of human suffering, catastrophe, and crisis. Schmemann's emphasis upon the joyous realization of the kingdom of heaven on earth in the eucharistic liturgy clearly provides support for much of what Metz seeks in sacramental practice. I am arguing, however, that we can expect more from the liturgy as the performative knowing and appropriation of the Christian faith in an "anticipatory memory" of both crisis and consolation.

Future Judgment, Present Transformation

Just as Metz has argued for the recovery of the dangerous, transformative potential of dogmatic formulae, so we might look for dangerous elements in the vast treasury of the Church's liturgical history and tradition. With specific regard to Metz's desire to recover and promote apocalyptic consciousness, Wainwright provides an informative presentation on the inclusion of the Second Coming and the final judgment in the anamnesis sections of classical Eastern anaphoras. The extent and manner of the apocalyptic element varied. The anaphora

---

individual (i.e., the poor soul awaiting release at this moment from purgatory). It is not difficult to recognize the dissonance of this particular doctrine with Metz's (as well as Schmemann's) concern that contemporary Northern Christians abandon an excessively individualistic notion of salvation for a more communal and eschatological approach to anthropology. In Metz's terms, an "anthropological revolution" is in order.

For a historical and theological analysis of the practice of Mass stipends, see Edward J. Kilmartin, *The Eucharist in the West: History and Theology*, ed. Robert J. Daly (Collegeville: The Liturgical Press, 1998) 205–37.

of St. James refers to Christ's "second glorious and dreadful *parousia* when he will come with glory to judge the quick and the dead, when he will reward every man [*sic*] according to his works," whereas the anaphora of St. Basil simply mentions Christ's "glorious and dreadful second coming."[19] The West Syrian liturgies attached even stronger importance to the final parousia, describing it at great length. Wainwright quotes the translation of one of these anamnesis formulas in full. The anamnesis in the anaphora of Severus of Antioch remembers Christ's "second appearance, glorious and full of dread," as follows:

". . . when Thou shalt sit upon Thy lofty and dreadful Throne, and around Thee shall stand thousands of Angels; and a stream of fire shall descend, and consume the wicked without mercy; and all men [*sic*] shall render an account of their works, having no need of accuser or advocate, but the very works which they have done shall be rehearsed, for their thoughts themselves shall accuse or acquit them. When fire shall test the work of every man [*sic*]; when there shall be no opportunity of excuse, even to the wise and learned, in that terrible time; when quaking and fear shall fall upon all reasonable creatures, and every mouth shall be stopped, and confusion shall seize the wicked and foolish; when a brother will not be an aid, and pity will not be of avail, nor will fathers be any protection; when vengeance without mercy will follow those who did not know mercy. In that day, turn not Thy face from us and despise not Thine heritage that it should be delivered to eternal torments. Let us not be heirs of darkness where is no ray of light, nor do Thou make us outcasts from Thy fellowship, O Lord; nor deny us and say to us, 'For I know you not'; place us not on Thy left hand, with those who saw Thee hungry and fed Thee not, sick and visited Thee not; but acknowledge us and number us in the company of those who have done Thy will. Therefore, Thy people and Thine heritage beseech Thee, and through Thee and with Thee, Thy Father."[20]

This lengthy description bears a striking resemblance to Metz's apocalyptic eschatology.[21] Both draw explicitly upon the final judgment nar-

---

[19] Wainwright, *Eucharist and Eschatology*, 63.
[20] Ibid., 63–4.
[21] See the section of Chapter 2 entitled "Mysticism I: Apocalyptic Eschatology."

rative in Matthew 25. Metz employs the narrative to assert that Christians' belief in the definite end of this world's history reveals the Gospel's demand for their *practical solidarity* with the suffering, "the necessity of active commitment to others, of 'the least of the brethren.'"[22] The West Syrian anaphora asserts the practical character of the faith when it describes the merciless vengeance that will be visited upon those "who did not know mercy." The mercy at the heart of the gospel which Christians receive, at the heart of the God whom they confess at baptism, at the heart of the Jesus whom they commemorate in the Eucharist, is only genuinely *known* by those who themselves *act* mercifully in history and society. The anaphora proclaims that unless one practices mercy, one does not know mercy. That, however, is to say that one does not know Christ, the very embodiment of God's mercy, no matter how much one might profess him at the Eucharist. Nor shall Christ know such a person at the parousia.

Reflection upon the mutual recognition of Christ and his followers returns our discussion to Paul's eucharistic teaching to the Corinthians: Those who eat and drink without "discerning the body" bring judgment upon themselves (1 Cor 11:29). The discernment of the body is multivalent. It entails an awareness and imitation of the person and mission of the Christ who is present in the eucharistic gifts, as well as an awareness of Christ's presence in each member of his body, the Church, especially in the poor and lowly.[23] Wainwright explains the lesson Paul intends:

"Even in the stern words of I Cor. 11:27-34 the fundamental optimism which is surely grounded in the Christian's baptismal incorporation into Christ breaks through: *present* judgement by the Lord (vv. 29-32a) is a gracious chastisement ([*paideuometha*], v. 32a), whose

[22] Metz, *Followers of Christ*, 79.

[23] Jerome Murphy-O'Connor explores what he calls the "community interpretation" of Paul's reference to the body that is to be discerned in the Eucharist. See Jerome Murphy-O'Connor, "Eucharist and Community in First Corinthians," *Worship* 51 (January 1977) 67–9. For a discussion of the multivalency of the body in relation to liturgy see Bruce T. Morrill, "Initial Consideration: Theory and Practice of the Body in Liturgy Today" and "The Many Bodies of Worship: Locating the Spirit's Work," *Bodies of Worship: Explorations in Theory and Practice*, ed. Bruce T. Morrill (Collegeville: The Liturgical Press, 1999) 1–37.

purpose is to (bring to repentance and so) save us from *final* condemnation (v. 32b)."[24]

Wainwright argues that the classical Eucharistic Prayers of the subsequent early centuries, in their petitions for the fruits of communion that follow upon the epicletic invocation of the Holy Spirit, demonstrate the same dual awareness of the present remittance of sin and hope for salvation at the final judgment. Such a "gracious chastisement" resonates with Metz's appropriation of Matthew 25 as a symbolic narrative that is at once both consoling and goading. Thus does the study of one aspect of the Eucharist's history offer a source from the liturgical tradition wherein anticipatory memory, narrative, and solidarity converge with practical, transformative implications for the contemporary believer.

The question still remains: How can this historical and scholarly knowledge about the eucharistic tradition be translated into some practical form for the Church at this point in history, in the context of late-modern society? Would it be reasonable, for example, to implement the inclusion of the West Syrian anaphora's extended anamnesis formula in the present performance of the Eucharistic Prayer? The length of the passage certainly poses a serious problem. Proclamation of such an anamnesis formula at the Lord's Table each Sunday would be susceptible to rushed recitation by presider and flagging attentiveness by assembly. On the other hand, a presider and assembly with some significant level of (Metzian) apocalyptic consciousness among them might find themselves engaged with this text. Perhaps it could be part of a particular Eucharistic Prayer that would be used only occasionally, on certain Sundays or seasons. For example, the scriptural readings for the Liturgy of the Word in the last few weeks of the liturgical year in both the Roman and several Protestant churches are eschatological, even apocalyptic, in theme and content.

On a more general note, the crucial lesson to be drawn from our brief study of this one aspect of the classical Eastern anaphoras is the possibility and value of including a stronger eschatological element in contemporary Eucharistic Prayers. This comment invites a study of the Eucharistic Prayers in the sacramentaries or ordos of the various churches, but such an analysis is beyond the scope of this book. As a general statement I would advocate that there be in the epiclesis-

[24] Wainwright, *Eucharist and Eschatology*, 83.

intercession movements of the prayers a strong measure of the language and images of the taste, pledge, or promise of the fulfillment of God's reign, the heavenly banquet, the peaceable kingdom. Engagement in the language-event of such imagery could heighten the sense of imperative (and hope) for engaging in the praxis of gospel faith (kenotic service) in the world. This proposal, of course, rings of Schmemann's own argument for the impact which a genuine participation in the Liturgy of the Lord's Day can achieve. And we have seen something of the difficulties or limits to his argument. Some inclusion of the images of a definite end and final judgment of this world and its history are needed to bring a dialectical sting to the assembly's great prayer of thanksgiving and intercession, as well. This, of course, rings of Metz's practical theological agenda.

The difficulty obviously lies in the effort to move from these *ideas* about apocalypticism to liturgical *practices* for today's Church that can effectively proclaim the symbols and messages, both consoling and goading, of the *eschaton*. Reflection on this particular problem in the theory and practice of the liturgy will draw this study to its conclusion. The theological issues for eucharistic worship raised here are offered as an invitation to further constructive thought about the theological implications—both theoretical and practical, both liturgical and ethical/political—of the scholarly and traditional sources we have marshaled in this study.

THEOLOGICAL IMPLICATIONS IN LITURGICAL PRACTICE

I begin these reflections with the Eucharistic Prayer or anaphora. Our study of liturgical anamnesis has focused on (1) the Supper narrative, which contains the dominical command to perform the commemoration, and (2) the ensuing anamnesis formula, with its statement that the assembled community is remembering Christ's death and resurrection and, therefore, offering the four-fold eucharistic action. To expand our discussion to the entire Eucharistic Prayer is to enter into a vast and complex topic which, as mentioned in Chapter 4, has been the subject of extensive research and debate among scholars of the liturgy. Even a basic survey of the issues is beyond the scope of this concluding section of our study.[25]

---

[25] For a summary of the basic structure of the Eucharistic Prayer, along with concise discussion of crucial issues related to its structure and parts, see

Our concern is with the basic shape of the Eucharistic Prayer and the purpose of its performance. These are summarized in the anamnesis section of the prayer: The remembrance of God's great and merciful deeds of creation and redemption, which reached their climax in the mission, death, and resurrection of Jesus, is the cause for offering to God the sacrifice of praise and thanksgiving in the covenantal meal. This summary reflects our basic study of Jewish and early Christian forms of remembrance and commemoration, wherein we found that the blessing of God or naming of Jesus in prayer or proclamation entailed a recital of at least some of the mighty deeds of God and (for Christians) the actions whereby Jesus was established as Messiah and Lord. When Christians perform remembrances of Jesus they do so with the desire of knowing Christ more deeply and thereby being empowered to imitate him in word and deed. In the case of the Eucharistic Prayer, the remembrance of Jesus leads into the petition for the Holy Spirit to sanctify both the gifts and the community. This, in turn, elicits further intercessions for the salvation of various members of the Church and, ultimately, the whole world. Thus, within the offering of the anaphora itself the community undertakes its vocation of service to the world in the image of Christ; it intercedes for the living and the dead and concludes by raising all up to God in doxological acclamation.

In the narrative performance of the Eucharistic Prayer we can discern the eschatological dialectic, the dialectic between the symbols of danger and crisis and the symbols of promise and consolation, that Metz has argued is essential to the praxis of faith. The dialectic of crisis and consolation is evident in all three temporal periods which the anamnetic character of the entire prayer articulates for its participants. The Eucharistic Prayer's remembrance of the past centers on the person of Jesus, but precisely in the dangerous, catastrophic memory of his death. The painful crisis of Jesus' abandonment and execution is

---

Edward J. Kilmartin, "The Catholic Tradition of Eucharistic Theology: Towards the Third Millennium," *Theological Studies* 55 (September 1994) 443–57. For a comprehensive historical and theological study of the major liturgical "families," as well as learned discussion of pastoral and theological issues in the present celebration of the liturgy, see Hans Bernhard Meyer, *Eucharistie: Geschichte, Theologie, Pastoral,* Gottesdienst der Kirche: Handbuch der Liturgiewissenschaft 4 (Regensburg: Friedrich Pustet, 1989).

the key to understanding the depth of his love for God and humanity, demonstrated in kenotic service and vindicated in his resurrection. The crisis of his death is, nonetheless, remembered in the consoling narrative and symbols of the supper he shared with his disciples—an intimate experience of covenant and an encouraging promise of presence in the sacramental meal and, ultimately, the heavenly banquet. The Church's remembrance of the past reaches further back in the history of salvation in the various forms of its prefaces and opening sections. Here again, while the tone of the prayer is one of joyous, thankful remembrance, nevertheless, mention is made in some way of humanity's plight or lack of faithfulness and God's interventions through crucial events and people, especially the Hebrew prophets.

When the assembled Church remembers with God the promises of the *future*, both in the anamnesis and intercessory sections of the anaphora, it should do so not only with the consoling images of the kingdom but also some traces of an apocalyptic sting. As we have seen, the Western medieval prayers and especially the Roman canon failed to associate the eucharistic anamnesis with Christ's Second Coming and the final judgment. In its liturgical reform the Roman Church has had to look to sources from the early classical period for models of (1) anamnesis formulas that mention anticipation of Christ's return and (2) intercessions which express more explicitly the expectation of a communal sharing in the kingdom and its banquet. The second Eucharistic Prayer for Masses of Reconciliation is especially notable in this regard. In its anamnesis section it describes the Eucharist as "this pledge of [Christ's] love," and it concludes its petitioning with the words, "In that new world where the fullness of your peace will be revealed, gather people of every race, language, and way of life to share in the one eternal banquet with Jesus Christ the Lord." None of the Eucharistic Prayers in the present Roman sacramentary, however, incorporate from the Eastern anaphoras the language and images of the dreadful aspect of Christ's glorious Second Coming; language or description of the final judgment is absent. Among the various Eucharistic Prayers, nevertheless, the petitions in remembrance of those who have died do ask God to be merciful. This request for mercy is extended to the living, who are gathered around the Lord's Table and who hope to join the saints in the kingdom of God. To be true to the dialectical character of Christian eschatology, however, these petitions need some stinging images of the apocalypse as well. The sting is needed to occasion a present moment of judgment in the participants, the possibility of a gracious chastisement (to borrow Wainwright's phrase) for those who, not unlike some in the Pauline community at Corinth, might hear a call in the prayer to discern anew their own lives as the *imitatio Christi*.

Our discussion of the intercessions has already introduced the focus upon the present time which occurs within the Eucharistic Prayer as well. Intercession is made that God might mercifully bring those now living finally into the heavenly kingdom, in the company of Mary and all the saints. Let us consider, however, the people whom the Roman anaphoras explicitly mention. In all of the current Eucharistic Prayers, petition is made in remembrance of the bishop of Rome, the local ordinary, and all the bishops. In some case mention is made of all the clergy and all God's people. While there is merit to leaving the language general so that the referents might be inclusive, still Metz's critique of the middle-class subject of religion leads me to question whether contemporary ecclesial communities might not need to be more explicit in their remembrance of those who are currently living in suffering, turmoil, or oppression.

If, again, we look East for assistance, we find in the Byzantine anaphora of St. Basil a generous remembrance of many in need:

"Remember, Lord, the people who stand around and those who for good reason are absent, and have mercy on them and on us according to the abundance of your mercy. Fill their storehouses with all good things, preserve their marriages in peace and concord; nourish the infants, instruct the youth, strengthen the old; comfort the fainthearted, gather the scattered, bring back the wanderers and join them to your holy, catholic, and apostolic Church; set free those who are troubled by unclean spirits; sail with those that sail, journey with those that journey; defend the widows, protect the orphans, rescue the captives, heal the sick. Be mindful, O God, of those who face trial, those in the mines, in exile, in bitter slavery, in all tribulation, necessity, and affliction; of all who need your great compassion, those who love us, those who hate us, and those whom commanded us, though unworthy, to pray for them.

"Remember all your people . . . Be mindful of those whom we have not mentioned . . . O God, you know the age and the title of each, you know every man [*sic*] from his mother's womb. For you, Lord are the help of the helpless, the hope of the hopeless, the savior of the tempest-tossed, the haven of sailors, the physician of the sick: yourself be all things to all men, for you know every man and his petition, his house, and his need.

"Rescue, Lord, this flock, and every city and country, from famine, plague, earthquake, flood, fire, the sword, invasion by foreigners, and civil war."[26]

The fundamental value of this extended petition (quoted here only in part) is its movement to particularity. The worshiping community does not raise up an abstract humanity or world but, rather, names the circumstances of crisis and danger in which so many struggle at this very time. In his own treatment of the intercessions from this anaphora (the full quotation of which spans three pages), Schmemann interprets their function as *"the gathering of the Church, the body of Christ,* her manifestation in all fulness" of the entire cosmos.[27] His concern is to correct individualistic piety by asserting the corporate nature of the eucharistic communion, a uniting of all the Church and all creation. While this interpretation is certainly valid, it is also consistent with the extremely realized eschatology which Schmemann asserts for the liturgy. The entire prayer and action does indeed, as Schmemann teaches, grant its participants a communal *vision* of the kingdom of God; it is the symbol that bears what is most real for the world. What I wish to assert, however, is that this vision is the symbol of a reality and truth which is itself a *praxis*. In the name of Christ and the power of the Spirit, the assembled Church blesses God for God's deeds of redemption and petitions God to remember again all those in need. Those assembled thereby perform a commemoration that enables them to remember *with* God, to see the world as God does, and thus to recognize their own mission as one of acting as God has revealed God's merciful action in the tradition of the prophets and the person of Christ.

These reflections on the narrative content of the Eucharistic Prayer, of course, raise again questions about actual performance in the contemporary context. One might, for example, strive to introduce contemporary terminology into the petitions, such as "refugees" in relation to civil war and invasion, or "child laborers" in relation to

[26] R.C.D. Jasper and G. J. Cuming, *Prayers of the Eucharist: Early and Reformed,* 3d ed. (Collegeville: The Liturgical Press, 1987, 1992) 121–2.

[27] Schmemann, *The Eucharist,* 235.

those who are enslaved. The issue of the length of the prayer recurs as well. There is a problem with trying to make any one part or even the entire prayer do too much. The temptation to focus myopically upon the Eucharistic Prayer or any one of its sections must be avoided. Remembrance of the suffering, for example, certainly occurs in the early part of the Eucharistic Prayer as well, in which the people bless God by remembering God's actions on behalf of the afflicted. To the extent that this occurs in the current Roman anaphoras this remembrance obtains a christological focus: "To the poor he proclaimed the good news of salvation, to prisoners, freedom, and to those in sorrow, joy" (Eucharistic Prayer IV). By remembering, with praise and thanksgiving, these actions and attitudes of Jesus, the worshiping community claims its desire to think and act in kind, to be conformed to the image of Christ.

If we move our attention away from the Eucharistic Prayer itself to the entire Liturgy of the Lord's Day, then elements of the Service of the Word bear opportunities in different genres and tonalities of prayer and proclamation for the assembled body of Christ to remember God as the Savior of the living and the dead, and thereby to participate in Christ's mission of kenotic service. We need to remember that the entire cultic or ritual action constitutes the Church's commemoration of Christ and that the nature of this memorial action is to bring about, in the words of Kevin Irwin, "a new act of salvation occur[ing] here and now for contemporary believers."[28] The participants experience anew God's redemptive action in Christ. This experience is constituted by the proclamation and manifestation of salvation through the symbolic media of word and ritual gesture. In turn, the people's response to and appropriation of this revelation occurs through these media for the transformation of their lives in service to the world. The proclamation of Sacred Scripture from several texts (including the Psalms), reaching its climax in a reading from one of the four gospels, is the primary way in which the content of the faith is conveyed to the worshiping community in the Liturgy of the Word.

The importance of the Second Vatican Council's recovery of an ample Service of the Word, especially in the three-year lectionary

---

[28] Kevin W. Irwin, *Context and Text: Method in Liturgical Theology* (Collegeville: The Liturgical Press, 1994) 47. For treatment of the ancient sense of the "today" of the salvation borne by the liturgy see 47–8, 93, 196, 320.

cycle and the requirement of a genuine liturgical homily, cannot be underestimated. Through the cycles of readings ecclesial communities encounter the whole range of the Scriptures' narratives and images of God's creative and redemptive action in history. If open to this word, people are not left to their own images of God or Christ but, rather, are confronted or consoled by narratives which at times gently invite and at other times strongly demand a decision to enter into God's life, to take up the way of imitation. This is the anamnetic character of the proclamation of God's word or message, about which Dahl instructed us in our fourth chapter. The homily is an integral part of the proclamation. The preacher's hermeneutical task is to throw together the worlds of Scripture and the contemporary community in the unique moment of a particular liturgical celebration. It is this *throwing together*, the meaning of the Greek root for symbol *(symbolein)*, that constitutes the homily as a liturgical act, manifesting the reality in the proclamation of the word. In the ensuing Prayers of the Faithful the people concretely respond through intercession on behalf of a world and Church that so greatly need divine grace.

Such is a normative description of the anamnetic and transformative character of the Liturgy of the Word. My concluding reference to the people's intercessions recalls Metz's admonition that these prayers must not degenerate into a "eulogistic evasion" of the community's mission of ethical and political praxis in society. The same charge can be brought to the preacher. This returns our attention to the actual subjects, both clerical and lay, who perform the liturgy at this time and in this society. In the case of the Roman Church, the eucharistic pieties and theologies of the hierarchical authorities, wider clergy, and laity alike largely continue to draw from the medieval ritual gestures and scholastic sacramental synthesis discussed intermittently in Chapter 3. While we cannot enter into a detailed treatment of those problems at this point, we can acknowledge that the Church's *reception* of the Vatican Council's mandate for liturgical renewal remains an enormous challenge. Some of the ambiguities and compromises in the Constitution on the Sacred Liturgy and the Mass of Paul VI directly contribute to the problem.

On the other hand, as Schmemann reiterated many times in his writings, the rites themselves cannot bear the onus of ecclesial renewal. To put this in Metz's terms, only if believers are engaged in the dialectical praxis of mysticism and politics can they experience the faith as an ongoing hunger and urgent desire for the just and loving God revealed in

the person and gospel of Jesus. Those who practice the ethical and political demands of the faith in the challenging and, at times, overwhelming context of late-modern society constantly turn to the liturgy,
among other mystical practices, for an experiential knowledge of the
memories and promises which reveal the presence of the God of Jesus.
The entire range of experiences in the concrete praxis of faith, from the
consoling and joyous to the catastrophic and painful, fosters the need
for many types of ritual and prayer. To turn *exclusively* to the eucharistic liturgy is to demand of it what it cannot alone provide. Other rituals in the cycle of the liturgical year and the sacramental pastoral care
of the Church, along with the Liturgy of the Hours and any number of
communal and individual devotional practices, afford different types
of opportunities for praise and lament, acclamation and contrition.
Moreover, the entire range of the Church's traditions of ritual and
prayer entail different postures and gestures by which the faith is
kinesthetically inscribed in human bodies. The celebration of the Eucharist is enriched by the complementarity of these other forms of
Christian mysticism. All of these mystical practices, in turn, function
as consolation and goad for believers who commit themselves to political and ethical praxis. Believers live within the eschatological dialectic of faith in this world as they remember the Christ whom they
imitate and watch for his glorious and dangerous return.

Index of Names

Adorno, Theodor, 24n.11, 27n.15, 29n.22, 31n.27, 32, 50–1n.79, 54n.87, 82
Aristotle, 146, 167, 176
Ashley, J. Matthew, xiv, 31n.27, 45n.69, 47n.72, 63n.112, 69, 73n.1
Athanasius of Alexandria, 119n.98
Augustine of Hippo, 68, 94

Baldovin, John, 12–4, 111n.80
Barth, Karl, xi, 41n.54, 74n.3
Basil of Caesarea, 94, 195, 202, 208
Baum, Gregory, 74n.4
Benjamin, Walter, 30n.25, 60n.108
Berger, Teresa, 63n.114
Bornkamm, Gunther, 158n.39, 197n.10
Botte, Bernard, 126
Bouyer, Louis, 76, 171n.61
Browning, Don, xv, 63n.112
Buber, Martin, 61
Bultmann, Rudolph, 41, 42

Cabié, Robert, 87n.31
Campbell, Stanislaus, 10n.21
Cardinal, Ernesto, 60n.106
Casel, Odo, 91n.40, 164, 195
Chauvet, Louis-Marie, 61n.110, 167n.52
Childs, Brevard, 151–4, 163, 176, 178
Chopp, Rebecca, xii, xvi, 43, 72n.140
Colombo, Joseph, 44n.63, 47n.72, 62, 68

Congar, Yves, 91n.41
Connerton, Paul, 24n.47
Cooke, Bernard, 136n.37
Cullmann, Oscar, 99

Dahl, Nils, 145–51, 155–67, 211
Dalmais, Irénée, 64n.116, 76, 89n.36, 91n.40
Daly, Robert, xvi
Daniélou, Jean, 76, 92–3n.44, 94
Davies, W. D., 168, 174
Dietrich, Donald, xvi
Dix, Gregory, 92, 92n.42, 171n.61
Duffy, Regis, 5n.13
Dunn, James D. G., 157n.36, 158n.39

Fagerberg, David, 63n.114, 75n.7
Fink, Peter, xi, 64n.115
Fiorenza, Francis, 78n.11
Fisch, Thomas, 75n.7

Gaillardetz, Richard, 13
Gelpi, Donald, 107n.68
Giraudo, Cesare, 177n.70
Gregg, David, 166–80, 186, 194, 196n.7
Gregory of Nyssa, 108n.73
Grimes, Ronald, 15n.35
Gustafson, James, 74n.3
Gutiérrez, Gustavo, 33n.30, 56n.95

Haight, Roger, xvi, 8–9
Häussling, Angelus, 153n.28
Hegel, G. W. F., 85

213

Saliers, Don, xvi, 14–5, 64n.115, 97n.53, 115–6n.92

Sawyer, J. F. A., 168

Schäfer, Philipp, 165n.48, 182n.78

Searle, Mark, 6–7n.15

Seasoltz, Kevin, xvi

Severus of Antioch, 202

Schillebeeckx, Edward, xi, 66n.120, 70n.137, 89–90n.37, 96–7n.53, 175

Schmemann, Alexander, xiv, 17, 63n.114, 64, 70, 73–138, 139–46, 149, 153–6, 159, 170, 172–5, 184, 185, 189, 191–3, 200, 205, 209, 211

Schneiders, Sandra, 81n.16

Soelle, Dorothee, 38n.46

Taft, Robert, 66n.122

Tannehill, Robert, 158n.39

Tanner, Kathryn, 44n.62

Teilhard de Chardin, 71

Theodore of Mospsuestia, 108n.73, 196

Thoma, Clemens, 150n.20, 152n.27, 171n.60

Thomas Aquinas, 70n.37, 96n.53

Thurian, Max, 150n.19, 173, 174

Vagaggini, Cyprian, 76

Wainwright, Geoffrey, 194–205, 208

White, James, 15–6n.36

Index of Subjects

of faith, xv, 38, 39n.50, 40, 42, 43,
48–9, 52, 53, 70, 85, 96, 100, 112,
120, 125, 131, 134, 142, 144, 145,
149, 161, 162, 164, 174–6, 200,
201, 205, 209, 212
mysticism and politics, xiv, 36,
38–40, 42, 53–6, 60, 63, 64, 80,
88, 107, 128, 129, 131, 140, 146,
158n.39, 162, 166, 171, 175, 190,
191, 199, 211
political, 12, 30, 40, 47, 53, 55, 60,
66, 69, 162
prayer, 50–6, 64, 87, 91, 116, 136, 147,
159, 162–3, 165, 170, 188, 190
preaching, 159–61, 163, 165, 188, 193
presence, personal, encounter, 180,
183, 185, 193, 203
priest, priesthood, 3, 66n.120, 71, 91,
130, 168, 204
private, privatism, 21, 22, 30, 38, 57,
64–5, 82, 123, 137, 172, 190
proclamation, 53, 105, 123, 132, 144,
163, 165, 166, 170, 187–8, 190–1, 210
prophet, prophetic, 107, 133, 146,
155, 170, 181, 183, 207, 209, 211–2
psalms, 50, 149–52, 210
psychology, 77

reason, 18, 20, 23, 26, 27, 68–70, 78,
84n.23, 86, 140
instrumental, technical reason, 22,
23, 27–9, 39, 50, 54, 57, 58, 64,
102, 117, 132, 137, 140, 148, 190
practical reason, 26–7, 34, 37, 140,
148, 189, 200
Reformation, 61, 109n.76
refugees, 209
religion, 20–5, 43, 49, 51, 57–9, 65, 77,
82, 83, 86, 88, 91, 111, 112, 149,
150, 155, 208
Religionswissenschaft, 90, 91
representation, 108–9, 112, 165,
177n.70

responsibility, 55, 56
resurrection, 31–3, 36, 49, 56n.95, 70,
88, 93, 94, 104, 114, 117–9, 139,
158n.39, 166, 175, 179, 191, 196, 207
revelation, 17–8, 25, 37, 89, 91, 96,
99, 126, 128–30, 135, 144, 192,
210, 211
ritual, 90, 91, 97, 106, 182, 212
action, performance, practice, xii,
xv, 7, 12, 15, 61, 85, 92, 93,
98n.55, 105, 108, 110–1n.80, 111,
112, 128, 134, 140, 143, 144, 150,
151, 163, 170–4, 176, 178, 180,
183, 192, 195, 205, 209
ritual theory, 65–6n.119
ritualism, 25, 59, 67, 70, 87
Roman Missal, 110–1n.80, 207, 210
romantic, romanticism, 83, 120

Sabbath, 93, 94, 96, 154, 168, 171
sacramental theology, xi, 67, 71,
89–93, 96, 107n.68, 112, 130, 133,
136–7, 171, 184, 185
sacraments, sacramentality, 12–4, 50,
57–61, 81, 89, 91, 96, 97, 99, 102,
111, 113, 130, 133, 135, 136, 165,
170–1, 175, 184, 185, 188, 190, 193,
196, 200
sacred and profane, 25, 86, 98–9, 105,
111, 142, 144, 154, 191
sacrifice, 2, 53, 91, 120, 122–4, 143,
150, 164, 168, 170, 183n.81, 195,
200
Sacrosanctum concilium, 1–4, 79n.12,
211
Saint Vladimir's Seminary, 125, 128
salvation, redemption, salvation history, 7, 18, 25, 37, 40–2, 48, 50, 53,
56, 59, 63, 70, 75, 91, 92, 97–100,
104, 111, 113, 114, 116, 118,
119n.97, 135, 139, 140, 150–5, 157,
165, 175, 176, 177n.70, 180, 183,
185, 192, 195, 205, 206, 210–1

54, 64–70, 72, 75–7, 79, 81, 83–5,
88, 109, 110n.80, 126, 132, 140, 141,
145, 149, 151–3, 156, 163, 175, 182,
190, 194, 199–201, 204
transcendence, transcendent, 9–10,
119, 131
transcendental theology, transcendentalism, xi, 18, 19, 44n.63, 53,
59, 118n.97
transformation, 56, 67, 75, 78, 85, 88,
89, 98–102, 107, 115–22, 124, 129,
133, 135, 136, 148, 154, 170, 185,
186, 194, 201, 204, 210
Trinity, trinitarian theology, 52n.82,
120, 130, 196
truth, 23, 32, 54n.87, 86, 87, 99, 115,
129, 130, 188, 209

unity, 77, 128–30

value(s)
 bourgeois, 50, 51, 57, 58, 117, 122,
 130, 137, 179, 201
 Christian ethical, 22, 39, 157
 cultural, 12
 exchange, market, 21–3, 38, 64,
 137, 148, 190
 national, nationalist, 12, 128–9
victims, the dead, 22, 29, 31, 33, 36,
 41, 43, 45, 51n.79, 67, 69, 101, 140,
 141, 148, 175, 179, 185, 189, 206
violence, 50
virtues, 22, 39, 40, 48, 54, 102, 116,
 190

witness, 75, 89, 95, 123, 131, 132, 192
Word, Liturgy of, 204, 210–1
World Council of Churches, 76
World War II, 45, 49